TOUGH-AS-NAILS
Flowers
FOR THE SOUTH

Norman Winter

UNIVERSITY PRESS OF MISSISSIPPI · JACKSON

www.upress.state.ms.us

The University Press of Mississippi is a member of the Association
of American University Presses.

05 04 03   3 2 1

Page i: 'Bluebird' nemesia, 'Compact Innocence' bacopa, and 'Tukana Scarlet'
verbena combine for a basket of patriotic color.
Page ii: The late spring garden comes alive with 'Bouquet Purple' dianthus,
'Honey Bee Blue' anise hyssop, and 'Cooler' periwinkles.

All photographs courtesy of Norman Winter, except photographs on the follow-
ing pages: 71, courtesy of Dr. Steve George, Texas Agricultural Extension
Service; 85, The John Henry Company; 96, All American Selections; 161,
Netherland Bulb Information Center; 180, Perennial Plant Association; 181,
Dr. James T. Cole, University of Arkansas

Library of Congress Cataloging-in-Publication Data
Winter, Norman.
   Tough-as-nails flowers for the South / Norman Winter.
      p. cm.
Includes bibliographical references and index.
   ISBN 1-57806-543-7 (cloth : alk. paper) —ISBN 1-57806-544-5 (pbk. : alk.
paper)
   1. Landscape plants—Southern states. 2. Landscape gardening—Southern
States. 3. Flowers—Southern States. I. Title.
   SB407 .W583 2003
   635.9'525'0978—dc21   2002014246

British Library Cataloging-in-Publication Data available

In memory of our daughter Lorie Kelly
who had a passion for flowers

"A man is what he thinks about all day long."
—Ralph Waldo Emerson

"As a man thinketh in his heart, so is he."
—Proverbs 23:7

This book is dedicated to southerners who indeed think and
dream passionately about the beautiful flowers God has created.
These dreamers become gardeners who reflect the Creator by
sharing their love, knowledge, and plants.

Contents

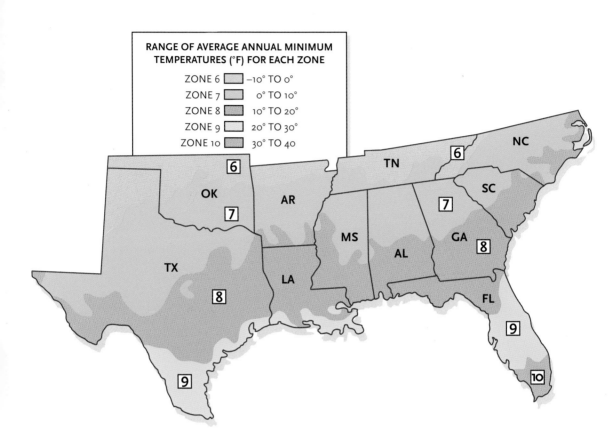

RANGE OF AVERAGE ANNUAL MINIMUM
TEMPERATURES (°F) FOR EACH ZONE

ZONE 6   −10° TO 0°
ZONE 7   0° TO 10°
ZONE 8   10° TO 20°
ZONE 9   20° TO 30°
ZONE 10   30° TO 40

Gardening Basics

At no time in the history of the United States have people wanted more flower color in the landscape. Sure, shrubs are the backbone and foundation of the yard, but flower power is the passion of today's gardener. With one child going to soccer practice and the other to drama rehearsal, Mom and Dad find it tough to give as much time to the garden as they would like. They want flowers that are indeed "tough as nails."

What are tough-as-nails flowers? Are they drought-tolerant in the summer? Can they take heat and humidity? Will they perform during the winter? The answer is an unequivocal yes, sort of. Pansies, for instance, are troopers in the winter, giving months of cool-season color. Cold almost never fazes them. They are tough! On the other hand, they fail in the sweltering heat of the southern summer.

'New Gold' lantana can thrive on a west-facing wall in the summer and is as tough a flower as there is on the market. It retreats to ground level, however, once winter sets in. So there are tough-as-nails flowers for all seasons. Some are annuals, some are perennials, and others are in between. Each plant featured in *Tough-as-Nails Flowers for the South* offers good value and performance for the dollar spent.

Plant Cultural Requirements

Key cultural requirements are given for each plant featured in this book. One of the most important is the amount of sunlight needed. Horticulturists like myself often make the statement that a plant needs "full sun." What does this mean? Full sun means a minimum of 8 hours of direct sunlight per day. Part shade means 4 hours of direct sunlight. Shade means approximately 2 hours of sunlight.

USDA Cold-Hardiness Zone Map

The USDA cold-hardiness zone map featured on page viii shows the minimum temperatures that can be expected in each zone. *Tough-as-*

Nails Flowers for the South was written for the area from Texas to Oklahoma east to North Carolina and south to Florida. This encompasses zones 6–10. If a plant is listed as zone 10 hardiness, this means zones 6–9 must treat it as an annual or give it sufficient winter protection. If there is a parenthesis around an indicated zone—such as (6)—the plant's hardiness in that zone is considered marginal. If you live in zone 6 where the plant is listed as marginal in your area, it should be planted in the most protected area of the landscape to have a chance of surviving the winter.

Soil Preparation: The Key to the Green Thumb

The key to the green thumb is how brown it gets first in soil preparation. With every plant in this book, soil preparation is targeted because very few plants can thrive by simply digging a hole and planting. Most of us do not have the ideal soil for bedding plants, annuals or perennials. Roots of bedding plants have to penetrate soils quickly, anchor plants, and absorb water and nutrients, often under adverse conditions. In many cases the lots where our homes are sitting have had the topsoil scraped off and a material that is hardly suitable for plant life brought in for the foundation—and unfortunately for the flower and shrub beds too!

If we give our plants a good home for their roots, we can have beautiful flowers that are tough.

But all is not lost. We can have beautiful flowers, and many are indeed tough in our climate, but we have to give them a good home for their roots. Since landscaping is so important, aesthetically and financially, to a home, it make sense to do the job right the first time.

Plants require oxygen, nutrients, and water for proper growth. Soil texture plays the most important role in determining whether or not those three needs are met sufficiently to allow the plant to become established and perform to expectations. Desirable soil holds water while allowing for adequate drainage. It also provides adequate oxygen for root development.

If you are unsure of your soil type but believe internal drainage is poor, you can do a simple test. Use a large (approximately 46-ounce size) coffee can with the top and bottom removed. Dig a 4-inch-deep hole and set the can on the floor of the hole. Firm the soil around the can so water cannot slip under the bottom edge. Fill the can to the top with water. Wait an hour and then measure the water level. If the water level drops at least 2 inches in 1 hour the drainage is considered normal. If the level drops more than 5 inches in 1 hour, it is considered excessive. If the level doesn't seem to drop at all, the soil drainage is poor.

Clay soils usually make for poorly drained planting sites unless steps are taken to correct the situation. Not only do they have a tendency to be poorly drained, they are also easily compacted, which prevents water penetration, oxygen exchange, and good root development.

Amending the planting area is one of the best ways to have success over these conditions. Add organic matter such as fine pine bark (pieces less than 1/2 inch), leaf mold, compost, peat, and sand. Incorporating a 3–4-inch layer of organic matter in with the native soil allows the bed to be built up and provides excellent drainage.

This same organic matter will be of benefit to gardeners with an excessively sandy soil structure. These sandier soils dry quickly and allow for rapid leaching of nutrients. The organic matter will greatly improve the water-holding capacity and will hold valuable nutrients.

Composting: Leaves to Treasure

Soil amendment is just one good reason for starting a compost pile. The piles of weeds, grass clippings, and leaves normally thrown away can be turned into a treasure in just a matter of weeks. A well-tended compost pile contains microorganisms that quickly process mounds of organic matter into rich soil amendments.

To get started, place your compost pile in a convenient but inconspicuous location. You will need easy access to water. The pile should be at least 3 feet wide and 3 feet high to retain heat and moisture and to decompose properly. Old loading pallets are just about perfect, but you can certainly go larger if you have access to the organic material. Many gardeners find that three piles are ideal, one finishing, one in the process of decomposition and one in which fresh materials are being added. Other good materials for enclosing the compost pile are chicken wire, wood slat fencing, cement blocks, and bricks. Many garden centers sell the drum-type compost bins that make for easy turning with a handle.

Under proper conditions, compost piles do not smell and can reach 150 degrees inside from the heat given off by the microorganisms. To make a compost pile, alternate 3–8 inches of plant material with 2–3 inches of soil. Do not put in any fat of any sort, including meat scraps, egg yolks, and vegetable oil. The fungi and microorganisms that decompose the pile cannot process the fat. The fat will also smell and attract insect and animal pests.

Reduce the size of the clippings or leaves as much as possible by shredding or running over them with a mower. Smaller pieces break down faster. Keep the compost pile moist and moved or turned. The pile should be damp, neither bone-dry nor soggy. Turn the pile so it can receive the oxygen needed to decompose. The pile should be turned every 2 months or sooner.

Another important element of thriving compost piles is proper nitrogen content, which microorganisms need to complete their life cycles. Grass clippings are an excellent source of nitrogen. If grass clippings are not used, add 1/2 cup of ammonium nitrate to each 8 bushels of leaves.

To test when the compost pile is done, stick your hand into the pile. If the center is cool, it's time either to use or to turn the compost. If the middle of the pile is totally broken down, it's time to use. A properly maintained compost pile containing leaves, grass clippings, and garden trimmings turned once or twice can be composted in 10–12 weeks. A pile containing small limbs, tree shavings, and leaves can take 6–9 months.

Planting

Next to soil preparation, planting depth may be the most important technique for bedding plants. Planting too deep can cause suffocation of the roots and rotting of the stem. Digging the hole too deep often causes the soil to settle, and the results end up being the same as planting too deep. The top of the root ball must be even with the soil surface. There are, of course, a few plants that can be planted deeper, in which case roots will form along the stem.

Proper Watering

Once in the ground the roots of the bedding plant must grow outside the root ball to get established. This must happen with even the toughest, most drought-tolerant plants. For this to happen there must be adequate soil moisture. Unless rains fall perfectly this means watering will be up to the gardener.

Once the plants are established, they must be trained to be tough. This is accomplished by watering deeply but infrequently. As the top layer of soil starts to dry, the roots will go deeper for the available moisture. The plants then become not only established but also drought-tolerant.

Fertilizing

Fertilization is a cultural practice that often gets ignored when it comes to the flower garden. The fact is that annuals and perennials need frequent light applications of fertilizer. There will always be those who do not believe in fertilization or those who believe in special concoctions resembling snake oil. It really is a simple matter: fertilizer is a substance that makes the soil more productive by supplying needed nutrients for growing your plants.

With each plant in *Tough-as-Nails Flowers for the South*, I suggest a fertilizer ratio most often with a formula that is controlled or slow released with minor nutrients and with a specific quantity based on 100 square feet of bed space or planted area. These are based on observations from my garden and represent some of the best in general all-purpose fertilizer blends. Your square footage and fertilizer requirements may be different. A soil test is always recommended to determine exactly what is needed in your particular bed.

Annuals and perennials benefit from frequent light applications of fertilizer.

Every state offers gardeners the opportunity to get a soil test done through its land grant university. This soil test is easy to do and comes with instructions about where to collect your soil and where to mail it. In a couple of weeks you will know precisely what is needed for the plants you want to grow.

There are sixteen chemical elements known to be essential for optimum plant growth. The three large numbers on bags of fertilizers refer to nitrogen (N), phosphorous (P), and potassium or potash (K). Nitrogen produces vegetative growth and gives the dark green color to plants. It increases the yield of foliage, fruit, and seed. Phosphorous stimulates early root formation and gives a rapid and vigorous start to plants. It stimulates bud set and blooming. It also lingers in the soil much longer than nitrogen. Potassium, the last of the big three, is important for increasing vigor and producing strong, stiff stalks. It also imparts winter hardiness.

The secondary and minor nutrients are also important. Calcium is part of a compound in the cell wall. Magnesium is present in chlorophyll, the green pigment in plants. Many gardeners apply Epsom salts, magnesium sulfate, to their plants. Sulfur affects cell division and formation. Manganese, iron, copper, zinc, and cobalt influence plant growth by serving as activators or catalysts. Boron is associated with calcium use, and molybdenum is essential in nitrogen use.

RECOGNIZING THE SYMPTOMS

NITROGEN: Plants with adequate nitrogen have a dark green color because of high concentrations of chlorophyll. Conversely, nitrogen deficiency leads to reduced chlorophyll concentrations and thus chlorosis (yellowing) of leaves. This appears first on the oldest leaves and then on younger leaves as the deficiency worsens.

PHOSPHORUS: The first indication of phosphorus deficiency is an overall stunted plant. Leaves may be unusually dark green at some stages, may have distorted shapes, and may become purple. Lower leaves may turn yellow between the veins. If stunting is suspected, confirm the visual symptom with plant tissue analysis.

POTASSIUM: Scorching, or firing, occurs along margins of older leaves. However, some plants under certain conditions will exhibit deficiency on younger leaves first. Growth rate is slow, root systems are poorly developed, stalks are weak, and lodging (falling over) often occurs. Disease resistance is very low.

CALCIUM: Deficiency symptoms commonly occur on the youngest tissues because calcium does not move within the plant. Root growth is poor, the growing point may die, and the roots turn black and rot. Leaf tips will turn jellylike and die. Maintenance of soil pH normally precludes calcium nutrition problems.

MAGNESIUM: Margins of older leaves curl. Leaves may show yellowish, bronze, or reddish colors while the veins remain green.

SULFUR: Leaves have a pale green color usually seen first on younger ones, though the whole plant may take on the pale green appearance. Sulfur deficiencies most commonly occur in sandy soils or other low-organic-matter soils.

IRON: Younger leaves yellow between veins, but yellowing spreads to whole leaf. Leaves die from the edges.

MANGANESE: Upper leaves become yellow between veins. Dead spots form in severe cases. The veins remain green, and young leaves get a checkered effect.

BORON: Plants become brittle, and growing tips may die.

It pays to be able to recognize when your plants are suffering from a fertilizer deficiency. The guidelines on page xv will help you diagnose your plants' symptoms.

Before applying fertilizer you need to have an understanding of what is in the bag. If the label on a 50-pound bag of fertilizer shows a formula of 10-20-10, that means that it has 5 pounds (10 percent) available nitrogen, 10 pounds (20 percent) available phosphorus, and 5 pounds (10 percent) potassium. If the bag has trace elements or minor nutrients, they will be listed on the bag, and the percentages are much smaller. The remaining 30 pounds in the bag is made up of filler or carrier for the nutrients.

Many gardeners, myself included, have killed plants by burning with fertilizer. Today fertilizers are available that are coated and released over an extended period of time from 2–12 months. These coated fertilizers, although more expensive, are worth the price for gardeners who are worried about burning plants or too busy to make repeated applications.

Color Creates Excitement in the Garden

There are few things that affect the overall look of a garden as much as color. Used effectively, color can create a feeling of calm, graciousness, spaciousness, excitement, or just about any mood a gardener wants to achieve. Used wrongly, it's "nightmare on your street."

Use flowers to complement the exterior color of the home. If your home is basically neutral—say, beige, gray, or white—the task is easy because you can use any color scheme you like. If, however, your home is accented with a colorful trim, you may want to pick colors that echo that color or complement it. Red, for example, is the direct complement of green. So red geraniums, salvia, or petunias would be a good choice for a neutral house with green trim.

By limiting ourselves to two or three colors that we repeat we can give a planned, unified look in all garden spots and avoid the hodgepodge look.

Look at the color wheel on page xviii to see which colors are complementary, analogous, triadic, and monochromatic.

A monochromatic color scheme means that all the flowers are the same color, or light or darker shades of the same color, such as red, pink, and burgundy impatiens. Color used in this scheme creates spaciousness because it is not broken or interrupted by another color.

There are few things
that affect the overall
look of a garden as
much as flowers.

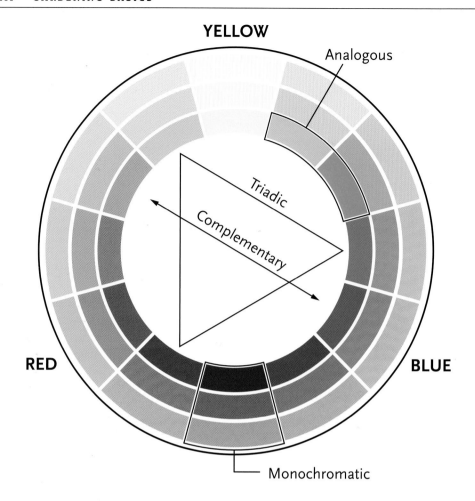

An analogous color scheme uses colors that are next to each other on the color wheel—red and orange, orange and yellow, yellow and green, for example.

The old adage "opposites attracts" may work with spouses sometimes, but it always works with plant colors. Just as different abilities and personalities make couples compatible, different colors can complement each other in a flowerbed. The complementary color scheme uses colors that are directly opposite each other on the color wheel. One color comes from the hot side of the wheel and one from the cool side. Examples are red and green, orange and blue, yellow and violet.

Some very striking uses of color can be made with complements. Blue ageratums and orange marigolds are one such combination. Lemon Twist coleus and fuchsia-colored impatiens make a winning combination.

An unusual but very attractive color scheme uses three colors that are equal distance on the color wheel. For example, yellow marigolds, blue

COMPLEMENTARY

ANALOGOUS

TRIADIC

MONOCHROMATIC

salvia, and red zinnias form a triadic harmony. This scheme gives you not only more color but more opportunity to use a greater variety of plants. Four colors will work too, as long as they are equal distances apart on the wheel. The result is called quadratic harmony.

White is one of the most overlooked colors. It is the last one to fade from view in the evening. In shady areas, white impatiens or caladiums stand out in the shadows and give form and focus to a garden that might otherwise be lost to view. Also, don't ignore the value of green. Green is restful to the eyes, so allow the foliage to be seen and admired.

If you still feel unsure about using the wheel, try this tip: Before making your purchases, place flats of plants beside each other at the garden center and see if you like the resulting combinations.

No matter what scheme you choose, massing of plants is the key to your success. Planting six here and six there just can't create the look of planting by the flat. Mass planting and spacing as recommended will give you that professionally designed look.

Container Gardening Can Be a "Barrel" of Fun

Growing flowers in containers can be as much fun as just about any other type of gardening. Containerized plants can give a special touch—stationed elegantly at the entrance to the front door, stair-stepped, or artfully arranged on the deck or patio.

Container gardening offers several advantages. First, containers are movable, which allows for winter protection or placing in the plant's required microclimate. Another plus is that you can select and modify the soil to grow almost any plant, whether it is an acid lover or one that needs more alkalinity. Container plants can be less work because you can place them close to the water source and at a height that can minimize bending for watering and tending.

The containers offered by nurseries and garden centers have changed dramatically over the last decade. New on the market are containers resembling those you might find at an old European villa, and other containers from around the world provide almost limitless possibilities for decorating outside entertaining areas.

But container gardening need not be just for those with expensive tastes in pots. It is fun growing plants in anything that holds soil and drains well. Having a whimsical approach to container gardening is often the most enjoyable. Recycling old household items and turning them into artful containers is the latest rage. When it comes to containers, one thing is sure: there is a size and shape to fit your desires as well as your budget.

Select a container that will give your plants' roots room to grow but not so much that they will never fill the pot. Consider the mature size of the plants you will be growing and follow spacing recommendations.

The deeper the pot, the less watering it will need. Pots with a small amount of soil will dry out faster and will require frequent watering. Small pots or hanging baskets may require watering twice a day during the summer heat.

The potting mix should be light and airy. This is one area where you should avoid skimping. Many bargain soils sold by the pound are heavy and don't drain well enough. Large containers with this type of soil would be extremely hard to move around. The peat, perlite, and vermiculite mixtures, with their moisture-holding capacity, are almost never a problem in containers. Today's best ready-made mixes have controlled-release fertilizers added.

Baskets aren't just for the Pacific Northwest. Choosing tough plants will let you have baskets like these photographed in August in Birmingham.

Be bold and use three to five species of plants in large containers.

It is not necessary to line the bottom of the pot with broken pottery, gravel, or rocks. If you are concerned about soil washing out, place a small piece of mesh screen over the drainage holes.

Planting in containers is much the same as in the landscape. Place large plants first, then plant smaller plants around the perimeter and in pockets created by greenery. The top of the root ball of the plants should be even with the soil line. Keep the container well watered as the plants get established. With frequent watering during the intense summer heat, nutrients quickly leach from the soil. To keep your plants well fed, use controlled-release granules or a diluted water-soluble fertilizer.

Bountiful Baskets

Beautiful, blooming baskets are popular across the country. A designer look can be achieved with several species of flowers blooming at once.

To make your own, choose a wire basket, preferably a large one. Next, get sphagnum moss and place it in a bucket of water. Remove the moss

Baskets don't have to be complicated to be beautiful. Two colors of 'Babylon' verbena and 'Mini Supertunias' petunias make for a dynamic combination.

and squeeze the water out. Line the basket by pressing the moss down and around the wires. You are actually creating a bowl to hold the potting mix. The sphagnum moss allows water to drain without the soil washing away. Once the basket has been lined, the plants can be inserted through the moss and wires into the bowl. Use your fingers to poke holes through the moss and wires starting at the bottom of the basket. Insert the plants in the holes. Space the plant 4–6 inches apart to give a full appearance. After the bottom layer of plants is in place, cover with the potting mix. Work your way to the top of the basket, creating more holes and inserting additional plants covering each layer with soil. The soil should be about 3/4 inch below the top of the moss. Plant flowers in the top of the basket as well.

Many gardeners prefer the new baskets lined with coconut coir. These are less messy but usually a little more expensive. Cut a slit or hole in the liner to allow the plant to be placed in the potting mix. The baskets will need frequent watering and feeding.

Designing the Container or Basket

As you consider flowers for your containers, keep in mind their color and leaf texture. Do they work harmoniously together? Do they have similar light and water requirements, and, most important, do their bloom periods coincide?

Don't underestimate the value of filler plants, foliage plants, and plants that cascade over the rim of the container. Be bold, be artistic, and have fun!

ANNUALS

Plants That Hustle

No other group of plants provides as much color as quickly and economically as annuals. True to their name, annuals sprout from seed, flower, set seed, and die within one season. There are many more plants that we treat as annuals that live longer in their native lands and in reality may be perennials, shrubs, or even small trees, but that will not survive the heat or cold associated with our climate.

Most annuals are planted in the spring and are killed by frost in the fall. Tough ones, however, such as cosmos, gomphrena, moss rose, marigolds, and zinnias, can be sown or transplanted in mid- or late summer with great success. Cool-season annuals like pansies, snapdragons, violas, and flowering kale and cabbage are tolerant of our winters and are best planted in the fall for color throughout the winter. These are usually killed by the heat of early summer.

Despite their one-year reputation, several annuals reseed with ease, offering a perennial-like performance in the landscape. Plants like cleome, cosmos, gomphrena, melampodium, and Texas sage return every year with an abundance of seedlings. The seedlings can be thinned and even transplanted throughout the flower border.

Annuals come in a variety of colors, heights, and textures, and their uses are almost unlimited. They can be exceptional when planted in bold drifts of single or mixed colors. They are also excellent for creating pockets of color in front of evergreen shrubs or as a welcoming display near the front door.

Many annuals are compact; others are trailing. They are great for the front of the flower border and also excel in baskets, containers, and window boxes. Large annuals work well when placed toward the middle or back of the border. Some annuals are vines that can climb a pergola or trellis in one season. Look for these in the vines chapter.

Page 1: Ornamental peppers and rudbeckias create a blaze of color.

Opposite: Annual salvias, *Salvia splendens*, lend a spiky texture to the garden.

Gardeners may find that they have great success growing flowers in containers yet continue to struggle when growing flowers in the landscape. The problem can usually be attributed to poor soil preparation. Roots of annuals have to penetrate soils quickly to get established and anchor the plants. They must absorb water and nutrients in one season under all kinds of weather conditions.

The first step in preparing a bed for annual plants is to remove unwanted vegetation using a nonselective herbicide or a hoe. The soil should then be turned to about the depth of the shovel. To prevent resprouting, remove grass and weed roots while turning the soil.

Add 3–4 inches of organic matter such as compost, humus, pine bark, or peat moss and an inch or two of sharp sand if the soil is really heavy. Many garden centers sell bulk or bagged landscape soil mixes and blends that are ideal for flower and shrub bed plantings. Such soil mixes provide excellent drainage and should allow you to plant in raised beds above the natural soil level. This has become a standard practice with commercial landscapers.

It is always best to get a soil test before adding fertilizer. If you are unable to get a soil test, you can simply broadcast 2 pounds of a slow-release 12-6-6 fertilizer containing minor nutrients per 100 square feet of bed space and till it in with the organic amendments.

Annual flowers can be grown from transplants or by direct seeding. Sowing seeds directly in the garden soil is a time-honored ritual that rewards a little work and patience with great returns. It is more economical than buying transplants. It also provides varieties you will never find as transplants.

There are also several advantages to buying transplants and planting them in the garden. Most of us have had those prized seedlings emerge and then virtually disappear within a couple of days. Did something eat them? Maybe. Young seedlings trying to get established in the garden are very susceptible to soil-borne pathogens. Setting out transplants, however, avoids most soil-borne seed or seedling diseases, thereby ensuring a good stand.

If you have sown a packet of seeds with a high percentage of germination, you face a dilemma that is hard for many gardeners. Within days they are competing for sunlight, and you realize they need thinning. This means killing these plants you so carefully grew from seed or carefully moving them to some other place in the garden—a backbreaking task. The crowded condition means a poor environment for growing and opens the door for catastrophe from disease pressure within the stand of seedlings. Planting transplants makes it easier to set them out at the proper spacing. The need for thinning is eliminated.

Setting out transplants also usually means a shorter time to harvesting those colorful bouquets of flowers. It may take 70 days or more from seeding before you have serious flower production, but if you set out transplants that are perhaps 4–6 weeks old, the time to flower is cut by half.

Setting out transplants reduces or avoids adverse environmental conditions affecting the growth of the plants. For instance, sowing seeds after the soil has warmed may mean your blooms are coming at the hottest time of the year. Setting out transplants, however, lets the bloom cycle get started during the cooler time of the year and results in a better and longer landscape performance.

It is a good idea to take advantage of both methods. Select nursery-grown transplants when available, and sow seeds for those varieties or plants that just aren't economical for the grower to produce.

Most garden centers have small greenhouses for seedlings to simplify your job. They come with a tray, plastic or peat planting cells, and a clear plastic dome cover that acts like a greenhouse. These will allow you to have transplants at the right time.

Set plants with the top of the roots just under the soil surface. If transplants are grown in pots made of compressed peat moss, crumble the top edge of the pot away from the plant so that it will not act as a wick pulling water away from the roots. Pinching off small flowers on brand-new transplants may be hard to do, but it will promote faster establishment, new growth, and more flowers sooner.

After planting, apply a good layer of mulch to conserve moisture, keep soil temperatures moderate, and discourage weeds. Keep flowers deadheaded (remove old flowers) to keep them looking their best and to increase production. Most annuals require a light monthly application of fertilizer to keep them growing. Those in containers will need frequent watering during the summer as well as frequent fertilizing.

Nothing beautifies the landscape like flowers, and every garden needs a healthy combination of both perennials and annuals.

Acalypha (ak-al-LY-fa) wilkesiana

Copper Plant

FAMILY: *Euphorbiaceae*
ORIGIN: Pacific Islands
RELATIVES: Poinsettia, Croton
PROPAGATION: Cutting
ZONE: All, perennial in 10
LIGHT: Sun to part shade
WATER: Average
SIZE: 4–6 feet
COLOR: Grown for variegated
foliage—bronze, burgundy,
pink, cream

The color of the copper plant's leaves intensifies in full sun.

TOUGHNESS The copper plant is one of several tropicals treated as annuals north of zone 10 that are rugged and vigorous in the landscape, putting on a show of near riotous color in the foliage when everything else is succumbing to the heat. Copper can be worth as much as gold when you use this plant in the landscape.

PLANTING To reach the most spectacular color, plant in full sun, although part shade is tolerated. In the bright light the copper-colored foliage with marbled red, pink, and purple will rival the croton or coleus.

Well-drained soil is an absolute must for the copper plant. If drainage is the least bit suspect, you will want to incorporate several inches of organic matter while preparing the bed. Since these plants grow quite large, give them adequate spacing. At 18 inches they will quickly form a hedgelike look. Depending on the look sought, 24–36 inches apart is ideal.

GROWING The copper plant responds well to a midsummer pinching or pruning that encourages lateral branching and a bushier look. To reach the maximum height potential side-dress monthly with light applications of a slow-release, balanced fertilizer.

LANDSCAPE USE Copper plants are great grouped in clusters among evergreen shrubs. The bold copper colors look striking in contrast with dark green. Combining with ornamental grasses such as 'Hameln,' a dwarf fountain grass that forms coppery pink flower spikes on 24-inch-tall clumps, creates some of the showiest beds. Purple fountain grass and 'Karl Foerster' feather reed grass also make nice companion plants.

Marigolds, in almost any size or color, were made to be grown with copper plants. 'New Gold' lantana, melampodium, and zinnias also work quite well. For an almost indescribable show of color, try combining with blue plumbago.

VARIETIES Look for 'Mardi-gras,' 'Moorea,' 'Tahiti,' 'Tri-color,' or the dwarf selection 'Godseffiana.'

Opposite: The colored foliage of the copper plant combines wonderfully with yellow flowers like the melampodium.

*Alternanthera
(al-ter-nan-THEE-ra) ficoidia*

Joseph's Coat

FAMILY: *Amaranthaceae*
ORIGIN: Mexico, Brazil
RELATIVES: Celosia, Gomphrena
PROPAGATION: Cuttings
ZONE: All, perennial in 10
LIGHT: Sun
WATER: Average
SIZE: 6–12 inches
COLOR: Grown for foliage—lime
green, burgundy, purple

TOUGHNESS The small tropical Joseph's coat livens up the landscape with its richly colored foliage. From late spring until frost it performs admirably in the garden, making it a favorite of home horticulturists and commercial landscapers. In fertile well-drained soil it is a problem-free plant.

PLANTING Joseph's coats thrive in full sun with fertile, loamy, well-drained soil. If this doesn't describe your soil, add 3–4 inches of organic matter and till to a depth of 8–10 inches. While tilling, incorporate 2 pounds of slow-release 12-6-6 fertilizer with micronutrients per 100 square feet of bed space. Set out nursery-grown transplants 6–10 inches apart in late spring.

GROWING Joseph's coats are easy to grow and look their best if kept sheared, to keep low growing and compact. These troopers are in the ground a long time, performing a valuable task, so water them during periods of drought and feed with a light application of fertilizer 3 times during the summer and early fall.

LANDSCAPE USE I looked forward each year to seeing Texas A&M spelled out in Joseph's coats on the campus in College Station. Whether you want to spell something or create an artistic design, Joseph's coat is among the best plants to use. Try growing in a tropical bed with cannas, impatiens, and coleus. Interesting combinations can be created with caladiums. The choices of companions are endless.

VARIETIES 'Filigree,' 'Magnifica,' 'Parrot Feather,' 'Tricolor,' and 'Versicolor' are just a few of the leading selections. Look also for the 'Purple Knight,' a selection of *A. dentata*.

Here lime green Joseph's coats and red begonias make for a showy display.

Amaranthus (am-ar-ANTH-us) tricolor

Joseph's Coat, Tampala, Summer Poinsettia

FAMILY: *Amaranthaceae*
ORIGIN: Africa, Southeast Asia
RELATIVES: Celosia, Gomphrena
PROPAGATION: Seed
ZONE: All
LIGHT: Sun to part shade
WATER: Average
SIZE: 2–4 feet
COLOR: Grown for foliage—red, yellow, burgundy, green

The brilliant color of the foliage makes the summer poinsettia a worthy addition to the tropical or cottage garden.

TOUGHNESS This Joseph's coat is so outstanding in color it is often called the summer poinsettia. It produces a blaze of flaming color on plants that grow with extreme vigor from seed. Green forms are eaten as a spinach substitute called tampala, which points out its one weakness: if humans find it tasty some critters will too! The plant grows so fast it is easy to keep multiple crops going, which can be a landscape enhancement.

PLANTING Select a site in full to part sun. Sow seeds in late spring or early summer in well-drained, fertile soil. Crops can be sown every 4–6 weeks, giving a variation in heights and color intensities. This layered look is striking in the tropical garden. Bedding plants are found at many local garden centers. Thin or space plants 12–18 inches apart.

GROWING Overwatering is one of the leading causes of problems with the summer poinsettia. Let the soil dry before the next irrigation. These are not heavy feeders, so fertilize lightly a month after transplanting and then admire the beauty that follows. The most tender leaves may fall prey to chewing insects, so watch and treat early with an approved insecticide.

LANDSCAPE USE Some of the most striking plantings use the summer poinsettia mixed with tall bananas, elephant ears, or castor bean. The brilliant foliage looks even more colorful when grown against a backdrop of evergreen shrubs.

VARIETIES If you aren't already convinced that this plant is bold and colorful, consider the names of the leading varieties: 'Aurora,' 'Early Splendor,' 'Flaming Fountain,' and 'Molten Fire.'

Angelonia (an-gee-LO-nia) angustifolia

Angelonia, Summer Snapdragon

FAMILY: *Scrophulariaceae*
ORIGIN: Mexico, West Indies
RELATIVES: Snapdragon, Diascia
PROPAGATION: Cutting, division
ZONE: All, perennial in (8) 9–11
LIGHT: Sun
WATER: Less than average
SIZE: 18–30 inches
COLOR: Purple, pink, blue, white, lavender, some two-toned

TOUGHNESS Relatively new, the angelonia amazes growers and gardeners alike for its durability. Few plants can bloom with such ease all summer long, taking on the temperatures of July and August without fail. Yet, incredibly, it is closely related to the snapdragon. The tall, spiky flowers are most welcome in the cottage garden or tropical garden or as the center plant in mixed containers.

PLANTING Select a site in full sun and plant anytime after the soil has warmed. Beds should be fertile, organically rich, and well drained. Incorporate 2 pounds of a 12-6-6 preplant fertilizer per 100 square feet of bed space. Set plants out 24–30 inches apart to the middle or back of the border.

GROWING Remove flower stalks as they complete their bloom cycle. This will stimulate more growth and flowers. Side-dress with a light application of fertilizer in midsummer and again in August. Angelonias are drought-tolerant but will appreciate supplemental irrigation during prolonged dry spells. Apply a good layer of mulch to increase chance of winter survival.

LANDSCAPE USE The tall flower spikes have the ability to give a larkspurlike performance all summer long. Plant blue or purple angelonia in a tropical cottage garden with allamandas. If this isn't your style, use with 'Profusion Orange' zinnia or 'New Gold' lantana. Blue and white striped varieties look exceptional with Shasta daisies, while pink angelonia combine well with purple heart or 'Blackie' sweet potato.

VARIETIES 'Hilo Princess' was the Florida Plant of the Year. Look also for a newer series called 'AngelMist,' 'Carita,' and 'Angel Face.'

White angelonias appear to glisten above annual red salvia.

Opposite: The blue-flowered 'Hilo Princess' angelonia is still performing well into chrysanthemum season.

White strawflower, yellow trailing snapdragon, and lavender-colored lamium make a colorful spring planter.

Antirrhinum (an-ti-RY-num) majus

Snapdragon

FAMILY: *Scrophulariaceae*
ORIGIN: Southwest Europe, Mediterranean
RELATIVES: Angelonia, Diascia
PROPAGATION: Seed
ZONE: All
LIGHT: Sun
WATER: Average
SIZE: 8–48 inches depending on variety
COLOR: All shades and blends except blue

The 'Crown' series of snapdragon reaches 12–18 inches tall.

TOUGHNESS Many gardeners may not think of the snapdragon as tough, but consider that it should be planted in the fall in zone 7 southward and that it blooms through May into June. That's pretty tough. Newer varieties have an even lengthier performance.

PLANTING If you plant in the fall the snapdragon will be in the ground 8 or 9 months, so it pays to do bed preparation. Incorporate 3–4 inches of organic matter along with 2 pounds of a slow-release 12-6-6 fertilizer per 100 square feet of planting area. Set out transplants in the early fall at the recommended rate for your variety. This may mean some selections should go toward the back of the border, others up front. Apply a good layer of mulch to keep soil temperatures moderate and give added winter protection.

GROWING Deadhead snapdragons to keep tidy and to keep the flowers producing. If unusually cold weather is forecasted, completely cover with pine straw until the temperatures have moderated. Pay attention to moisture levels during the winter. While soggy feet can be lethal, many cold fronts in the south dry out beds to a severe level. As growth becomes more active in late winter or early spring, side-dress with a light application of fertilizer.

LANDSCAPE USE Snapdragons are ideal companions with pansies, violas, flowering cabbage and kale, as well as bulbs like daffodils. Don't forget to use in mixed containers.

VARIETIES The variety list seems endless. New series that look outstanding are the 'Montego' (8–12 inches), 'Crown' (12–18 inches), 'Liberty Classic' (24–30 inches), and 'Sonnet' (24–30 inches). New trailing series 'Lampion,' 'Chandelier,' and 'Lumenaire' offer additional heat tolerance by virtue of hybridization with *A. hispanicum* and *A. molle* from Spain.

Begonia (beg-O-nia)
semperflorens-cultorum hybrids

Wax Begonia

FAMILY: *Begoniaceae*
ORIGIN: South America
RELATIVES: Other begonias
PROPAGATION: Cutting, seed
ZONE: All
LIGHT: Part shade to sun
WATER: Above average
SIZE: 8–10 inches
COLOR: Red, pink, white, rose

TOUGHNESS The wax begonia is a continuous flower producer during spring, summer, and fall. In mild years it returns to generate its colorful blossoms once again. The foliage is striking and may be green, bronze, or variegated. The waxy coating imparts good drought tolerance. It is one of the best flowers to plant in shady areas. Many can tolerate full sun, and all are low maintenance.

PLANTING Plant your wax begonias in the spring, after the last frost. The soil should be fertile and organic rich, so amend with 3–4 inches of compost or humus. While preparing the bed incorporate 2 pounds of a slow-release 12-6-6 fertilizer with minor nutrients per 100 square feet of planting area. Space plants 8–12 inches apart. Bronzed-leafed varieties can tolerate full sun. Most other selections thrive in part shade.

GROWING Keep the wax begonias growing vigorously with supplemental water during prolonged dry periods and light monthly feeding of the above fertilizer. Should the foliage become unattractive in late summer, shearing will stimulate new growth and blossoms for fall.

LANDSCAPE USE Wax begonias are perfect for creating pockets of color among evergreen shrubs or using in a tropical garden under large foliage like bananas and elephant ears. Mass planting can create a bold, colorful look while spot planting seldom yields enough flowers to be noticed.

VARIETIES The 'Cocktail' series is among the most popular with 'Brandy' (pink), 'Rum' (white with rose), 'Vodka' (scarlet), 'Gin' (rose), and 'Whisky' (white). The 'Ambassador,' 'Inferno,' and 'Victory' are also industry leaders.

Wax begonias perform from spring through fall with little effort from the gardener.

Begonia (beg-O-nia) x hybrida

'Dragon Wing' Begonia

FAMILY: *Begoniaceae*
ORIGIN: South America
RELATIVES: Wax Begonia
PROPAGATION: Cutting, seed
ZONE: All, perennnial in 9–10
LIGHT: Part shade
WATER: Above average
SIZE: 2–3 feet
COLOR: Red, pink

TOUGHNESS The 'Dragon Wing' has changed begonia growing for most of the gardening public. Large panicles of scarlet or pink blooms cascade downward from lush, glossy, green, angel-winged-shaped foliage. The plants grow with an incredible vigor from spring until frost, making it one of the best buys in annual bedding plants.

PLANTING Select a site in partial shade for a tropical-looking plant. 'Dragon Wing' can be grown in full sun, but the look is entirely different: the plants are more compact and the foliage turns slightly golden with red margins. While this look is entirely acceptable, the part shade appearance is preferred by most. The bed should be fertile and organic rich. Performance suffers greatly in tight, heavy soil, so improving with compost will pave the way for the 'Dragon Wing' to reach 24–36 inches in height with a spread nearing 36–42 inches. Space the plants 12–18 inches apart.

GROWING Feed monthly with light applications of a slow-release 12-6-6 fertilizer containing minor nutrients. Once canes have passed their prime, pruning at the base of the plant will generate new growth. The 'Dragon Wing' also excels in large containers and baskets, adding wonderful color to the porch patio or deck. Containerized plants watered daily will need feeding more often with a diluted water-soluble 20-20-20 fertilizer every other week or controlled-release granules per label recommendation.

LANDSCAPE USE Grow as a mounding border plant with the yellow shrimp plant, or in front of tall plants like gingers, candlestick plants, cannas, bananas, and elephant ears.

VARIETIES The 'Dragon Wing' red was chosen as a Mississippi Medallion winner in 2002. Look also for the pink version.

'Dragon Wing' begonia gives a tropical look to the garden.

Brassica (BRASS-ik-a) oleracea

Kale and Cabbage

FAMILY: *Brassicaceae*
ORIGIN: Western Coastal Europe
RELATIVES: Broccoli, Stock
PROPAGATION: Seed
ZONE: All
LIGHT: Sun
WATER: Average
SIZE: 6–12 inches
COLOR: Grown for foliage—pink,
lavender, maroon, white, green

TOUGHNESS Flowering kale and cabbage produce foliage in brilliant colorful shades of lavender, green, purple, pink, and white from October through April, bringing the winter garden alive. Once acclimated by cool weather, kale and cabbage can withstand temperatures in the mid-teens. The Chicago Botanic Garden has actually seen them survive minus 10 degrees.

PLANTING Select a site in full sun with fertile, organic-rich soil. If planting area is tight, heavy clay, amend with compost or humus to loosen. While preparing the soil incorporate 2 pounds of a slow-release 12-6-6 fertilizer with minor nutrients per 100 square feet. Set out nursery-grown transplants in the fall 12–18 inches apart and add a layer of mulch. In northern regions they can also be planted in early spring.

GROWING Keep kale and cabbage growing vigorously with supplemental water during dry cold periods and light applications of the fertilizer every 4–6 weeks. Should abnormally cold weather be in the forecast, completely cover with a layer of pine straw, removing once temperatures have moderated. The real enemy of flowering kale and cabbage is warm, fall weather followed by horrific cold. Cabbage loopers can be a problem but are easily controlled with the organic insecticide B.t.

LANDSCAPE USE Combine flowering kale and cabbage with other cool-season annuals like pansies, violas, snapdragons, and spring-blooming bulbs like daffodils. Plant two or three varieties boldly next to each other in large informal drifts to make a real impact. Ornamental grasses and fall chrysanthemums make great companion plants.

VARIETIES The 'Chidori,' 'Feather,' 'Ka-mome,' 'Nagoya,' 'Osaka,' 'Pigeon,' and 'Tokyo' series are among the best. Try also 'Redbor' and 'Winterbor' kale as well as 'Red Giant' mustard.

Flowering kale and cabbage excel for winter color, offering foliage in shades of pink, lavender, maroon, and white.

Capsicum (KAP-sik-um) annuum

Ornamental Pepper

FAMILY: *Solanaceae*
ORIGIN: Tropical America
RELATIVES: Angel Trumpets, Eggplant
PROPAGATION: Seed
ZONE: All
LIGHT: Sun to part shade
WATER: Average
SIZE: 4–24 inches
COLOR: Grown for fruit—red, yellow, ivory, purple, orange

Ornamental peppers and flowers make nice partners.

TOUGHNESS Ornamental peppers have reached a new level of popularity, with more than 35 varieties for the landscape. Tough and tropical, the colorful fruit are produced from late spring until frost. Ornamental peppers, many of which are edible, can present a look that is as appealing as any flower in the border.

PLANTING Select a site in full sun for best performance. The soil should be fertile and well drained. Space plants at the recommended distance for the variety. Choose healthy growing transplants with dark green, strong foliage (some new varieties have purple leaves). Yellow leaves and spindly foliage indicate the plant is not thriving and will probably fail in your garden. When planting, place the plant at the same depth it is growing in the container.

GROWING Peppers are heavy feeders. To keep peppers blooming and producing, feed with 2 tablespoons of a 10–20–10 fertilizer per plant at 3–4-week intervals. Diluted water-soluble fertilizer every other week will also work satisfactorily. Keep plants watered and mulched through the long growing season and they will give an unfailing performance.

LANDSCAPE USE Ornamental peppers can make an impressive impact in the flower border. Use purple-leafed varieties like 'Explosive Ember,' 'Black Prince,' or 'Royal Black' with bold yellow or orange marigolds or lantana. Pink flowers like verbenas or coral nymph salvia also make nice companions. The multicolored varieties like 'Medusa,' 'Chili Chili,' 'Explosive Blast,' and 'Treasures Red' look great with yellow or red 'Dreamland' zinnias as well as marigolds.

VARIETIES 'Chili Chili' is a multicolored selection, producing chartreuse, orange, and red peppers all at one time. This 2002 All America Selections winner is not hot! Try 'Medusa,' with peppers that change from ivory to yellow, orange, and crimson as they mature. 'Explosive Ignite' has ivory, green, and orange fruit. Purple-leafed forms are 'Explosive Ember,' 'Black Prince,' and 'Royal Black.'

Catharanthus (ca-thar-AN-thus) roseus

Madagascar Periwinkle

FAMILY: *Apocynaceae*
ORIGIN: Madagascar
RELATIVES: Mandevilla,
Allamanda, Plumeria
PROPAGATION: Seed, cutting
ZONE: All
LIGHT: Sun
WATER: Less than average
SIZE: 1–2 feet
COLOR: Blue, pink, white, red,
lavender, coral, salmon

The Madagascar periwinkle is one of the most loved summer annuals because of its rugged nature.

TOUGHNESS Although tropical in nature, the Madagascar periwinkle has become one of the most loved bedding plants in the United States. If planted at the right time, it is rugged, durable, and able to withstand heat and humidity all summer, while producing a show of color that is hard to beat.

PLANTING Cool soil temperatures are lethal to these wonderful flowers, and many an anxious gardener has planted them too early. Do not plant zone 8 until May 1; wait until May 15 in zone 7. The soil must be very well drained. Before planting, loosen tight soils by amending with 3–4 inches of organic matter, compost, or humus and 2 pounds of slow-release 12-6-6 fertilizer containing minor nutrients per 100 square feet of bed area. Mulching is critical to prevent splashing of water from the ground to stems and leaves. This will lessen your disease pressure.

GROWING Don't overwater! Hand watering with a wand or soaker hose is preferred to overhead irrigation. Side-dress with a light application of fertilizer in midsummer. Maintain a good layer of mulch.

LANDSCAPE USE Mass periwinkles in mixes or with two colors planted in irregular drifts. Use a pocket color in front of evergreen shrubs. Glossy green foliage, coupled with bright cheerful flowers, allows these beauties to work in tropical settings. Plant white periwinkles with mandevillas, or violet selections with allamandas. 'Pacifica Red' looks at home underneath tall banana trees.

VARIETIES The 'Pacifica' and 'Cooler' series are still considered the best, although 'Sunstorm' and 'Victory' have gained positive press in university trials, as has the trailing 'Mediterranean' series. The 'Heatwave' series and 'Blue Pearl' are the only F1 Hybrid periwinkles and are also worth a try.

Celosia (sell-O-sia) argentea

Celosia

FAMILY: *Amaranthaceae*
ORIGIN: Tropics
RELATIVES: Joseph's Coat,
Gomphrena
PROPAGATION: Seed
ZONE: All
LIGHT: Sun
WATER: Less than average
SIZE: 8–36 inches
COLOR: Pink, orange, yellow, red

TOUGHNESS Feathery plumes, cockscombs, or wheatlike flowers are produced from summer through fall, withstanding drought and extreme summer temperatures. Celosia is a valuable source of color in the landscape when summer has flowers looking tired. They are also among the most popular cut flowers for drying and floral arrangements.

PLANTING Wet soggy soils are lethal to celosia, so amend if soil drainage is suspect. Select healthy growing transplants with few buds showing, or direct seed into warm soil. Prior to planting, incorporate 2 pounds of a slow-release 12-6-6 fertilizer with minor nutrients per 100 square feet of bed area. Space plants 10–15 inches apart.

GROWING Celosia is mostly a trouble-free plant. In abnormally wet summers a fungicide application may prove helpful. Side-dress with a light application of fertilizer every 6–8 weeks to keep the plant growing vigorously. To dry for winter arrangements, harvest before seed-set; strip foliage and hang upside down in a cool, dark, well-ventilated place.

LANDSCAPE USE Celosia is not a flower to be spot planted. Mass plant celosia for the most effective landscape display. Plant in combination with other drought-tolerant flowers. The colorful plumelike flowers are showiest in front of a backdrop of green shrubbery. The wheat-formed selections give a light and airy, native prairie look to the landscape. Combine with gomphrena and ornamental grasses.

VARIETIES Popular Crista or cockscomb varieties are the 'Bombay' and 'Chief' series. 'Fireglow' was an All America Selections winner in 1964 and 'Prestige Scarlet,' a multiflora type, was an All America Selections winner in 1997. In the Plumosa group, the 'Castle,' 'Century,' and 'Kimono' series are among the most recognized. 'New Look' was an All America Selections winner and a Georgia Gold Medal winner too. In the Spicata group, 'Flamingo Purple' and 'Pink Candle' are two of the best.

Celosias are terrific in the garden and are superb for cutting and drying.

Cleome (klee-O-mee) hassleriana

Cleome, Spider Flower

FAMILY: *Capparidaceae*
ORIGIN: Paraguay, Argentina, Brazil
RELATIVES: Common Caper
PROPAGATION: Seed
ZONE: All
LIGHT: Sun to part shade
WATER: Less than average
SIZE: 3–6 feet
COLOR: Pink, white, lavender,
violet, rose

TOUGHNESS Tropical-looking colorful flowers with long delicate stamens are produced all summer on plants that are durable in heat and humidity. The spidery blossoms are a delight to hummingbirds and can be used for cut flowers.

PLANTING Select a site in full sun and plant in soil that is fertile and well drained. Nursery-grown transplants have become popular in recent years, giving the gardener choices in color and size. Plant when the soil has warmed, planting at the same depth they were growing in the container. Cleome is also easy to grow from seed, although varieties may be limited.

GROWING Cleomes are drought-tolerant but respond to supplemental irrigation during prolonged dry periods to keep the flowers pristine-looking. Mulch to conserve moisture and keep weed-free. Pruning just before blooming will encourage branching and a bushier plant. One light application of a 5-10-5 fertilizer in midsummer will keep cleomes happy. Saying they reseed may be an understatement. If this poses a problem, remove seedpods as they form.

LANDSCAPE USE The cleome works in any style garden. Combined with mandevillas, allamandas, and bananas to form the tropical look, or salvias and petunias for the cottage garden look.

VARIETIES New varieties in the past few years have dramatically changed cleome growing in the United States. The 'Sparkler' series is a new dwarf bush form with large flowers. The 'Sparkler Blush' was named an All America Selections winner, although all colors are good. From Georgia comes the Athens Select variety 'Linde Armstrong,' tiny and compact by cleome standards, pink, and thornless. This one is super! Try the 'Queen' series and 'Helen Campbell,' a white selection.

The 'Queen' series of cleome comes in an array of colors.

'Sparkler' cleomes are bushy and compact with large flowers.

Blue and white larkspur combine with burgundy hollyhocks for a cottage garden appeal.

Consolida (con-SOL-i-da) ambigua

Larkspur

FAMILY: *Ranunculaceae*
ORIGIN: Mediterranean
RELATIVES: Delphinium, Clematis
PROPAGATION: Seed
ZONE: All
LIGHT: Sun
WATER: Average
SIZE: 1–5 feet
COLOR: Blue, pink, white, some
two-toned

In a world dominated by round flowers, larkspurs give a welcome spiky look.

TOUGHNESS Each spring we see beautiful larkspur blooms in pink, bluish purple, and white on long flowering spikes that inspire the words, "I wish I had those in my garden." Once you get larkspurs started you will have them around for years to come. They reseed quite prolifically, even in the cracks of sidewalks.

PLANTING Growing larkspurs is an issue of timing. To grow beautiful spring larkspurs, plant in the fall. Lightly sow the seeds on top of loosened, well-drained soil and tamp with a garden hoe. The seeds will germinate with the cool rains of fall and form small plants. These tiny plants are not the least bit intrusive, and can be transplanted in late winter or very early spring, if handled with care. Plant them in bold drifts within your flower border.

GROWING Some gardeners frown at thoughts of reseeding annuals, but in the case of the larkspur, it is a blessing. Larkspurs should be thinned to about a 12-inch spacing to allow for best garden performance. With a plant as pretty as the larkspur, the sadness doesn't come with plucking unwanted seedlings but with the end of their bloom. Leave some larkspurs in the garden until seeds have matured for next year's garden.

LANDSCAPE USE The spring bloom of the larkspur gives several great choices for companion plantings. Among the best is 'Early Sunrise' coreopsis, as the bright gold looks exceptional with blue-flowered varieties. Ox-eye daisy, gold or pink yarrow, and hollyhocks also make nice partners for the cottage garden.

VARIETIES Most garden centers have seeds available in their seed racks. They are also available in many catalogs. Look for 'Dwarf Hyacinth Hybrids,' 'Giant Double Hyacinth Hybrids,' and 'Thompson and Morgan Improved Hybrids.'

Cosmos (KOS-mos) bipinnatus

Cosmos

FAMILY: *Asteraceae*
ORIGIN: Mexico
RELATIVES: Rudbeckia, Coreopsis
PROPAGATION: Seed
ZONE: All
LIGHT: Sun
WATER: Less than average
SIZE: 2–4 feet
COLOR: Magenta, rose, pink, white, lilac

'Sensation' cosmos is an All America Selections winner from 1938.

TOUGHNESS It's time to take a stand! Bring back the cosmos! These daisylike flowers, 2–4 inches wide in burgundy, pink, lilac, and white with orange centers, are born on stems of airy fernlike foliage for weeks on end during the growing season. They are so easy to grow from seed, you will want to sow succession plantings to have blooms the entire growing season. Superior flower for cutting!

PLANTING Cosmos are so colorful and effortless to grow, it is a wonder we don't plant them everywhere. Plant seeds or nursery-grown transplants in loose, well-drained planting bed. Fertility need not be high. Seeds germinate in 5–7 days, and you will be cutting bouquets in 8 weeks! Thin seedlings or space transplants 12–36 inches apart, depending on variety. Plant a mid-summer crop too!

GROWING Deadheading old flowers keeps those gorgeous blooms coming. Maintain nitrogen levels on the low side or too much foliage and top growth will be produced at the expense of flowers. The cosmos gives a perennial-like performance by reseeding, although the resulting flower may be different than the parent. Water sparingly but deeply when necessary.

LANDSCAPE USE Plants grow 2–4 feet, so plant to the back of the border. Use in cottage gardens against a white picket fence. Tall forms may need a garden wire to help uphold, or better yet use salvias, such as 'Victoria' blue, indigo spires, or the large blue anise sage to give the support. The spiky flowers of the salvias will combine perfectly with the more rounded cosmos. Try also with cleome.

VARIETIES The 'Sonata' series, a Flueroselect Award Winner, may be the most popular. These are dwarf, 2-foot-tall plants in four colors and a mix. The 'Psyche' series is an old favorite with large 4-inch semi-double blooms on 4½-foot-tall plants. 'Sensation,' an All America Selections Winner from 1938, is still impressive in display gardens thoughout the south. 'Seashells,' 'Early Wonder,' and 'Versailles' are also worthy.

Cosmos (Kos-mos) sulphureus

Sulphur Cosmos

FAMILY: *Asteraceae*
ORIGIN: Mexico, Central America
RELATIVES: Purple Coneflower,
Shasta Daisy
PROPAGATION: Seed
ZONE: All
LIGHT: Sun
WATER: Less than average
SIZE: 1–7 feet
COLOR: Yellow, orange, red

TOUGHNESS Brilliant orange and yellow double, or semidouble flowers are produced prolifically most of the growing season, attracting bees, butterflies, and passersby who gaze at your blossoms. It is not uncommon to see the old-fashioned strains, reaching 6–7 feet by the time fall arrives.

PLANTING Sow seeds or set out nursery-grown transplants in a weed-free, loose, well-drained bed. Seeds germinate quickly and will be blooming in 8 weeks. Thin seedlings or transplants to 12–36 inches depending on variety. Add a good layer of mulch around young plants to help keep in moisture and keep weed free.

GROWING Deadheading old flowers will pay dividends with this plant as it gives the impression of wanting to bloom itself to death. Water the plant deeply during long dry periods and give a mid- to late summer pick-me-up with a light application of a slow-release 12-6-6 fertilizer. Plant a midsummer crop in front or around the current bloomer.

LANDSCAPE USE Although the *Cosmos bipinnatus* is considered the taller of the two species, it is the sulfur that is at the 6- or 7-foot level in September. If you are growing a tall variety, plant at the back of the border. Blue or violet flowers make the best companions. Salvias and angelonias are among the best taller flower partners. 'Blue Daze' evolvulus, 'New Wonder' scaevola, and verbenas like 'Biloxi Blue' or 'Homestead Purple' would be showy planted in front.

VARIETIES 'Bright Lights,' a taller form in orange and yellow, is highly recommended. 'Cosmic Orange,' a 2000 All America Selections Winner, and its counterpart 'Cosmic Yellow' are shorter selections. 'Sunny Red,' an All America Selections winner from 1988, and the yellow version 'Sunny Gold' are excellent dwarf forms but are getting harder to find. The 'Lady Bird' series is also dwarf.

The sulphur cosmos is a prolific bloomer.

Cuphea (KEW-pea) hyssopifolia

Mexican Heather, False Heather

FAMILY: *Lythraceae*
ORIGIN: Mexico, Guatemala
RELATIVES: Crape Myrtle,
Loosestrife
ZONE: All, perennial in (8) 9–10
PROPAGATION: Cutting, seed
LIGHT: Sun to part shade
WATER: Average
SIZE: 6–24 inches
COLOR: Violet, pink, white

TOUGHNESS Incredibly, this small plant never stops blooming, with scores of small lavender, purple, or white flowers. The leaves are glossy green and worthy of a spot in the garden even if the plant didn't bloom. Heat and humidity doesn't faze it, and there are virtually no insect or disease problems with this plant. Mexican heather was very popular in the 1980s and needs widespread planting again. The yellow sulfur butterflies love it.

PLANTING This tough plant is tolerant of poorer soils but not wet feet. If the planting area is heavy, poorly drained soil, improve by amending with 3–4 inches of compost or humus. Plant nursery-grown transplants in full sun to part shade, spacing 8–12 inches apart; then apply a good layer of mulch.

GROWING The Mexican heather is a low-maintenance plant. If growing as a perennial, prune frost-damaged stems back. Feed established plants with a light application of a slow-release, balanced fertilizer in late spring and again in midsummer. In annual plantings, feed in midsummer. Pruning will keep the plant bushier. Cuttings can be easily rooted for over-wintering.

LANDSCAPE USE Any type garden can be made more beautiful with Mexican heather. Plant using informal drifts in front of yellow flowers like lantana, melampodium, or rudbeckia. The glossy leaf texture works well in tropical gardens as small understory plantings to bananas, elephant ears, cannas, bush allamandas, and yellow shrimp plants.

VARIETIES Often sold generically, but look for improved selections like 'Alba' (white), 'Allyson' (pink-purple), 'Lavender' (lavender), and 'Compacta' (dwarf). Try also *C. rosea,* similar to *C. hyssopifolia* 'Lavender Lace' and 'New Light Lavender.'

The lavender-purple flowers of the Mexican heather gently cascade over the wall.

Cuphea (KEW-pea) llavea

Bat-Faced Cuphea

FAMILY: *Lythraceae*
ORIGIN: Mexico
RELATIVES: Crape Myrtle,
Cigar Plant
ZONE: All, perennial in (8) 9–10
PROPAGATION: Cutting, seed
LIGHT: Sun to part shade
WATER: Average
SIZE: 2½–3 feet
COLOR: Red with purple

Children will love the colorful flowers that look like bat faces or purple faces with red mouse ears.

TOUGHNESS Once the heat of summer arrives so does nonstop flower production. The blossoms resemble little bat faces, or purple faces with little scarlet red mouse ears. The stems become slightly woody, arching, and weather tough. These are low-maintenance, drought-tolerant, heat-loving plants.

PLANTING Select a site in full sun and plant in well-drained soil. Set out plants 12 inches apart, planting at the same depth as in the container. Apply a good layer of mulch and water to get established and then enjoy. Your children or grandchildren will love looking at flowers that remind them of Mickey Mouse.

GROWING If growing as a perennial, prune frost-damaged stems back. Feed established plants with a light application of a slow-release, balanced fertilizer in late spring and again in midsummer. In annual plantings, feed in midsummer. Pruning or pinching will keep the plant bushier. Cuttings can be easily rooted for over-wintering.

LANDSCAPE USE Even though the plant reaches 2 feet in height, make sure and place it where children can see it and watch it through the growing season. This is one plant that will get them interested in gardening. Bat-faced cuphea is best used informally. Scarlet 'Dreamland' zinnias make for one of the better combination plantings. Try in front of bright red cannas, in mixed containers.

VARIETIES Bat-faced cuphea is most often sold generically, but 'Georgia Scarlet' and 'Tiny Mice' are well known selections in the industry. Try also *C. x purpurea* 'Firefly,' another good-looking rugged cuphea, with magenta-colored blossoms. This one is an Athen's Select release.

Cuphea (Kew-pea) micropetala

Cigar Plant

FAMILY: *Lythraceae*

ORIGIN: Mexico

RELATIVES: Crape Myrtle, Mexican Heather

ZONE: All, perennial in (8) 9–10

PROPAGATION: Cutting, seed

LIGHT: Sun to part shade

WATER: Average

SIZE: 3–5 feet

COLOR: Red, orange, pink with yellow

Cigar flowers are a delight to the ruby-throated hummingbird.

TOUGHNESS This cuphea is a must for the midsummer-to-fall garden. The plant loads up with 2-inch-large flowers in an exotic combination of reddish-orange, yellow, and green, proving a delight to the darting ruby-throated hummingbird. Heat and humidity don't even cause a pause in its vigorous growth.

PLANTING The number one enemy to having thousands more gardeners enjoying this plant is instant gratification. Most often, when it is for sale, there isn't even a bud, although the foliage is texturally an asset in the garden. Hence, the shopping gardener who may not be familiar with the plant chooses something in bloom, perhaps its cousin the Mexican heather. Buy it and plant it in full sun in well-drained soil. Buy it once and you will be hooked forever. Plant at the same depth it is growing in the container.

GROWING Nothing is difficult about growing this plant other than being patient. By midsummer the rewards begin and by fall your friends and neighbors are jealous. In early summer give it a little pinch and more branching will follow. Feed in midsummer and again in early fall with a light application of a balanced, slow-release fertilizer. The cigar plant is drought-tolerant but watering during long dry periods will pay dividends in the fall.

LANDSCAPE USE Remember, the potential size of the cigar plant is 3–5 feet. Plant in the middle or back of the border. Use in combination with the yellow forms of the firebush *Hamelia patens*. Try also with variegated cannas like 'Bengal Tiger' or 'Tropicanna.' Lantanas like 'Sonset,' 'Patriot Firewagon,' or 'Radiation' make nice companions.

VARIETIES The cigar plant is sold generically, but there are several named varieties of its much smaller cousin, *C. ignea,* often called cigarette plant.

Evolvulus (ee-VOLV-yew-lus) pilosus

'Blue Daze'

FAMILY: *Convolvulaceae*
ORIGIN: South Dakota, Montana to Texas, Arizona
RELATIVES: Morning Glory
PROPAGATION: Cutting
ZONE: All
LIGHT: Sun to part shade
WATER: Average
SIZE: 8–12 inches
COLOR: Light blue

TOUGHNESS This Mississippi Medallion winner proved to the South how resilient it is, flowering from spring through frost without ceasing. The blue shade is most rare in the garden and complemented by the olive gray-green hairy leaves. Although related to the morning glory, the 'Blue Daze' needn't cause fear, as this is a mounding compact plant that is well behaved.

PLANTING The 'Blue Daze' will be in your bed a long time, so give it a proper home. Loosen heavy soil with the addition of 3–4 inches of organic matter such as compost or humus and a pre-plant fertilizer. Apply a slow-release fertilizer such as a 12-6-6 with minor nutrients at a rate of 2 pounds per 100 square feet. Till the soil 6–8 inches deep and you are ready to plant. Set out nursery-grown transplants 12–24 inches apart, planting at the same depth as in the container.

GROWING This is a carefree plant that requires little maintenance. Keep the 'Blue Daze' mulched, with a little supplemental water during dry periods and light applications of fertilizer about 3 times during the growing season. There are no insects or diseases to fight, so enjoy! 'Blue Daze' does over-winter well as a houseplant and can be propagated by cuttings for spring planting.

LANDSCAPE USE The unique blue color of the flowers works well with oranges like 'Profusion Orange' zinnia, or pink flowers such as petunias, verbenas, or salvias. The leaf color and flower color both work very well with purple heart, *Tradescantia pallida*. The 'Blue Daze' is a perfect filler plant in large mixed containers and looks nice in hanging baskets.

VARIETIES 'Blue Daze' continues to be the leading variety; 'Hawaiian Blue Eyes' is another very good selection.

The icy blue flowers of 'Blue Daze' are most welcome in the summer garden.

Gomphrena (gom-FREE-na) globosa

Globe Amaranth, Bachelor's Button

FAMILY: *Amaranthaceae*
ORIGIN: Panama, Guatemala
RELATIVES: Joseph's Coat
PROPAGATION: Seed
ZONE: All
LIGHT: Sun to part shade
WATER: Less than average
SIZE: 9–24 inches
COLOR: Red, purple, pink, white, rose

'Gnome' gomphrenas are dwarf and compact.

TOUGHNESS Most gardeners don't realize the gomphrena is such a staunch performer in the flower border, nor do they realize how beautiful and bold the colors can be in companion plantings. The gomphrena could be the poster picture for tough plants. Few pests, drought tolerance, and blooms until frost are just a few of its outstanding traits.

PLANTING Plant nursery transplants in fertile, well-drained, warm spring soil or anytime in the summer. Incorporate 2 pounds of a slow-release 12-6-6 fertilizer with minor nutrients per 100 square feet of bed space. Space plants 6–12 inches apart, depending on variety selected. Plant at the same depth as in the container. Gomphrena can be grown from seed for transplanting later or directly sown into the bed. Germination usually takes about 20 days, which makes most of us willing to buy transplants.

GROWING Keep the gomphrena mulched to conserve moisture. Although it is drought-tolerant, give it supplemental water during dry periods. Deadhead flowers as needed to keep more blooms coming. Feed with light applications of the fertilizer about 6–8 weeks apart in the summer. Gomphrenas are excellent for cut flowers or dried flowers for winter bouquets, and the colorful balls make a wonderful addition to potpourri dishes.

LANDSCAPE USE The gomphrena comes in several colors. The purple forms are ideal in combination with yellow flowers like lantana, melampodium, and rudbeckia. All colors work well with purple heart, *Tradescantia pallida,* which is an equally tough plant. Use pink, lavender, or rose-colored varieties with burgundy-leafed coleus, 'Blackie' sweet potato, 'Coral Nymph' salvia, or purple coneflower.

VARIETIES Gomphrena is still often sold generically by color. 'All Around' is a new, tall, purple variety that looks very impressive. The 'Gnome' series is dwarf and offers 3 colors and a mix. *G. haagena* selections 'Lavender Lady' (lavender) and 'Strawberry Fields' (red) are also popular.

Hamelia (ham-EE-lia) patens

Firebush

FAMILY: *Rubiaceae*
ORIGIN: Florida, West Indies, Mexico
RELATIVES: Gardenia, Ixora
PROPAGATION: Cutting, seed
ZONE: All, perennial in 9–10
LIGHT: Sun
WATER: Less than average
SIZE: 18–30 inches to 20 feet in frost-free areas
COLOR: Orange-red, yellow-orange

The tubular flowers of the firebush are loved by hummingbirds.

TOUGHNESS The firebush received the Texas Superstar award and the Florida Plant of the Year award. It blooms all season, producing terminal clusters of orange to yellow blossoms, attracting hummingbirds, and enhancing the landscape. The firebush is drought-tolerant once established and is virtually pest-free. Blood-red fall foliage only adds to its attributes.

PLANTING Select a site in full sun with well-drained soil. Before planting incorporate 2 pounds of a slow-release 12-6-6 fertilizer per 100 square feet of planting area. Set out nursery-grown transplants in late spring through summer, planting at the same depth they were growing in the container. Space plants 2–3 feet apart.

GROWING Keep the firebush mulched to conserve moisture and keep weed-free. Shearing occasionally will keep flowers producing through fall. Feed with the slow-release fertilizer every 6–8 weeks during the growing season. In southern areas of zone 8 apply extra mulch going into winter to enhance the chances of a spring return.

LANDSCAPE USE Use in a hummingbird garden with the cigar plant *Cuphea micropetala,* orange mountain sage *Salvia regla,* forsythia sage *Salva madrensis,* and lantanas in the orange and yellow shades. The firebush also works extraordinarily well in a tropical-looking garden with bananas and cannas like 'Tropicanna' and 'Wyoming.'

VARIETIES The firebush is mostly sold generically, although 'Compacta,' a dwarf selection, and 'Africans,' with yellow orange flowers, are occasionally seen.

Impatiens (im-PAY-shiens) walleriana

'Mosaic' impatiens

Impatiens

FAMILY: *Balsaminaceae*
ORIGIN: East Africa
RELATIVES: Touch-Me-Not
PROPAGATION: Seed, cutting
ZONE: All
LIGHT: Part shade to shade
WATER: Average to above average
SIZE: 8–24 inches
COLOR: Several shades and
patterned blends

TOUGHNESS When someone asks what flower they can plant in the shade, the first answer is, unequivocally, impatiens. Some may not consider toughness a virtue of impatiens, but consider that they bloom from late April or May through the first frost. This means in an average year they will bloom about 210 days, and longer on the coast. There are not very many flowers that you can say that about.

PLANTING Impatiens do best in part shade or full shade in a soil that is organic-rich, fertile, and well drained. Not everyone has such wonderful soil. Composted pine bark and humus mixtures are available at garden centers everywhere; these mixtures can improve the native soil or give the option to plant on raised beds, which is becoming the norm in commercial landscaping. When tilling in the organic matter, incorporate 2 pounds of a slow-release fertilizer per 100 square feet of bed space. An all-purpose blend like a 12-6-6 with minor nutrients is ideal. Space the impatiens 8–12 inches apart or at the spacing recommended for the variety. Plant at the same depth as in the container. Then apply a good layer of mulch.

GROWING Impatiens' needs are fairly simple. Keep them watered and fed with light applications of fertilizer every 4–6 weeks through the growing season. If they get leggy in midsummer, cut back to about six inches, and they will quickly revive, producing more foliage and flowers. Taking care of them during July and August pays with a fall display that usually can compete with the beauty of the spring azalea bloom.

LANDSCAPE USE Impatiens give the best show of color in the shade garden. Use with caladiums that have similar colors. Plant in front of gingers and in combination with hostas and ferns. Try lilac or fuchsia impatiens with lime green coleus like 'Lemon Twist.'

VARIETIES The choices of impatiens are almost mind-boggling. 'Accent' (14–16 inches), 'Cajun' (12–15 inches), 'Dazzler' (12–16 inches), 'Showstopper' (20–24 inches), 'Super Elfin' (12–15 inches), and 'Tempo' (20–24 inches) series are all very good. There are several patterned series like 'Mosaic' (12–16 inches), 'Swirl' (12–16 inches), and 'Stardust' (12–16 inches). There are dwarf or miniature series like 'Firefly' (8–10 inches), 'Little Lizzy' (8–10 inches), and 'Pixie' (8–10 inches). Rose-form or double impatiens are much improved with the 'Cameo' (20–24 inches), 'Fiesta' (20–24 inches), and 'Tioga' (20–24 inches) series.

'Super Elfin' impatiens

'Fiesta' double impatiens

Ornamental sweet potatoes are great cascading over a wall.

Ipomoea (eye-po-MEE-a) batatas

Ornamental Sweet Potato

FAMILY: *Convolvulaceae*
ORIGIN: Tropical America
RELATIVES: Morning Glory
PROPAGATION: Seed, cutting
ZONE: All, perennnial in 9–10
LIGHT: Sun
WATER: Average
SIZE: 6–8 inches
COLOR: Grown for foliage—lime green, purple, rust, variegation

TOUGHNESS If you had told most garden center managers in the early 1990s that they would be selling hundreds or perhaps thousands of sweet potatoes for the landscape each year, they would have laughed hysterically. Now they are laughing all the way to the bank, as the ornamental sweet potato has become a tremendous success story in just a few short years. Why? It is because they bring color and pizzazz to the landscape the entire season and cover space almost as quickly as kudzu. Other than an insect or two, the ornamental sweet potato is foolproof.

PLANTING Select a site in full sun, although a little afternoon shade is quite acceptable. A farmer will tell you the sweet potato likes fertile, well-drained soil. In the landscape it does too, and this usually means amending with 3–4 inches of organic matter. Incorporate 2 pounds of a slow-release 12-6-6 fertilizer per 100 square feet of bed space while preparing the bed. Plant nursery-grown transplants at the same depth as in the container, spacing 24–48 inches apart, depending on variety.

GROWING Give supplemental water during the long growing season. Flea beetles are known to make them unsightly, so treat with a recommended insecticide at the first sight of damage. Prune as needed to keep contained to their allotted space.

LANDSCAPE USE The ornamental sweet potato is the best annual groundcover today. The different colors intermingle for an effective display. They are unbeatable for cascading over walls and are easily capable of hanging down 8–10 feet, if needed. Grow in mixed containers and baskets too. Combine them with coleus or cannas.

VARIETIES 'Blackie' (purple, deep lobes), 'Black Heart' (purple, heart-shaped leaves), and 'Margarita' (lime green, heart-shaped leaves) have been among the most common. 'Sweet Caroline' is a new series with rust, lime green, bright green, and purple, all with deep lobes. 'Pink Frost' is not as vigorous, but it is still outstanding (3-lobed leaves in variegated pink, green, and white).

'Sweet Caroline' rust

*Melampodium
(mel-am-PO-dee-um) paludosum*

Melampodium, Butter Daisy

FAMILY: *Asteraceae*
ORIGIN: Mexico, North America
RELATIVES: Rudbeckia
PROPAGATION: Seed
ZONE: All
LIGHT: Sun
WATER: Less than average
SIZE: 9–36 inches
COLOR: Yellow, orange

TOUGHNESS The melampodium, a Mississippi Medallion winner, is the ideal beginner plant. Small, bright yellow daisies bloom from spring through frost. The plant is self-cleaning, needing no deadheading, and thrives in the heat and humidity of summer as long as the soil is well drained. And—surprise!—there is an added bonus! Although the plant is an annual, it gives a perennial-like performance by reseeding. Next spring pluck the ones you don't want and give them to me.

PLANTING Select a site in full sun and plant in fertile, well-drained soil. If this doesn't describe your bed, amend with 3–4 inches of organic matter like compost or humus and till to a depth of 6–8 inches. While tilling incorporate 2 pounds of a slow-release fertilizer per 100 square feet of bed space. A 12-6-6 blend containing minor nutrients would be a good selection. Space the melampodium transplants 8–16 inches apart, depending on the variety. Plant at the same depth as in the container. Apply a good layer of mulch after planting.

GROWING Feed with a light application of fertilizer a month after transplanting and again in midsummer. Although the plant is drought-tolerant, a deep soaking during prolonged dry spells will maintain the appearance and vigor. In the spring, when volunteer seedlings emerge, thin to the proper spacing.

LANDSCAPE USE The bright yellow flowers combine wonderfully with violet to purple. Use with 'Purple Wave' petunias, 'Black Knight' buddleia, or 'Homestead Purple' verbena. Red flowers also work well with melampodium. Try 'Dreamland Scarlet' zinnias, or use in front of the Turk's cap hibiscus. Grow them in front of ornamental grasses.

VARIETIES 'Derby' (8–10 inches), 'Million Gold' (8–10 inches), and 'Lemon Delight' (light yellow 8–10 inches) are the leading compact varieties. 'Showstar' (24–30 inches) and 'Medallion' (36 inches) are choice taller selections.

'Million Gold' melampodium

Pachystachys (pak-ISS-tak-iss) lutea

Yellow Shrimp Plant

FAMILY: *Acanthaceae*
ORIGIN: Peru
RELATIVES: Ruellia
PROPAGATION: Cutting
ZONE: All, perennial in (9) 10–11
LIGHT: Part shade
WATER: Average
SIZE: 3–6 feet
COLOR: Yellow

The white flowers protruding from the yellow bracts are loved by hummingbirds.

TOUGHNESS This is the first tropical plant to win the Mississippi Medallion award. Dark green leaves serve as the perfect contrast for bright yellow 5–6-inch spikes of bracts. From the yellow bracts emerge white flowers that are irresistible to the ruby-throated hummingbird. The yellow shrimp plant, sold usually in bloom in the late spring, blooms profusely until the first freeze of the fall.

PLANTING The yellow shrimp plant prefers fertile organic-rich beds with morning sun and afternoon shade. Amend the soil with 3–4 inches of organic matter like compost or humus and till to a depth of 8–10 inches. While preparing the soil incorporate 2 pounds of a slow-release 12-6-6 fertilizer per 100 square feet of bed space. Plant the shrimp plants at the same depth as in the container. Water thoroughly and apply a layer of mulch.

GROWING Even after the white flowers are open, the yellow spike of bracts remains attractive for a long period. Once the bract starts to deteriorate, deadhead. Keep the shrimp plant growing vigorously by maintaining moisture and feeding every 4–6 weeks with light applications of the above fertilizer. If growing in containers, feed with a diluted water-soluble 20-20-20 every other week. Cuttings root easily for over-wintering.

LANDSCAPE USE The yellow shrimp plant can be massed for a showy display or grown as the center plant in large containers. Use them with other hummingbird flowers such as violet-colored impatiens, Brazilian sage, and *Salvia van houttei*. Plant underneath upright elephant ears, *Alocasia macrorrhiza*.

VARIETIES The yellow shrimp plant is mostly sold generically, although 'Golden Candle' is a named selection. Try the red shrimp plant, *Justicia brandegeana*.

Pentas (pen-TAS) lanceolata

Pentas

FAMILY: *Rubiaceae*
ORIGIN: Tropical Arabia, East Africa
RELATIVES: Gardenia
PROPAGATION: Seed, cutting
ZONE: All, perennial in 9–11
LIGHT: Sun to part shade
WATER: Average to above average
SIZE: 12–48 inches
COLOR: Red, pink, lavender, cranberry, white, violet

'Butterfly' pentas

TOUGHNESS Butterflies, hummingbirds, and gardeners everywhere love pentas. The deep green, glossy foliage serves as the perfect backdrop to the colorful flower clusters. While we call them pentas, much of the world calls them Egyptian Star Cluster. In fact, the name "pentas" comes from the Latin word for five, because of the five floral petals. These are not only colorful, long-blooming flowers that thrive during the sweltering summers in the South, they are also great in the vase as cut flowers.

PLANTING Choose a site in full sun for best flower production. Prepare the bed by incorporating 3–4 inches of organic matter and till to a depth of 8–10 inches. While tilling, incorporate 2 pounds of a slow-release 12-6-6 fertilizer. The next step may be the most crucial to happiness with your pentas. If your soil is acidic and you grow azaleas, camellias, or blueberries with ease, then add lime to your pentas' planting area. While preparing the soil, add 5 pounds of pelletized lime per 100 square feet in sandy soil or 10 pounds in clay-based soil. This is recommended because pentas prefer a soil pH of 7.

GROWING Feed every 4–6 weeks with a light application of a balanced 8-8-8 fertilizer. Remove old flowers to increase flower production. Keep the plants well watered and mulched through the long growing season. In lower zone 8 and zone 9, apply extra mulch going into winter and they may return in the spring.

LANDSCAPE USE Pentas give a lush tropical look to the garden when planted in front of bananas and upright elephant ears *(Alocasia macrorrhiza)*. In a traditional garden use them in bold drifts in front of evergreen shrubs such as hollies, ligustrums, wax myrtles, or junipers. They are well suited to the garden dedicated to butterflies and hummingbirds.

VARIETIES The 'Butterfly' series (20–24 inches with six colors and a mix) was chosen as a Mississippi Medallion winner. The 'New Look' series (12–15 inches) is another good choice. 'Cranberry Punch' (2–4 feet), 'Nova' (2–3 feet), and 'Pink Profusion' (15–18 inches) are good selections.

Petunia (pet-YEW-nia) integrifolia

Wild Petunia

FAMILY: *Solanaceae*
ORIGIN: Argentina
RELATIVES: Angel Trumpets
PROPAGATION: Cutting
ZONE: Annual all zones, often
returns 7–10
LIGHT: Sun
WATER: Average
SIZE: 12–18 inches
COLOR: Violet

TOUGHNESS This species petunia not only is of great importance in the history of petunia hybridizing but is certainly outstanding itself. The small purple petunias are produced in profusion and without ceasing during the entire season. *Petunia integrifolia* was chosen as a Texas Superstar because it is cold-tolerant, takes heat, and is disease-resistant. It has found the same kind of success throughout the South.

PLANTING Select a site in full sun to part shade. The soil should be fertile, organic-rich, and very well drained. Amend the soil with 3–4 inches of organic matter and till to a depth of 6–8 inches. While you are preparing the bed, incorporate 2 pounds of a slow-release 12-6-6 fertilizer per 100 square feet of bed space. Plant the petunias at the same depth as in the container and space 24–36 inches apart. Water thoroughly and apply a layer of mulch.

GROWING To keep the petunias growing vigorously and in constant bloom, feed with light applications of fertilizer every 4–6 weeks. Pinch or cut back the petunia by as much as 20 percent to generate growth and blooms. Maintain a layer of mulch to keep soil temperatures cooler and prevent rapid loss of moisture through evaporation.

LANDSCAPE USE The *Petunia integrifolia* makes an excellent ground cover and is perfect for window boxes and mixed containers, as well as hanging baskets. The violet color combines wonderfully with rudbeckia, lantana, melampodium, as well as pink verbena, 'Coral Nymph' salvia, and pink angelonia.

VARIETIES The *Petunia integrifolia* is sold generically or by regional names. In Texas it is marketed as 'VIP Petunia' (violet in profusion), in Mississippi it is often sold under the name 'Lake Tiak o'khata Petunia,' and in Alabama it is 'Polly Petunia.'

The wild petunia, *Petunia integrifolia,* is very cold-hardy often surviving winter temperatures.

Petunia (pet-YEW-nia) x hybrida

Petunia

FAMILY: *Solanaceae*
ORIGIN: Tropical South America
RELATIVES: Peppers
PROPAGATION: Cutting, seed
ZONE: All
LIGHT: Sun
WATER: Average
SIZE: 6–30 inches
COLOR: All shades and blends

TOUGHNESS The petunia wasn't a flower that was considered tough until the mid 1990s. This changed with a group called the 'Wave' series. As good as these have been, their larger relatives the 'Tidal Wave' series may have surpassed them. The 'Waves,' 'Easy Waves,' and 'Tidal Waves' now give the gardener a petunia that will probably bloom from spring through frost. Some are showing remarkable cold toler-ance, allowing them to either bloom during the fall and winter or return in the spring. These petunias make this an exciting time to be a gardener.

PLANTING To maximize the potential of your petunia purchase, prepare the soil like commercial landscapers. Amend the native soil with 3–4 inches of organic matter and till to a depth of 6–8 inches. While you are preparing the bed, incorporate 2 pounds of a slow-release 12-6-6 fertilizer per 100 square feet of bed space. Plant the petunias at the same depth as in the container and space as recommended for your variety. Water thoroughly and apply a layer of mulch.

GROWING To keep the petunias growing vigorously and in constant bloom, feed with light applications of fertilizer every 4–6 weeks. Pinch or cut back the petunia to generate growth and blooms. Maintain a layer of mulch to keep soil temperatures cooler and prevent rapid loss of moisture through evaporation.

LANDSCAPE USE Petunias should be massed to create a show that will stop traffic. Use in front of ornamental grasses. Plant boldly, massing petunias of one color with those of another color. Think about the complementary color

'Mini Pastel Pink Supertunia' gives months of color.

'Marco Polo' double petunias cascade over the window planter.

scheme; when looking for companion flowers, remember opposites do attract. 'Purple Wave' petunia with 'New Gold' lantana and 'Blue Wave' petunias with 'Bonanza Gold' marigolds are winning combinations.

VARIETIES The 'Waves' are now offered in three categories. The 'Easy Wave' series is new, and the plants are spreading—but more mounding—reaching 12 inches in height (cherry, pink, shell pink, and white). The original 'Waves' were designated as Mississippi Medallion winners and also include three All America Selections winners and two Flueroselect Gold Medal winners (blue, lavender, misty lilac, pink improved, purple, and rose). The 'Tidal Waves' are larger, reaching 24–30 inches in height when spaced 12 inches apart (cherry, hot pink, silver AAS winner, and purple). Look also for the 'Kahuna,' 'Supertunia,' 'Surfinia,' and 'Suncatcher' series.

'Pink Wave' petunias look exceptional with blue plumbago.

Portulaca (por-tew-LAY-ka) grandiflora

Moss Rose

FAMILY: *Portulacaceae*
ORIGIN: Brazil
RELATIVES: Purslane
PROPAGATION: Cutting, seed
ZONE: All
LIGHT: Sun
WATER: Less than average
SIZE: 6 inches
COLOR: Several shades and blends

'Margarita Cream' moss rose offers an heirloom look to the flower garden.

TOUGHNESS Moss rose is one of the first flowers children fall in love with because of the lush succulent leaves and flowers that are unbelievable in their color and texture. The flowers that are ever so soft yet tough enough for children to sit in posing for pictures are durable for the hottest streets and the driest years.

PLANTING Select healthy, growing transplants and space them 6–8 inches apart in a bed with well-drained soil and full sunlight. Moss rose does not tolerate wet feet or waterlogged soil. Amend tight clay soils with 3–4 inches of organic matter and till to a depth of 8–10 inches. Incorporate a preplant fertilizer at a rate of 2 pounds per 100 square feet of planting area. A fertilizer blend such as a 12-6-6 or 8-8-8 is recommended. Plant at the same depth as in the container, spacing plants 6–8 inches apart.

GROWING Water the plants to get them established and then only sparingly. Once they are established in the bed, they are considered among the top plants for drought-tolerance. Feed with a light application of fertilizer a month after transplanting, and again in 4–6 weeks. A light shearing in midsummer will generate more growth and blooms.

LANDSCAPE USE Grow with other drought-tolerant plants such as lantana or purple heart. Use in rock gardens or in beds located next to sidewalks or pavement. Mass-planting a single color of moss rose can literally stop traffic with the brilliant color. They are ideal filler plants for mixed containers.

VARIETIES The 'Sundial,' 'Sundance,' and 'Margarita' series are known for large double or rose form flowers that stay open longer into the day. *P. oleracea* 'Yubi,' a Texas Superstar winner, and the bicolored 'Duet' series are single-petaled flowers with brilliant colors that are almost iridescent.

Ricinus (RISS-in-us) communis

Castor Bean

FAMILY: *Euphorbiaceae*
ORIGIN: Northeast Africa,
Middle East
RELATIVES: Copper Plant,
Poinsettia
PROPAGATION: Seed
ZONES: All, perennial in (8) 9–11
LIGHT: Sun
WATER: Average
SIZE: 5–15 feet
COLOR: Grown for foliage—red,
bronze, brown, burgundy

Huge colorful palmate leaves of the castor bean give a tropical appearance in the lanscape.

TOUGHNESS The castor bean is an old heirloom plant that produces huge colorful palmate leaves, giving the landscape the look of the tropics. It is treated as an annual in most locations but can put on astounding growth, reaching 8–10 feet in just one season from seed. Red stems and burrlike seedpods are equally attractive.

PLANTING Before planting, know that the castor bean is poisonous if eaten and the seeds are considered deadly. The castor bean is extremely easy to grow. Select a site in full sun with fertile, well-drained soil. Plant nursery-grown transplants at the same depth as in the container, spacing 4–6 feet apart. Apply a layer of mulch after planting.

GROWING If growing as a perennial, remove frost-damaged foliage in the fall and add extra mulch. It often resprouts in zones 8 and 9 but grows so fast from seed that an annual planting may be the best option. Growth is usually vigorous enough to skip fertilization. If needed, feed with a light application of a slow-release 12-6-6 fertilizer a month after transplanting and again in midsummer. To prevent the development of

the poisonous seeds pinch either the flowers or immature seedpods and discard.

LANDSCAPE USE The castor bean makes an ideal specimen grown in combination with cannas, buddleias, bananas, elephant ears, or the bird-of-paradise bush, *Caesalpinia gilliesii*. The foliage has the ability to transform the perennial garden into a Jamaica garden.

VARIETIES The castor bean is often sold generically, by transplants, or by seed. Named selections are 'Black Beauty' (dark brown leaves turning green), 'Coccineus' (bronze), 'Impala' (maroon), 'Red Spire' (stems red, leaves bronze), 'Sanguineus' (deep red), and 'Scarlet Queen' (burgundy).

Rudbeckia (rood-BEK-ia) hirta

Black-eyed Susan, Gloriosa Daisy

FAMILY: *Asteraceae*
ORIGIN: Central United States
RELATIVES: Ox-eye Daisy
PROPAGATION: Seed
ZONE: All
LIGHT: Sun to part shade
WATER: Average
SIZE: 1–4 feet depending on variety
COLOR: Yellow, orange, burgundy

Gloriosa daisies make great cut flowers.

TOUGHNESS The gloriosa daisy is normally considered an annual, although they do return occasionally. Reseeding is likely to occur, however, giving a perennial-like performance. During the summer growing season this will no doubt be the prettiest plant in the garden with brilliant golden yellow blossoms that may be larger than softballs, as in the variety 'Indian Summer' or 'Prairie Sun.'

PLANTING Gloriosa daisies perform with breathtaking beauty if planted in fertile, well-drained soils in full sun. Amend tight soil with 3–4 inches of organic matter, and till to a depth of 6–8 inches, adding 2 pounds of a slow-release fertilizer per 100 square feet of bed space. A 12-6-6 or a balanced 8-8-8 blend with minor nutrients included is a good choice. Space 18–24 inches apart, planting at the same depth as in the container, or grow from seed. Apply a layer of mulch after planting or when seedlings are 6–8 inches tall.

GROWING Deadhead spent flower stalks to keep the plant tidy, increase production, and eliminate a potential site for disease. Keep well watered and fed with frequent light applications of fertilizer. Although considered an annual or biennial, it will often reseed if some seeds are left toward the end of the season. The resulting seedlings will most likely not be true to type but will be attractive nonetheless.

LANDSCAPE USE Don't let the thought of this being annual disturb you. Its beauty is as though it were created for the perennial border. The softball-sized flowers look even better when combined with spiky blue or violet flowers from salvias, angelonias, or veronicas like 'Sunny Border Blue.' Saturated red flowers from zinnias or annual salvias also combine well.

VARIETIES 'Indian Summer' produces 6–9-inch flowers on 18-inch stems. This was an All America Selections winner, an American Society of Specialty Cut Flower Growers flower of the year, and a Mississippi Medallion award winner, and was surely awarded elsewhere. 'Green Eyes' and 'Irish Eyes' have green disks or centers. 'Sonora,' 20 inches tall, has a dark mahogany inner ring. 'Toto,' 10 inches tall, is regarded as the best dwarf form. 'Prairie Sun,' the most recent All America Selections winner, produces 5-inch blooms with green eyes, circled by yellow-orange with primrose tips.

'Indian Summer' yields extra large flowers.

Salvia (SAL-via) splendens

Scarlet Sage

FAMILY: *Lamiaceae*
ORIGIN: South America
RELATIVES: Coleus, Agastache
PROPAGATION: Division,
cutting, seed
ZONE: All
LIGHT: Sun to part shade
WATER: Average
SIZE: 1–3 feet
COLOR: Red, white, pink, lavender,
coral, yellow, blue, some two-toned

TOUGHNESS The scarlet sage comes in a variety of colors, including two-toned. As you drive through neighborhoods in late spring salvias bring a brilliance of color to the landscape. As you drive through those same neighborhoods in the fall the same salvias are twice as large and even more dazzling. Color from spring through frost means this annual form of salvia is an exceptional buy and ranks as a stalwart performer.

PLANTING The ideal site would be morning sun and afternoon shade. The soil should be very well drained. Plant on raised beds or amend heavy soils with the addition of compost or humus. While preparing the soil incorporate 2 pounds of a slow-release 12-6-6 fertilizer per 100 square feet of planting area. Space the plants 10–12 inches apart, planting at the same depth as in the container.

GROWING Water deeply once a week, particularly during long dry periods. Mulching rewards the gardener with happier plants by keeping the root zone cooler and the moisture from quickly evaporating. Prune spent flowers to encourage branching and blossoms. Feed a month after planting with a light application of fertilizer and every 6–8 weeks through September.

LANDSCAPE USE For the best landscape impact, plant salvias in mass. The scarlet sage comes in almost any color, including two tones, so it helps to know your color combinations. Try a red variety like 'Vista Red' in front of bush allamanda or with yellow marigolds. Try lavender to purple forms with the two-toned petunias of the same colors. Use underneath cleome of the same color. They are well suited to large mixed containers.

VARIETIES Red forms like 'Vista Red,' 'Red Hot Sally,' 'St. John's Fire,' and 'Flare' are still among the most popular. The 'Salsa' series, which includes red, is popular because of its bicolored varieties. Another that is most unique and beautiful is called 'Sangria' and features white to creamy yellow bracts and a scarlet tube floret.

Annual salvias offer an exceptionally long blooming season.

Scaevola (skay-VO-la) aemula

Fanflower, Scaevola

FAMILY: *Goodeniaceae*
ORIGIN: Australia
RELATIVES: Goodenia
PROPAGATION: Cutting
ZONE: All, perennial in 9–11
LIGHT: Sun to part shade
WATER: Less than average
SIZE: 6–12 inches
COLOR: Blue, purple, pink, white

TOUGHNESS The purple, blue, lavender, or white fan flowers of the scaevola are produced from the instant you plant it in the garden to the first hard freeze. This persevering annual from Australia is versatile enough to grow in a part shade bed with impatiens and caladiums or to be planted by the street, where ground temperatures have escalated off the chart. It has received numerous awards in the South.

PLANTING Select a site in full sun to part shade in a bed that is fertile, organic-rich, and well drained. Amend heavy soils or those poorer drained locations by adding 3–4 inches of organic matter and tilling to a depth of 6–8 inches. Plant nursery-grown transplants at the same depth as in the container, spacing 12–18 inches apart, depending on variety. Apply a layer of mulch after planting.

GROWING Plants in the landscape are very drought-tolerant, but those in containers will need watering daily during the summer. Feed every 4–6 weeks with light applications of fertilizer. Pinch or prune to keep compact and improve branching.

LANDSCAPE USE Planting the scaevola will enhance almost any flower border. It is superior for containers or baskets where the stems are allowed to cascade over the rim. Some of the better companions in the sun are lantana, lysimachia, purple heart, melampodium, and zinnias like the 'Profusion Orange.' In filtered light areas, grow with red impatiens and white caladiums for a patriotic look.

VARIETIES 'New Wonder' scaevola has been given the Georgia Gold Medal, Louisiana Select, Mississippi Medallion, and Texas Superstar award. Others to try are the 'Sapphire Blue' and the 'Outback' series, which features several colors.

'New Wonder' scaevola, the purple fan flower from Australia, is the most awarded flower in the South.

Senecio (sen-EE-sio) cineraria

Dusty Miller

FAMILY: *Asteraceae*
ORIGIN: Italy
RELATIVES: Yarrow, Artemisia
PROPAGATION: Seeds, cutting
ZONE: Mostly treated as
an annual; perennial in 7–10
LIGHT: Sun to part shade
WATER: Less than average
SIZE: 1–3 feet
COLOR: Grown for silver-gray foliage

TOUGHNESS The striking gray foliage of the dusty miller stands out in the world dominated by dark green foliage. The leaves are white to gray and appear as if coated with velvet. This Mediterranean plant is low-maintenance and can endure summer's heat and drought conditions.

PLANTING The soil must drain freely. Plant on raised beds or amend the planting area with 3–4 inches of organic matter to improve drainage. While tilling soil, incorporate 2 pounds of a 5-10-5 fertilizer per 100 square feet of bed space. If planting seed, do not cover with soil but lightly tamp. Seeds will germinate in 7–21 days. Nursery-grown transplants are easier. Space plants 6–8 inches apart. Apply only a thin layer of mulch after planting.

GROWING These are drought-tolerant plants. Water the transplants to get them established and then only sparingly or during prolonged dry periods. Golden yellow flowers appear in summer, although they are not really considered an asset. Prune back during or after blooming to stimulate new growth.

LANDSCAPE USE This is a wonderful companion used as a border plant with other drought-tolerant selections like gomphrena, salvias, purple heart, pink lantanas, and yarrow. Use for spot planting with sweeping beds of petunias, sweet alyssum, and dianthus. Plant dusty miller with 'Fragrant Delight' heliotrope for a bed that will be worthy of a photograph.

VARIETIES To say that dusty miller can be confusing is a gross understatement. In addition to *Senecio,* consider also that *Centaurea, Artemisia,* and even *Tanacetum* species are also called dusty miller. 'Cirrus,' 'Silverdust,' 'Silver Feather,' and 'Silver Queen' are popular selections of dusty miller under the genus *Senecio.*

Dusty miller stands out in this garden where it is surrounded by sweet alyssum.

Senna (SEN-na) alata

Candlestick

FAMILY: *Fabaceae*
ORIGIN: Tropical America, Africa, Southeast Asia
RELATIVES: Hyacinth bean
PROPAGATION: Seed
ZONE: All, perennial in 10
LIGHT: Sun
WATER: Average to less than average
SIZE: 8–12 feet
COLOR: Yellow

Tall candlestick plants topped by yellow blossoms can make the late summer garden look like the West Indies.

TOUGHNESS Bright yellow blossoms are borne in candelabra spike-like fashion and accompanied by large compound leaves that also offer added landscape interest. The spring-planted candlestick reaches 8–12 feet in height and is eye-catching when in bloom. This tropical is drought-tolerant and weather-tough.

PLANTING Select a site in full sun with fertile, well-drained soil. Plant nursery-grown transplants at the same depth as in the container, spacing 4–6 feet apart. If planting by seed, sow in containers for transplanting later. Transplant to the garden once the seedlings have reached 10–12 inches tall. Remember the plants will reach 8–12 feet high.

GROWING Feed the candlestick plants monthly during the growing season with a complete and balanced fertilizer to encourage them to reach that 8-foot-high and -wide stature. Even though they are considered drought-tolerant plants, keep them watered during prolonged dry periods and maintain a good layer of mulch. Harvest mature seeds in the fall and save for spring planting.

LANDSCAPE USE Plant two or three candlestick plants in front of large bananas. In front of the candlesticks use several tropical hibiscus or brightly variegated coleus, such as 'Solar Sunrise,' 'Solar Eclipse,' or 'Mississippi Summer.' Grow also with the royal purple princess flower, *Tibouchina urvilleana.*

VARIETIES The candlestick plant, *Senna alata,* is often sold by the old name *Cassia alata.* There are no named selections of the candlestick plant. The wild senna, *Senna marilandica,* is often grown in native perennial gardens. It reaches 4–6 feet in height and bears brownish-yellow flowers in late summer. It is perennial in zones 4–9.

*Solenostemon
(sol-en-OST-emon) scutellariodes*

Coleus

FAMILY: *Lamiaceae*
ORIGIN: Malaysia, Southeast Africa
RELATIVES: Salvia, Mint
PROPAGATION: Cutting, seed
ZONE: All
LIGHT: Sun to shade determined
by variety
WATER: Average to above average
SIZE: 1–3 feet
COLOR: Grown for variegated foliage

Coleus works well in the tropical garden.

TOUGHNESS Since the early 1990s the coleus has gone from an obscure plant to one of unprecedented popularity. The colors are richer and more highly variegated, and many varieties are now able to withstand full sun all growing season. New vegetatively produced varieties of coleus are resistant to blooming, thereby providing nonstop vibrant, colorful foliage from spring until frost.

PLANTING Coleus prefers fertile, organic-rich, well-drained soil. Amend tight, heavy soil with 3–4 inches of organic matter, tilling to a depth of 6–8 inches. It pays to know your varieties, as some can thrive in full sun while others will need mostly shade. Some are seed-produced and by their nature produce flowers, when it is the foliage that is desired. Cutting-produced coleuses are superior. Space plants as recommended per variety purchased.

GROWING Keep the coleus watered and mulched during the growing season. Feed with a light application of a slow-release 12-6-6 fertilizer a month after transplanting and again in mid-summer. Too much nitrogen has been known to cause excessive greening. Pinch in mid- and late summer to keep the plant bushy.

LANDSCAPE USE The coleus is a tropical plant and can certainly give a carnival-like atmosphere to the garden. Grow in the shade garden with ferns, gingers, and hostas. Use in the tropical garden in front of bananas and elephant ears. Use bright red selections with bush allamanda. Try burgundy or maroon varieties with bright gold or yellow flowers such as 'New Gold' lantana and 'Indian Summer' rudbeckia, or with the glistening white Shasta daisy. Most sun coleus varieties also work in shade as well.

VARIETIES Four sun coleuses, all with maroon to burgundy red, have been recognized as award winners in the South. 'Plum Parfait' and 'Burgundy Sun' were chosen as Texas Superstars. 'New Orleans Red,' a Louisiana Select winner, and 'Mississippi Summer,' a Mississippi Medallion winner are equally outstanding. The Solar series, with several variegated selections, is truly outstanding. 'Solar Sunrise' and 'Solar Eclipse' are the most popular. Unique selections like 'Kiwi Fern,' 'Tilt a Whirl,' 'Ducks Foot Red,' and 'Swiss Sunshine' have now become more than a novelty.

'Alabama Sunset' coleus

Use coleus boldly in the flower garden.

Mass-plant marigolds for a traffic-stopping display.

Tagetes (ta-JEE-tees) patula
and *T. erecta*

Marigolds

FAMILY: *Asteraceae*

ORIGIN: Mexico, Guatemala

RELATIVES: Shasta Daisy,
Rudbeckia

PROPAGATION: Seed

ZONE: All

LIGHT: Sun

WATER: Average

SIZE: 6–30 inches

COLOR: Yellow, orange, cream, red,
combinations

Marigolds also come in rusts and reds.

TOUGHNESS If there were a poster child—or, in this case, poster plant—dedicated to the title "Taken for Granted" it would have to be the marigold. Incredibly, marigolds can be planted just about anytime from spring until fall all across the United States and will give what is arguably the showiest color in the landscape, if planted in mass. They are storm troopers in the face of heat and humidity.

PLANTING Fertile, well-drained soil and full sun are all that is needed to make you look like you are the world's garden guru. Well, there might be a couple of other things. First, plant enough to make a real show. One jumbo six pack isn't enough! Marigolds are also easy to direct-seed. The best idea is to buy a healthy, grown transplant, but keep a few seeds around for a fresh mid- to late summer crop. August-planted marigolds can compete with chrysanthemums for fall splendor!

GROWING To keep that flower production at full speed, feed with light applications of a 12-6-6 or balanced fertilizer about every 6 weeks. Deadheading the old flowers will keep them look-ing tidy and the flower production higher. Watering during long dry periods pays with a happier plant, producing more flowers.

LANDSCAPE USE When growing marigolds, remember blue and violet. These are marigold's complementary colors. If you are growing orange to red colors, consider a blue flower as a companion plant. If you are growing marigolds in the yellow range, violet to purple colors may be the best, such as 'Purple Wave' petunia. But don't forget the oranges and yellows also work well together. Marigolds are also great for mixed containers. Try using 'New Wonder' scaevola as a great cascading companion plant and dwarf fountain grass as a taller plant.

VARIETIES French marigolds *(Tagetes patula)* and African marigolds *(Tagetes erecta)* and their hybrids offer power to the flower border. In the French marigold group are French dwarf crested types like 'Aspen,' 'Bonanza,' and the 'Janie' series; French dwarf anemone series such as 'Durango' and 'Troubadour'; and French fully double types, such as the 'Aurora' series. No matter which you choose, the colors are rich and vibrant. Choice African selections are 'Inca,' 'Marvel,' 'Antigua,' and 'Perfection.'

Tecoma (te-CO-ma) stans

Yellow Bells, 'Gold Star' Esperanza

FAMILY: *Bignoniaceae*
ORIGIN: United States, Mexico, Venezuela, Argentina
RELATIVES: Cross-vine
PROPAGATION: Cutting, layering, seed
ZONE: All, perennial in 9–11
LIGHT: Sun
WATER: Average
SIZE: 3–4 feet as an annual, 15–20 feet in frost-free areas
COLOR: Yellow

'Gold Star' esperanza produces flowers from spring through frost.

TOUGHNESS This tropical was chosen as a Texas Superstar, and it performs like it throughout the South. This evergreen shrub produces yellow, bell-shaped flowers from spring through frost, laughing at the full sun heat in July and August. The striking flowers are complemented by dark green, glossy foliage. Butterflies and hummingbirds relish the nectar from the yellow bells.

PLANTING Grow in large containers around the porch, patio, or deck, or plant in fertile, well-drained soil in the tropical garden. Amend heavy, poorly drained soil, with the addition of 3–4 inches of organic matter and till to a depth of 8–10 inches. While preparing the soil, incorporate 2 pounds of a slow-release 12-6-6 fertilizer per 100 square feet of planting area. Dig the planting hole 2–3 times as large as the root ball and plant at the same depth it is growing in the container.

GROWING Feed container-grown plants with a diluted water-soluble 20-20-20 fertilizer every other week or use controlled-release granules as per the formula recommendation, keeping in mind that daily watering and high temperature usually means fertilizing more often. Feed those in the landscape every 4–6 weeks with light applications of the 12-6-6 fertilizer. Remove seedpods as they form to keep flowers producing.

LANDSCAPE USE Use the 'Gold Star' around the pool for the look of the islands. Grow under tall bananas or upright elephant ears. Combine with other hummingbird plants like the Brazilian sage or bog sage. Try in front of dark purple forms of buddleia.

VARIETIES Yellow bells are often sold generically, but the variety name 'Gold Star' esperanza from the Texas Superstar program is spreading across the country.

Viola (VY-o-la) cornuta

Johnny Jump-up, Viola

FAMILY: *Violaceae*
ORIGIN: Pyrenees, Spain
RELATIVES: Violets
PROPAGATION: Seed
ZONE: All
LIGHT: Sun to part shade
WATER: Average
SIZE: 6–12 inches
COLOR: All shades and blends

TOUGHNESS This old-fashioned garden favorite is the wild ancestor of the pansy and is even called wild pansy. Another common name is "hearts ease," which originated in England where the brightly colored flowers spring up in the meadows. They are very cold-tolerant and transplant to the garden with ease. They also last longer into the warm season. Plants will grow 6–8 inches tall and are prolific bloomers that may have dozens of dime-sized flowers at one time.

PLANTING Select a site with full sun or partial shade that has organically rich soil. Before planting your violas prepare the bed. Amend the soil with the addition of 3–4 inches of organic matter and till to a depth of 6–8 inches. Organic matter helps loosen the soil for better water penetration and aeration, leading to good root development. While preparing the soil, incorporate 2 pounds of a slow-release 12-6-6 fertilizer per 100 square feet of bed space. Set out plants 6–8 inches apart, planting at the same depth as in the container.

GROWING Maintain a layer of mulch to keep soil temperatures moderate. Johnny jump-ups are heavy feeders. Feed every 4 weeks with a light application of the fertilizer or every other week with a diluted water-soluble fertilizer like a 20-20-20. Deadheading old flowers encourages more flower production.

LANDSCAPE USE There are colors to suit every palette and color combination. For a really showstopping display, plant a large group of single-colored 24-inch-tall snapdragons such as yellow 'Sonnet' or 'Liberty Classic' to the back of the bed, with a mass of the purple and yellow violas in front. At the time of planting, drop in bulbs of smaller flowered narcissus with the Johnny jump-ups. Use also with flowering kale and cabbage.

VARIETIES The 'Sorbet' series is one of the best and offers 24 colors or blends. Equally impressive is the 'Penny' series with 16 color selections. Try the Mississippi Medallion award-winning 'Panola' series that is now offered in 18 colors and reflects the best of both the pansy and the viola.

This 'Panola' represents the best traits of pansies and violas.

Viola (VY-o-la) x wittrockiana

Pansy

FAMILY: *Violaceae*
ORIGIN: Garden origin 1830s
RELATIVES: Violets
PROPAGATION: Seed
ZONE: All
LIGHT: Sun to part shade
WATER: Average
SIZE: 6–12 inches
COLOR: All shades and blends

'Dynamite Wine Splash'

TOUGHNESS If you call someone a pansy, the term suggests he's wimpy, but this is absolutely not the case with the flower known as the pansy. Throughout the South pansies bloom from fall until May, withstanding bone-chilling temperatures. There are a staggering number of varieties of pansies. In fact, one major seed supplier alone lists 180 varieties and various mixtures. The reason there are so many is simple: the pansy sits on the throne as the most popular fall and winter flower.

PLANTING Select a site with full sun or partial shade that has organically rich soil. Before planting your violas, prepare the bed. Amend the soil with the addition of 3–4 inches of organic matter and till to a depth of 6–8 inches. Organic matter helps loosen the soil for better water penetration and aeration, which leads to good root development. While preparing the soil incorporate 2 pounds of a slow-release 12-6-6 fertilizer per 100 square feet of bed space. Set out plants 6–10 inches apart, planting at the same depth as in the container. Be sure and mulch after planting.

GROWING Pansies are heavy-feeders, something many gardeners don't consider in the winter. Feed every 4 weeks with a light application of fertilizer or every other week with a diluted water-soluble fertilizer like a 20-20-20. Deadheading old flowers encourages more flower production. Cold fronts often have a drying effect on winter flowers and available soil moisture. Maintain moisture and mulch during the winter growing season.

LANDSCAPE USE Your happiness with pansies may very well hinge on how aggressive you are in using them in the landscape. Massing the beds with one color gives the most dramatic impact. Massing the bed, even if a mixture is used, is still far better than spot planting. The South is also ideally suited for spring bulbs, and they make an excellent combination with pansies. When the bulbs emerge in the spring with the large pansy plants, the bed is a sight to behold. Use with flowering kale and cabbage, snapdragons, and dianthus.

VARIETIES New series that are causing the most excitement are the 'Majestic Giants II,' an improvement over the old 'Majestic Giants,' 'Dynamite,' and 'Karma.' 'Ultima,' 'Crown,' 'Crystal Bowl,' 'Delta,' 'Maxim,' and the 'Nature' series are industry leaders. 'Purple Rain,' the first and only mounding, cascading pansy, is also one of the most popular varieties.

Zinnia (ZIN-nia) angustifolia

Narrow-Leaf Zinnia

FAMILY: *Asteraceae*
ORIGIN: Mexico
RELATIVES: Purple Coneflower
PROPAGATION: Seed
ZONE: All
LIGHT: sun
WATER: Average
SIZE: 18–24 inches
COLOR: Yellow, orange, white

TOUGHNESS This is the award-winning zinnia that doesn't get leaf-spotting diseases and blooms from spring through frost. The quarter-sized flowers, produced in abundance, are bright and bold in orange, yellow, and white. They are low-maintenance and self-cleaning, meaning no deadheading.

PLANTING Select a site in full sun with fertile, well-drained soil. These drought-tolerant zinnias cannot survive with wet feet. Prepare the planting area by tilling in 3–4 inches of organic matter along with a slow-release 12-6-6 fertilizer. Incorporate 2 pounds of fertilizer per 100 square feet of planting area. Plant nursery-grown transplants at the same depth as in the container, spacing 10–12 inches apart. Apply a layer of mulch after planting.

GROWING Feed the narrow-leaf zinnia with a light application of fertilizer a month after transplanting and again in midsummer. Shear lightly in late summer to generate more growth and blooms for the fall garden.

LANDSCAPE USE The narrow-leaf zinnia excels in rock gardens and is the perfect complement in the cottage garden. The yellow, orange, and gold selections combine wonderfully with 'Biloxi Blue' verbena, 'Homestead Purple' verbena, 'Dark Knight' caryopteris, and 'Victoria' blue salvia. Use also with 'Blue Wave' petunia. White varieties stand out with burgundy or purple foliage plants like 'Mississippi Summer' or 'Solar Eclipse' coleus and 'Purple Knight' alternanthera.

VARIETIES The narrow-leaf zinnia was chosen as a Mississippi Medallion award winner. 'Crystal White' was chosen as an All America Selections winner and is now joined by 'Crystal Orange' and 'Yellow.' The 'Star' series also offers the same colors.

Narrow-leaf zinnias are self-cleaning, needing no deadheading.

Zinnia (ZIN-nia) elegans

Zinnia

FAMILY: *Asteraceae*
ORIGIN: Mexico
RELATIVES: Purple Coneflower
PROPAGATION: Seed
ZONE: All
LIGHT: Sun
WATER: Average
SIZE: 12–42 inches
COLOR: All shades and blends except blue

TOUGHNESS No annual flower is loved as much as the zinnia. The flowers are brilliant in color, many almost as large as a mum in a homecoming corsage. As a cut flower the zinnia is unsurpassed. If all of that weren't enough, consider that butterflies absolutely adore them. They relish summer heat and will thrive for months. Zinnias are susceptible to leaf-spotting diseases, certain varieties more so than others, so choose your varieties with prudence.

PLANTING Select a site in full sun with fertile, well-drained soil. Zinnias are drought-tolerant but cannot survive with wet feet. Prepare the planting area by tilling in 3–4 inches of organic matter along with a slow-release 12-6-6 fertilizer. Incorporate 2 pounds of the fertilizer per 100 square feet of planting area. Plant nursery-grown transplants at the same depth as in the container, spacing at the recommendation per your variety. Spacing is critically important in zinnia disease prevention, allowing for maximum air circulation around the leaves. These are also among the easiest plants to grow from seed. Try growing succession crops or sowing a midsummer crop for fall. Apply a layer of mulch after planting.

GROWING Feed with a light application of fertilizer a month after transplanting and every 4–6 weeks. It is important to keep the flowers deadheaded. In the cut-flower types once you remove one stem, two more will take its place, hence the need for adequate spacing and fertilization. If you grow roses or tomatoes or any other plant that you do spray with a fungicide, take advantage of the moment and douse the zinnia. Tall cut-flower types can be staked or allowed to fall over. They will still produce tall, upright stems that are attractive in the landscape and produce loads of cut flowers.

LANDSCAPE USE The *Zinnia elegans* offers short varieties perfect for the front of the border and, of course, the giants that look best grown to the middle or back. Try the large dahlia-shaped 'Dreamland' zinnias toward the front, planting with tall elephant ears, cannas, and salvias. The tall cut-flower types look best with something planted in front like lantanas or rudbeckias. Other good companions are buddleias and ornamental grasses.

VARIETIES The 'Dreamland' series, a 2-foot-tall landscape-type zinnia with dahlia-shaped flowers, has proven to be one of the best. Some years leaf spotting is apparent, but for the most part this zinnia is of great value. Other good short landscape zinnia series are 'Peter Pan' and 'Short Stuff.' The 'Benary Giant' series was outstanding in Mississippi trials. The plants reached 39–42 inches tall, produced flowers 4–5 inches in width, and had minimal leaf spots. The American Association of Specialty Cut Flower Growers designated the 'Oklahoma' series as an award winner. The 'Oklahoma' series is tall with 1½–2-inch flowers and was also excellent in Mississippi trials. 'State Fair,' 'Ruffles,' and 'Burpee Mix' (cactus flowers) are other tall selections.

'Eldorado' is one of several colors in the 'Benary Giant' series.

'Scarlet Flame' offers one of the showiest flowers in the 'Benary Giant' series.

'Dreamland' zinnias

Zinnia (ZIN-nia) hybrida

Hybrid Zinnia

FAMILY: *Asteraceae*
ORIGIN: Mexico
RELATIVES: Purple Coneflower
PROPAGATION: Seed
ZONE: All
LIGHT: Sun
WATER: Average
SIZE: 15 inches
COLOR: Orange, pink, white

TOUGHNESS The hybrids known as the 'Profusion' series have put the zinnia back in the mainstream garden of America. All three colors in the series received the All America Selections Gold Medal award and deservedly. The 'Profusion' series is disease-resistant and blooms from spring until frost. The plants form dense, compact mounds and are drought-tolerant. The flowers are only 2 inches wide, but when you have 50 of them on the plant they stand out like beacons.

PLANTING Select a site in full sun with fertile, well-drained soil. They are drought-tolerant but cannot survive with wet feet. Prepare the planting area by tilling in 3–4 inches of organic matter along with a slow-release 12-6-6 fertilizer. Incorporate 2 pounds of the fertilizer per 100 square feet of planting area. Plant nursery-grown transplants at the same depth as in the container, spacing 10–12 inches apart. Apply a layer of mulch after planting.

GROWING Feed with a light application of fertilizer a month after transplanting and every 4–6 weeks through the season. If the shape becomes less than desirable, prune lightly; this will generate more growth and blooming for the fall garden. The 'Profusion' series is also outstanding as a fall crop and loves September and October.

LANDSCAPE USE The 'Profusion' zinnias are 15 by 15 inches and perfect for the front of the border. 'Profusion Orange' is outstanding with 'Dark Knight' caryopteris, 'Victoria' blue salvia, or indigo spires salvia. 'Profusion White' and 'Profusion Cherry' excel with purple- or burgundy-leafed plants, such as purple heart, 'Mississippi Summer' coleus, and 'Purple Knight' alternanthera. Use all of them with ornamental grass, such as 'Purple Majesty,' millet *Pennisetum glaucum,* or purple fountain grass.

VARIETIES The 'Profusion' series is offered in cherry, orange, and white.

'Profusion' zinnias are available in three colors and are among the most disease-resistant.

PERENNIALS
Plants That Persevere

I t seems like only yesterday that garden centers had just a few perennials that took a lot of searching to find. They may or may not have been appealing enough to warrant purchasing. Today the perennial section of the local garden center is as large as the annual one and just as busy with shoppers. The quality and uniformity of the plants is impeccable.

The reasons for this change are simple: perennials are beautiful, fun to grow, and engaging. What first seemed like work with the soil preparation and designing quickly becomes a hobby as the flowers start to bloom. By the second or third year the hobby becomes a passion.

In *Tough-as-Nails Flowers for the South* you will see that perennials can range from the old cottage garden favorites like four-o'-clocks to natives growing at the roadside like the Joe Pye weed. But they may also be new, improved varieties like the lime green 'Sweet Kate' spiderwort or new species of plants like the 'Outback Sunset,' *Lysimachia congestiflora,* being brought to us by modern-day plant explorers.

Some gardeners are mistaken in thinking that a perennial is a plant that thrives for a lifetime without any maintenance. This is not the case, but perennials are easy to care for. The most important rule in selecting a perennial is to make sure it is appropriate for the site you have in mind. Because it is a perennial, it will occupy that space for some time.

Make sure the plant is appropriate for the light requirements, soil type, and hardiness for your area. Consider whether or not it will be a good companion plant in soil, light, and water requirements, as well as color, for flowers that are nearby.

Soil preparation for perennials is about the same as for annuals. Before you ever lift the shovel, consider what your expectations are for the perennials you have purchased. Do you have a vision of what you want that purple coneflower to look like in the third year? Once the goal

Page 61: Old-fashioned yarrow, coreopsis, and larkspurs combine in a cottage garden.

Opposite: The yellow flowers of the threadleaf coreopsis, *Coreopsis verticillata*, give a bold yet airy look to the garden.

is in place, remember that proper soil preparation is essential. Most often gardeners find that making major soil improvement corrections in the second or third year can be virtually impossible without completely redoing the bed.

Designing

Perennials look best when grown in a border, whether they border a fence, wall, or driveway. When planting a border against a fence or wall leave space between it and the taller backdrop plants. This allows for better air circulation, more light penetration and ease of maintenance from the rear of the bed.

Island beds in the middle of the lawn have become very popular as they allow for viewing from all sides. In these types of beds, the taller plants are used in the middle and layered downward to the perimeter. The island bed normally requires a little more effort to keep it looking attractive since it can be viewed from so many angles.

When creating the perennial border, plant in large, bold, informal drifts of color. In other words, plant in groups rather than spot planting. In addition to considering the colors, group differing textures or shapes of flowers. For instance, the large blooms of daylilies combine wonderfully with the spiky blossoms of salvias. The coarse-textured foliage of cannas or irises add interest to the garden.

A mixed border of annuals, perennials, and woody evergreens is one of the best styles for gardeners in urban neighborhoods. Woody evergreens like hollies serve as the foundation of the border. Green is the most important color in the winter landscape. Very few perennials bloom for the entire summer, and annuals can give quick, immediate, and long-lasting color as perennials come and go with their bloom.

Planting and Maintenance

As you read this book the importance of planting at the correct depth will become quite apparent. Set perennial plants in their permanent home so their roots are completely covered with the prepared soil, but avoid burying the stem or the crown. Place container-grown plants at the same depth they were grown; place dormant plants at the depth at which they grew the previous season. To encourage side root growth, make the planting hole twice as wide as the root ball. With bare-root perennials, spread the roots outward as well as downward. For container-grown plants, loosen encircled roots and shake some of the potting soil into the hole. Do not let the roots dry out during transplanting.

Water the plants thoroughly to force out any air pockets and to settle the soil. Mark and label the plantings. You may not remember where the plants are during the dormant season. Mulch the bed surface with pine straw or bark to keep the soil from drying and crusting, which prevents water and nutrient penetration during the summer. This will also make weeding less of a chore.

If you have tall plants that need staking do so early in the season using wire strands or bamboo canes. The risk of root damage will be greater later on in the season. In the fall, cut the old plant stalks to the ground after the leaves have fallen. Apply an added layer of mulch to protect crowns and roots from the harsh extremes of temperatures in the 60s or 70s one day and the low 20s or teens the next. Before applying the mulch remove any winter weeds that might have germinated.

As you grow perennials you will not only get hooked, you will also treasure the season where you can divide and multiply your plants for other parts of the landscape and to share with friends (save some for me). A general rule of thumb is to divide the perennials during the time opposite their season of bloom. Plants like daylilies, phlox, black-eyed Susans, purple coneflowers, and Shasta daisies are easy to clump divide. Other plants like salvias, lantana, and verbena are easy to root from cuttings for additional plants.

The South has a rich heritage in gardening. You will enjoy seeing these plants our ancestors grew and realize they need to be used again. Then your heart will start pounding when you see the new perennials just brought in from overseas. Whether you have a formal garden, a cottage garden, or the look of the tropics, your garden can't reach its true potential without perennials.

Acanthus (ak-AN-thus) mollis

Bear's Breeches

FAMILY: *Acanthaceae*
ORIGIN: Southern Europe,
Northwest Africa
RELATIVES: Ruellia, Shrimp Plant
PROPAGATION: Division,
root cutting
ZONES: 6–10
LIGHT: Sun to part shade
WATER: Average
SIZE: 3 feet
COLOR: White with purple bracts,
yellow

Bear's breeches offers attractive flowers and foliage.

TOUGHNESS Bear's breeches achieves the tough label for a number of reasons. First it can be slightly invasive, but the 3-foot-tall spikes of white flowers and purple bracts make it all worth it. Do not mishandle the bloom, or you will be greeted painfully with spines. Well after the plant has bloomed the colorful bracts persist. Many believe bear's breeches can't be grown in the South, but we can thanks to the new variety, 'Summer Beauty.' Give it a try!

PLANTING Bear's breeches can be difficult to find, so take advantage of the opportunity when it arises. It is ideally planted in the spring and divided in the fall. Get a start whenever you can because the plant will grow vigorously. Fertile, well-drained soil with morning sun and afternoon shade are the ideal growing conditions for this lush, green plant. Wet, soggy conditions are not tolerated.

GROWING The deep green, glossy, toothed foliage makes this plant an asset in the garden. To maintain the health of the foliage throughout the growing season remove flower spikes after the bloom cycle. Pay attention to remove unwanted suckers that may arise several feet away from the parent. Let the vigor of the plant dictate whether a light application of a slow-released, balanced fertilizer is needed.

LANDSCAPE USE Bear's breeches looks as tropical as any plant in the garden with its 2-foot-long foliage. Use it with ferns, bananas, and umbrella plants for a tropical garden. The purple and blue flower spikes allow it to be wonderfully combined in the perennial garden with purple coneflower, as well as the white flowered ox-eye daisy.

VARIETIES The plant itself can be hard to locate, but look for the golden yellow 'Holland's Lemon' and 'Summer Beauty,' which is known for excellent heat tolerance. Try also the spinier species *A. spinosus,* as well as the 'Spinosissimus,' a hybrid between the two species.

Opposite: *Salvia van houttei* and 'Stella d'Oro' daylily

Achillea (ak-il-EE-a) millefolium and *A. filipendulina*

Yarrow

FAMILY: *Asteraceae*
ORIGIN: Europe to West Asia
RELATIVES: Echinacea, Rudbeckia
PROPAGATION: Division, seed
ZONES: 3–10
LIGHT: Sun
WATER: Less than average
SIZE: 2–4 feet
COLOR: Red, golden yellow, pastels

TOUGHNESS Yarrow is a carefree perennial with heat- and drought-tolerance, providing colorful flowers for cutting and drying. In France it was called carpenter's herb in the belief that it had healing properties when used on the hands of working folks. The leaves have a peppery taste and are used finely chopped in salads; the flowers are used to flavor liqueurs.

PLANTING Yarrow doesn't require the most luxuriant of soils to perform and put on a show but does require good drainage. Plant in full sun for best flower production, and should your drainage be suspect, plant on raised beds.

While preparing the bed incorporate a pound of a 5-10-5 fertilizer per 100 square feet of bed space. Plant boldly in drifts 18–24 inches apart or as recommended per your selection. This may mean planting to the middle or back of the border. Yarrow is also easy to grow from seed.

GROWING After spring bloom, cut stalks down to the ground to encourage new growth and another bloom. For dried flowers, harvest while still in bloom and before browning. Hang upside down in a well-ventilated room until dry.

Yarrow is a prolific spreader, an attribute loved by most gardeners. Pluck unwanted plants and deadhead before flowers have a chance to reseed. If you want to divide, do so in the fall.

LANDSCAPE USE Use yellow yarrow as a buffer between ox-eye or Shasta daisies and verbenas. Try combining with Russian sage *(Perovskia)*, perennial blue salvias, or the old-fashioned larkspur. They also work well with drought-tolerant plants like lantana and gomphrena. The gray to green leaves with a fernlike texture are an added asset in the garden.

VARIETIES 'Fire King,' 'Debutante,' 'Summer Pastels' (AAS winner), and 'Cerise Queen' with its cherry-red blooms are among the most popular. 'Coronation Gold' is a superior variety of *A. filipendulina.*

'Coronation Gold' yarrow with the French hollyhock is a winning combination.

Agastache (a-GAH-sta-kee) foeniculum
and *A. urticifolia*

Anise Hyssop

FAMILY: *Lamiaceae*
ORIGIN: North America, China,
Japan
RELATIVES: Salvia, Coleus
PROPAGATION: Seed
ZONES: 5–9
LIGHT: Sun
WATER: Less than average
SIZE: 20–36 inches
COLOR: Lavender-blue, white

'Honey Bee Blue' anise hyssop and 'Bonanza' marigold make nice companions.

TOUGHNESS Anise hyssop is a rugged, drought-tolerant plant, giving months of colorful licorice to mint-scented, salvia-like blue flowers. Low maintenance plants producing an abundance of flowers are great for cutting and drying. These attributes make this popular herb the rage in perennial gardens too.

PLANTING Select a site in full sun for best flower production and to keep plants compact. Soil should be fertile and well drained. Wet feet will spell doom for the anise hyssop during the winter, so incorporate organic matter to loosen soil or plant on raised beds. Plants are easy to grow from seeds that germinate in 7–14 days. Bountiful bouquets of blooms will be produced the first year. Set out transplants in the spring 12–18 inches apart, or thin seedlings to spacing per variety recommendation.

GROWING Though this plant is drought-tolerant, watering during dry periods will pay dividends with added flower production. Feed with a light application of a slow-release, balanced fertilizer when spring growth has resumed. A mid-summer application will keep the plants at peak for the fall. Once freeze damage has occurred, cut back and add a protective layer of mulch.

LANDSCAPE USE Anise hyssop is a great choice for butterfly and nature gardens, enticing bees and butterflies by the dozens. In this type of garden, group anise hyssop as a lower level planting, under buddleias, and in combination with lantanas of all shades. In the flower garden plant boldly in drifts adjacent to gold, yellow, and orange marigolds. Purple heart *(Tradescantia pallida)* and pink shades from petunias or periwinkles also work well.

VARIETIES 'Honey Bee Blue,' a self-cleaning Flueroselect Award Winner, and 'Blue Fortune' are the leading varieties. Try 'Licorice Blue,' 'Licorice White,' 'Honey Bee White,' and 'Alabaster' (white).

Ajuga (aj-OO-ga) reptans

Bugle Weed

FAMILY: *Lamiaceae*
ORIGIN: Europe, Iran, Caucasia
RELATIVES: Salvia, Coleus,
Anise Hyssop
PROPAGATION: Division
ZONES: 3–9
LIGHT: Part shade
WATER: Average
SIZE: 4–12 inches
COLOR: Grown for variegated
foliage—purple, pink, cream, gold;
flowers—blue, pink, white

TOUGHNESS Ajuga is aggressive and persevering, allowing it to be used in a wide variety of soils and light conditions. It quickly spreads by runners, forming a dense mat of colorful foliage, accompanied by showy blue or pink spring flowers.

PLANTING Despite its durability, ajuga does best in fertile, well-drained soil. A site in morning sun and afternoon shade, or high-filtered light, allows ajuga to really look its best, although it is not uncommon to find exceptional plantings in full sun. Nursery-grown plants can be set out anytime during the growing season, with early spring or fall being choice. Space plants 6–12 inches apart.

GROWING Ajuga is very easy to grow. You may find keeping it confined to the designated area to be the biggest challenge. After the spring bloom, deadhead the flowers for a tidy look and to maximize air circulation. This can be accomplished with a string trimmer or mower or by hand pruning. Dividing every 2–3 years will also increase air movement. Reduced air circulation can accentuate crown rot.

LANDSCAPE USE Most often ajuga is used as a groundcover, particularly in areas where grass is shade-challenged. Use as a border; be bold and grow ajuga in a perennial bed. Try combining with plants such as alyssum, bacopa, petunias, and verbenas.

VARIETIES 'Bronze Beauty' (metallic bronze foliage), 'Burgundy Glow' (silvery green and burgundy foliage), 'Catlin's Giant' (large bronze/green leaves), and 'Multicolor' (red, pink, and gold leaves) are just a sampling of around 20 choice selections available.

The marbled foliage of the ajuga makes it an attractive groundcover.

Aquilegia (ak-wil-EE-jia) chrysantha
var. *hinckleyana*

Texas Gold, Columbine

FAMILY: *Ranunculaceae*
ORIGIN: Texas, Southwestern
United States
RELATIVES: Clematis, Helleborus
PROPAGATION: Seed
ZONE: 4–8
LIGHT: Part shade
WATER: Average
SIZE: 18–24 inches
COLOR: Yellow, white

'Texas Gold' is one of the best columbines for the South.

TOUGHNESS The *Aquilegia chrysantha* var. *hinckleyana*, known as 'Texas Gold' columbine, is native to the Big Bend area of Texas and brings the word "durable" to the world of columbines in the South. The golden yellow blossoms brighten the shade garden from late March through May. What makes the plant a real winner is that the scalloped bluish-gray foliage is compact and rounded and a garden asset year-round.

PLANTING Select a site with partial shade under the canopy of large deciduous trees. This allows the plant to get needed sunlight during the cooler months of the winter when the trees have lost their leaves, yet afford protection from intense heat during the summer. The soil should be fertile, organically rich, and well drained. If not, incorporate 3–4 inches of organic matter or plant on raised beds. Prior to planting apply 2 pounds of a slow-release 12-6-6 fertilizer per 100 square feet of bed area. Space plants 18–24 inches apart.

GROWING After the bloom cycle, deadhead flower stalks for a tidy look. Should spider mites or leaf miners make the foliage unattractive in mid- to late summer, use hedge shears or string trimmers and cut back down to a few inches above the crown of the plant. Remove the cut foliage. With fall temperatures, the foliage will heartily return. Feed established plantings with the same blend of fertilizer in October, December, and February.

LANDSCAPE USE Plant the columbine in informal drifts for the best appearance. Blue pansies and violas make exceptional partners for the 'Texas Gold' columbine. Try with the grape hyacinth.

VARIETIES The 'Texas Gold' columbine *Aquilegia chrysantha* var. *hinckleyana* is an award winner under the Texas Superstar program. Look also for other *A. chrysantha* varieties, 'Alba-Plena' (pale yellow tinged with pink), 'Floro Pleno' (yellow), 'Silver Queen' (white), and 'Yellow Queen' (yellow).

Artemisia (ar-tem-IS-ia) arborescens

'Powis Castle'

FAMILY: *Asteraceae*
ORIGIN: Mediterranean
RELATIVES: Yarrow, Echinacea
PROPAGATION: Division
ZONE: 6–8
LIGHT: Sun
WATER: Less than average
SIZE: 3 feet
COLOR: Grown for silver-gray foliage

TOUGHNESS Beautiful, silvery-filigree, evergreen foliage withstands summer temperatures and becomes an eye-catching focal point in the garden. While other cultivars of artemisia melt in the summer, 'Powis Castle' keeps on performing, maintaining a dense, compact shape. 'Powis Castle' and other artemisia are deer-resistant.

PLANTING Select a site in full sun. This Mediterranean native doesn't need luxuriously rich soil, but good drainage is an absolute must. Improve drainage by planting on raised beds or incorporating 3–4 inches of compost or humus into clay soils. Plant nursery-grown 'Powis Castle' in the spring or summer, 18 inches apart. If mulch is used, apply only a thin layer.

GROWING Water to get established, but then only sparingly. Overhead irrigation is not recommended. Mature plants become somewhat woody and may develop a spindly look. If this occurs, cut back in the spring, with the resuming of new growth. Dividing can be done in the fall or early spring.

LANDSCAPE USE The silvery foliage makes a dramatic statement against deep green shrubs like hollies, ligustrums, or junipers. The foliage is handsome in rock gardens and can be grown in combination with purple coneflowers, gomphrena, Shasta daisies, or purple heart. Try with salvias such as 'Victoria' blue or indigo spires.

VARIETIES In addition to 'Powis Castle' try *A. ludoviciana* varieties 'Silver King' and 'Silver Queen' and *A. stellerana* 'Silver Brocade.' The new artemisia hybrid 'Oriental Limelight' with cream and green variegation is an outstanding choice for mixed containers and the landscape too.

Silver foliage of 'Powis Castle' can become a focal point when grown among traditional green foliage.

Asclepias (ass-KLEE-pias) curassavica

Blood Flower, Indian Root

FAMILY: *Asclepiadaceae*
ORIGIN: South America
RELATIVES: Milk Weed, Butterfly Weed
PROPAGATION: Seed, cutting
ZONE: 8–11, reseeding annual elsewhere
LIGHT: Sun
WATER: Average
SIZE: 4–5 feet
COLOR: Red, orange, yellow

The blood flower is attractive to Monarch butterflies and hummingbirds.

TOUGHNESS Bright, bold orange and red flowers attract monarch butterflies like no other plant. The blood flower blooms all summer in the face of intense heat and humidity. After the monarch lays eggs and caterpillars strip the plant, the leaves and flowers magically reappear. In addition to butterflies you'll also notice hummingbirds feasting on the flowers. Although once considered a zone 9 plant, its performance is sur-prising gardeners in colder zones. We see blood flower returning in zone 8 from the roots and at times reseeding. It has been reported even reseeding in zone 7.

PLANTING Select a site in full sun for best blooming. Plants perform best in fertile, organically rich beds that are very well drained. Select healthy, growing nursery transplants in late spring, spacing 12–14 inches apart. Plants are easy to grow from seed.

GROWING Feed with a slow-release, balanced fertilizer in late spring and again in midsummer. Aphids will most likely attack, but resist spraying. Ladybugs and beautiful monarch butterflies will feast on your plants. Your children and grandchildren will love watching the butterflies and their colorful larvae feeding on the plants. Blood flowers make excellent cut flowers when immediately conditioned by placing them in warm water. Some suggest flaming the basal end of the stem.

LANDSCAPE USE The blood flower should be a mainstay in the butterfly garden, combining with buddleia like 'Black Knight,' lantanas like 'Sonset' or 'New Gold,' and 'Homestead Purple' verbenas. Aesthetically speaking the indigo spires *(Salvia farinacea x S. longispicata)* and 'Costa Rica Blue' *(S. guaranitica)* make for showy companion plantings.

VARIETIES Look for 'Red Butterfly' and 'Silky Gold' with gold and yellow flowers, reaching only 30 inches in height. These are often sold generically.

Asclepias (ass-KLEE-pias) tuberosa

Butterfly Weed

FAMILY: *Asclepidaceae*
ORIGIN: United States
RELATIVES: Milk Weed,
Blood Flower
PROPAGATION: Seed, root cutting
ZONE: 3–10
LIGHT: Sun
WATER: Less than average
SIZE: 2 feet
COLOR: Orange, red, yellow

TOUGHNESS This outstanding orange-to-red-flowered native is tough enough to exist on its own in the wild without your help. Once you get it established in your garden it will do the same. The bold, colorful flowers are produced in mid- to late summer and serve as a magnet to monarch butterflies. The butterfly weed is native over a broad area of the United States and is cold-hardy to zone 3.

PLANTING Unfortunately the native version is not as readily available at garden centers as the South American import. Nurseries specializing in natives, however, usually have a good supply, and there are several named selections. Digging from the wild and transplanting is usually not successful due to the long taproot and ultimate harm to natives. You can, however, collect seeds in midsummer, clean, and plant immediately. You might notice plants thriving in the wild under a variety of soil conditions, from sandy to loamy, but drainage is always very good. Make sure it is good in your garden.

GROWING If planting from seed keep evenly moist until germination. Once planted in the garden, water to get established, then water sparingly. Fertilizing isn't normally an issue. If needed, apply a light application of a slow-release, balanced fertilizer to established plantings with the emergence of spring growth. Spring growth is somewhat late, so it pays to mark your planting so as not to disturb by cultivation. Be tolerant of monarch caterpillars feasting on the plants. They will do no ultimate harm.

LANDSCAPE USE Create a butterfly garden, planting in front of buddleias such as 'Empire Blue,' 'Nanho Blue,' or 'Black Knight' for a striking combination. Grow with blue salvias, 'Dark Knight' caryopteris, or 'Biloxi Blue' verbena.

VARIETIES 'Gay Butterflies' (orange, red, and yellow mix), 'Orange Flame' (orange), and 'Vermillion' (red) are the leading selections. Try *A. incarnata*, known as milkweed. Look for 'Ice Ballet' with bright white flowers.

Native butterfly weed is brilliant on the roadside and in the garden too.

Buddleia (BUD-lia) davidii and hybrids

Butterfly Bush

FAMILY: *Loganiaceae*
ORIGIN: China, Japan
RELATIVES: Carolina Jessamine,
Spigelia (Indian Pinks)
PROPAGATION: Cutting
ZONE: 5–9
LIGHT: Sun
WATER: Average
SIZE: 5–10 feet
COLOR: Blue, pink, purple, white,
orange-yellow

Tall butterfly bush and lantana make perfect partners in the butterfly garden.

TOUGHNESS With well-drained soil, the butterfly bush is rock solid, regardless of pH. Many consider the butterfly bush a herbaceous plant. Others consider it a shrub or even a tree. The bright, almost iridescent colors of the 4–12-inch fragrant blooms stand out in the garden. The flowers are among the best nectar sources for butterflies. The unique gray-green foliage also gives an added texture to the garden.

PLANTING Select a site in full sun with a soil that is fertile and well drained. Incorporate 2 pounds of a 5-10-5 fertilizer per 100 square feet of planted area. Plant healthy, nursery-grown transplants in late spring, planting at the same depth as in the container. These are large plants and will need spacing of 4–6 feet.

GROWING Feed in late winter with a light application of a slow-release 12-6-6 fertilizer. Flowers are formed on new growth, so pruning hard in late winter is a common practice to generate good, strong growth. In extreme winters the buddleia may be killed to the ground but will return in the spring. Although drought-tolerant, it needs enough water to keep growing and bloom-ing. Removing spent flowers will keep the plant tidy and will generate more blooms.

LANDSCAPE USE The butterfly bush works perfectly in almost any style garden, butterfly, perennial, cottage, or tropical. For the showiest garden, select companions that are opposite or complementary in color to the buddleia. For instance, use 'New Gold' lantana in front of 'Black Knight' or 'Nanho Purple.' Try 'Samson' lantana (orange) in front of 'Empire Blue.' White-flowered forms such as 'White Bouquet' excel with blue salvia or 'Homestead Purple' verbena.

VARIETIES 'Black Knight' (dark violet), 'Dartmoor' (purple), 'Empire Blue' (blue), 'Pink Delight' (pink), 'Purple Prince' (fragrant violet purple), and 'White Prince' (white) are just a few of the best. Try *B.* 'Lochinch' varieties 'Nanho Alba' (white), 'Nanho Blue' (blue), 'Nanho Purple' (purple), and *B. x weyeriana* variety 'Sungold' (orange-yellow).

Caesalpinia (ceye-sal-PEYE-nia) gilliesii

Bird-of-Paradise

FAMILY: *Fabaceae*
ORIGIN: Argentina, Uruguay
RELATIVES: Mimosa
PROPAGATION: Seed
ZONE: 7–10
LIGHT: Sun
WATER: Less than average
SIZE: 4–8 feet
COLOR: Golden yellow

TOUGHNESS Long, deep red stamens protruding from golden yellow flowers that attract hummingbirds, combined with delicate mimosa-looking foliage, make this a plant all can enjoy. Many references suggest it is a zone 9 or higher plant, but it may be found growing along fence-rows in North Texas. This bird-of-paradise will return from temperatures below zero and survive out west with only the available rainfall.

PLANTING Unfortunately the plant is not readily available, but hope endures. The good news is it is easy to grow from seed, and seeds are readily available through specialty catalogs. Scratch the seed lightly a few times with sandpaper to speed up germination. Sow the seeds in later winter in containers indoors for transplanting later. Plant after the soil has warmed in the spring. Garden soil that is well drained and loamy is ideal.

GROWING In zones 7 and 8 cold winter temperatures may take the plant back to the ground. This is really a benefit as more shoots and, hence, more blooms will appear throughout the summer. Cut back hard in early spring to induce branching. Feed with a light application of a slow-release 12-6-6 fertilizer in early spring. Although very drought-tolerant, supplemental water during prolonged dry periods will keep the plant looking great.

LANDSCAPE USE The bird-of-paradise looks best in a tropical setting because of the foliage and long stamens. It does, however, work well in gardens with buddleia, lantanas, and salvias. Place with plants that are not heavy water users.

VARIETIES No known selections exist. In zone 9, try also *C. pulcherrima* 'Pride of Barbados.'

Long, delicate red stamens make the bird-of-paradise one of the most exotic-looking flowers in the garden.

Caryopteris (ka-ri-OP-ter-is) x clandonensis

Bluebeard, Blue Mist

FAMILY: *Verbenaceae*
ORIGIN: East Asia
RELATIVES: Verbena, Duranta
PROPAGATION: Cutting
ZONE: 7–10
LIGHT: Sun
WATER: Less than average
SIZE: 3–4 feet
COLOR: Blue, lavender-blue

'Dark Knight' caryopteris and the 'Profusion Orange' zinnia complement each other in the flower garden.

TOUGHNESS Considered a small shrub or returning herbaceous plant from cold winters, the bluebeard provides welcome blue color from summer through fall. The gray foliage is added texture in the world dominated by dark green leaves. Few insect or disease pressures make this plant a joy to grow. It is much underused in the South.

PLANTING With full sun and well-drained soil, a few bluebeard will make you look as though you have the ultimate green thumb. Wet, soggy winter soil is the number one enemy. Nurseries and garden centers usually sell caryopteris in gallon containers. Dig your hole twice as large as the root ball and plant at the same depth as it is growing in the container. The top of the root ball should be even with the soil profile.

GROWING Prune hard in early spring to generate vigorous new growth. Blooms are produced on current season's growth. During the growing season lightly prune after each bloom cycle to encourage more growth and blossoms. Feed with a light application of a slow-release, balanced fertilizer after each cycle. Although the plant is drought-tolerant, giving supplemental water during dry periods will keep it producing those colorful blue flowers.

LANDSCAPE USE The bluebeard combines wonderfully with flowers like 'Profusion Orange' zinnia, lantana, salvias, and purple heart. Plant large drifts of bluebeard in front of purple coneflowers, rudbeckia, or tall selections of gomphrena.

VARIETIES 'Azure,' 'Blue Mist,' 'Dark Knight,' and 'Longwood Blue' are the leading varieties. 'Dark Knight' has the darkest of the blue flowers and seems to have garnered a larger share of the market. Try also *C. incana* that is taller and has lavender-blue flowers.

Clerodendrum (kler-o-DEN-drum)
bungei

Cashmere Bouquet, Mexicali Rose

FAMILY: *Verbenaceae*
ORIGIN: Mexico, South America
RELATIVES: Verbena, Duranta
PROPAGATION: Suckers
ZONE: 7–10
LIGHT: Part shade
WATER: Average
SIZE: 4–6 feet
COLOR: Pink

TOUGHNESS The cashmere bouquet is either loved or hated, but all will agree it is rugged. Large, fragrant, pink flowers, loved by butterflies and suitable for arranging, measure approximately 8 inches in width. The large blossoms, in contrast with large, dark green foliage with a bronze-purple cast, give this plant a wonderful exotic shrublike appeal in the landscape.

PLANTING This plant can be purchased, but you'll have to search for it. More than likely a friend or a gardening neighbor will get you started. Once you have it, your next job will be controlling it. The cashmere bouquet performs best in fertile, well-drained soil in partial shade. Space plants 3–4 feet apart.

GROWING Many gardeners say the foliage is malodorous when touched, but not everyone's nose concurs. The cashmere bouquet is vigorous and spreads by suckers to the point of being invasive if not managed. Those who love it have no problem plucking unwanted sprouts. If you have a large area to fill in partial shade, you can't beat it. This plant almost never needs fertilizer but does appreciate supplemental water during long dry periods. Remove old flower heads to keep your cashmere bouquet looking its best. In colder areas, go into winter with an added layer of mulch.

LANDSCAPE USE Combine with elephant ears and bananas to give understory color. Try planting caladiums and impatiens with pink or pastel colors in front of the cashmere bouquet.

VARIETIES There are no named selections of the *Clerodendrum bungei*. Try also *C. ugandense* butterfly bush clerodendrum, *C. trichotomum* harlequin glorybower, and *C. paniculatum* pagoda flower.

Cashmere bouquet is one of several clerondendrums well-suited to the South.

Clerodendrum (kler-o-DEN-drum)
trichotomum

Harlequin Glorybower

FAMILY: *Verbenaceae*
ORIGIN: Japan
RELATIVES: Lantana,
Bleeding Heart
PROPAGATION: Suckers, division
ZONE: 6–10
LIGHT: Sun to part shade
WATER: Average
SIZE: 10–15 feet
COLOR: Cream with dark pink

TOUGHNESS The small deciduous tree or herbaceous perennial produces fragrant cream-colored blossoms with pink calyces. Swallowtail butterflies will adorn the tree when in bloom. Following the bloom, a steel-blue fruit will remain inside a hot-pink-to-red calyx. The harlequin glorybower can withstand cold, heat, and humidity and, as typical to the genus, will offer suckers or volunteers as well.

PLANTING The harlequin glorybower is a little easier to find than the cashmere bouquet, but not much. This plant does well in full sun but looks even better if given a little protection from afternoon sun. The soil should be organically rich, well drained, and slightly acidic. Amending soil with compost will reward you with a better specimen. Plant nursery-grown plants or volunteers from a friend at the same depth they are currently growing, no deeper.

GROWING Fertilizer is not normally required, as the harlequin glorybower is usually vigorous and aggressive. If previous years' growth is less than expected, give a light application of 12-6-6 fertilizer in late spring. Keep the plant well mulched in summer and winter. Pay attention to volunteers and remove as needed.

LANDSCAPE USE The harlequin glorybower is a great addition to the butterfly garden, tropical garden, or cottage garden. 'Costa Rica Blue' or 'Black and Blue' Brazilian sage, indigo spires salvia, and 'Victoria' blue salvia make nice companion plants. Try with purple fountain grass, buddleias, burgundy-leafed coleus, and purple coneflowers.

VARIETIES *C. trichotomum* var. *fargesii* is a smaller, more cold-hardy selection.

Harlequin glorybower becomes a small tree and is delightfully fragrant when in bloom.

Coreopsis (ko-rea-OP-sis) grandiflora

Bigflower Coreopsis

FAMILY: *Asteraceae*
ORIGIN: North America
RELATIVES: Rudbeckia, Yarrow
PROPAGATION: Division, seed
ZONE: 4–9
LIGHT: Sun
WATER: Less than average
SIZE: 1–2 feet
COLOR: Yellow, orange

TOUGHNESS Brilliant golden yellow flowers are borne on long stems all summer on plants that return next year. *Coreopsis grandiflora* is cold-tolerant, heat- and drought-tolerant, and tough enough to be planted streetside. This is one of the best perennials for the beginning gardener. A green thumb is sure to follow.

PLANTING Select a site in full sun. Well-drained soil is a must, but high fertility is not nec-essary. Improve drainage by adding 3–4 inches of organic matter and till to a depth of 8–10 inches. Set out nursery-grown transplants in early spring after the last frost at the same depth as in the container. Hybrid seed can also be planted with blooms in the first season. Space plants 12–15 inches apart.

GROWING It is essential to remove old flowers. This keeps the plant tidy and blooms producing and reduces the possibility of old flowers getting pathogens that can infect the rest of the plant. Seeds saved will not come true to type. The *Coreopsis grandiflora* will need dividing by the third year to keep the quality of the plant its best. Clumps may be divided in spring or fall.

LANDSCAPE USE The coreopsis has un-beatable color for the perennial or cottage garden. Combine with old-fashioned blue larkspurs or blue salvias like indigo spires and 'Victoria' blue. Try planting with 'Bouquet Purple' dianthus, angelonias, ox-eye daisies, and ornamental grasses.

VARIETIES The All America Selections Gold Medal winner 'Early Sunrise' is superior. Other good choices are 'Baby Sun,' 'Sunray,' and 'Sunburst.'

Coreopsis and ox-eye daisy are wonderful spring companions in the perennial garden.

Coreopsis (ko-rea-OP-sis) verticillata

Threadleaf Coreopsis

FAMILY: *Asteraceae*
ORIGIN: Maryland, West Virginia
RELATIVES: Yarrow, Rudbeckia
PROPAGATION: Division
ZONE: 5–9
LIGHT: Sun
WATER: Less than average
SIZE: 2–3 feet
COLOR: Yellow, gold

TOUGHNESS Words like worry-free, heat-tolerant, drought-tolerant, and beautiful describe the threadleaf coreopsis. Its wispy, airy foliage is as attractive as an asparagus fern, yet the plant loads up with hundreds of yellow flowers in summer and fall.

PLANTING Purchase nursery-grown transplants and place into soil that is very well drained. Organically rich soil or fertilizer isn't a prerequisite. Space plants 12–15 inches apart in the garden after the last frost in the spring. Set out at the same depth as in the container. Add a layer of mulch after planting. Water the transplants to get them established in your garden and then only sparingly or in drought conditions.

GROWING Feed established plantings with a light application of a 5-10-5 fertilizer in the spring. Divide the plants every 2–3 years in spring or fall to encourage vigorous growth. Shear back after the initial bloom cycle to generate growth and reblooming for fall.

LANDSCAPE USE Use in bold, informal drifts with blue flowers like Russian sage *(Perovskia)*, angelonias, or salvias like the indigo spires. Grow also with gomphrena or purple heart. Ornamental grasses make nice companion plants.

VARIETIES 'Moonbeam,' the 1992 Perennial Plant of the Year, is still the most popular, but 'Zagreb' is regarded as the best by many horticulturists. 'Golden Showers' produces the largest flowers. Try also the annual coreopsis *C. tinctoria*.

Threadleaf coreopsis produces incredible flowers on fern-like foliage.

Dendranthema (den-DRANTH-e-ma)
zawadskii

'Clara Curtis,' 'Country Girl' Chrysanthemum

FAMILY: *Asteraceae*
ORIGIN: Russia, Carpathians
RELATIVES: Purple Coneflower,
Rudbeckia
PROPAGATION: Division
ZONE: 4–9
LIGHT: Sun to part shade
WATER: Average
SIZE: 18–24 inches
COLOR: Pink

'Clara Curtis' chrysanthemum will return for years in the perennial garden.

TOUGHNESS The new botanical name will most likely be unfamiliar, but everyone in the South knows the common name. 'Clara Curtis' or 'Country Girl' chrysanthemum has stood the test of time. It is not only heirloom but still in production. Why is it in production? A glorious fall display of large, rose-pink flowers with orange disks is the main reason. Returning year after year, putting on a show that is unrivaled, is just one more reason.

PLANTING Whether you call it 'Clara Curtis' or 'Country Girl' this plant has the potential of being around quite a while, if you do your part. Your children can grow up with this flower. Plant them in full sun to produce the most floriferous compact plants. A little afternoon shade is tolerated. The soil must be fertile, organically rich, moist, but very well drained. If plagued by tight, heavy soil that doesn't drain, amend with 3–4 inches of organic matter and till to a depth of 6–8 inches. While tilling, incorporate 2 pounds of a slow-release fertilizer per 100 square feet of bed space. A 12-6-6 or balanced 8-8-8 blend with minor nutrients included is a good choice. Space

plants 15–18 inches apart. Plant at the same depth as in the container. Apply a layer of mulch after planting.

GROWING As great as the old-time plants are, rampant growth can make them leggy. Pinching in early June, July, and August develops a bushier plant that still reaches its full height but produces even more bloom. Maintain moisture through the long, hot summer and feed with a light application of fertilizer every 4–6 weeks. Divide in the spring, spacing as recommended.

LANDSCAPE USE One of the prettiest displays I have seen of 'Clara Curtis' was growing with tall purple gomphrena. The pink flowers combine wonderfully with purple fountain grass and muhly grass. Grow with burgundy-leafed coleus selections. The fall bloom cycle matches up well in the perennial garden with the Mexican bush sage and indigo spires.

VARIETIES Many growers believe 'Ryan's Pink' is similar to if not the same as 'Clara Curtis' or 'Country Girl.' 'Mary Stoker' has pale yellow blossoms with a pink blush.

Dianthus (dy-AN-thus) barbatus
interspecific hybrid

'Bouquet Purple'

FAMILY: *Caryophyllaceae*
ORIGIN: Southern Europe
RELATIVES: Bouncing Bet,
Rose Campion
PROPAGATION: Division, seed
ZONE: 3–9
LIGHT: Sun to part shade
WATER: Average
SIZE: 18–24 inches
COLOR: Purple-pink

'Bouquet Purple' dianthus and 'Early Sunrise' coreopsis make an attractive display.

TOUGHNESS When a plant is chosen as a Mississippi Medallion winner and the Minnesota Select Perennial Plant of the Year, it must be tough. 'Bouquet Purple' is a tall cut-flower-type dianthus that is cold-tolerant and yet endures a Mississippi summer. The flowers are a bright, bold, and cheerful hot-purple-pink color. It will be a short-lived perennial but is truly outstanding.

PLANTING 'Bouquet Purple' prefers well-drained, well-worked beds, rich in organic matter. When preparing a bed, incorporate 2 pounds of a slow-release 12-6-6 fertilizer with minor nutrients per 100 square feet of bed space. Plenty of sun is needed for full bloom potential. Plant at the same depth as in the container, in fall or spring. Space plants 8–12 inches apart.

GROWING Lightly side-dress with fertilizer once a month to keep them growing and producing. There are two important steps to achieving happiness with the 'Bouquet Purple.' The first is to mulch to conserve moisture, deter weed growth, and keep summer soil temperatures cooler. The other is to deadhead to keep the plant looking tidy and the flower stems coming. For cut flowers, harvest stems when three flowers are fully open.

LANDSCAPE USE To create the prettiest display, set out in large drifts of 3–4 plants per square foot. The hot-pink-purple color allows combination with a number of plants. Some of the best companion plants are pansies such as 'Purple Rain,' 'True Blue Panolas,' and flowering kale and cabbage with pink overtones. 'Early Sunrise' coreopsis combined with 'Bouquet Purple' makes for a spring display that is hard to beat.

VARIETIES No additions have been made to the 'Bouquet' series. Another new *C. barbatus* interspecific hybrid that does look promising is 'Amazon Neon Duo.' It is just as cold-hardy and slightly taller.

Dianthus (dy-AN-thus) chinensis x barbatus

Hybrid Pink Dianthus

FAMILY: *Caryophyllaceae*
ORIGIN: Hybrid China x
Southern Europe
RELATIVES: Bouncing Bet,
Rose Campion
PROPAGATION: Division, seed
ZONE: Short-lived perennial in 5–8,
annual all zones
LIGHT: Sun to part shade
WATER: Average
SIZE: 8–20 inches
COLOR: Red, pink, white, blends

Known as hybrid pinks, these plants give outstanding color in red, pink, white, and every blend of the three. In addition to their cheerful colors they have a delightful fragrance.

PLANTING Hybrid pinks prefer well-drained, well-worked beds rich in organic matter. When preparing a bed, incorporate 2 pounds of a slow-release 12-6-6 fertilizer with minor nutrients per 100 square feet of bed space. Give plenty of sun for bloom to full potential. Plant at the same depth as in the container in the fall or spring. Space plants 6–8 inches apart.

GROWING Lightly side-dress with fertilizer once a month to keep them growing and producing. Keep hybrid pinks mulched to conserve moisture, deter weed growth, give added cold protection, and keep summer soil temperatures cooler. Deadhead to keep the plant looking tidy and the flower stems coming.

LANDSCAPE USE Dianthus colors allow for partnering with cool season crops like pansies, violas, snapdragons, and flowering kale or cabbage. The door is also open for patriotic combinations of red and white varieties with plants like blue lobelia. Use with dusty miller, early spring petunias, and alyssum.

'Ideal' dianthus and blue lobelia.

VARIETIES The 'Telestar' Series was chosen as a Louisiana Select award winner. The 'Ideal' series has proven the best in University of Georgia trials. 'Ideal Carmine' and 'Ideal Rose' were chosen as Flueroselect Quality Mark winners, and 'Ideal Violet' was an All America Selections award winner. The 'Melody' series offers several choices, and the 'Melody Pink' was chosen as an All America Selections winner.

TOUGHNESS Many gardeners haven't given this group of plants a fair shake. These are tough, cold-tolerant plants, many times enduring the summer and becoming short-lived perennials. How tough? Louisiana Select winner, Flueroselect Quality Mark winner, All America Selections award winners, as well as the outstanding performers from the University of Georgia trials.

Dianthus (dy-AN-thus)
gratianopolitanus

Cheddar Pink

FAMILY: *Caryophyllaceae*
ORIGIN: West and Central Europe
RELATIVES: Bouncing Bet,
Rose Campion
PROPAGATION: Division,
cutting, seed
ZONE: 3–9
LIGHT: Sun to part shade
WATER: Average
SIZE: 8–12 inches
COLOR: Pink shades

'Bath's Pink' is exceptional in flower and foliage, making a great groundcover.

TOUGHNESS The cheddar pinks are among a handful of plants that make a significant landscape impact 12 months a year. In the spring this dianthus sends up an abundance of bright pink to magenta flowers 1–2 inches across that last for over a month. These blooms are borne on stalks about 12 inches high yet cover over the foliage, like a cloud of pink. After the bloom cycle is over, the gray to blue grassy-looking foliage forms a dense groundcover. This groundcover remains attractive throughout the year and really wows gardeners.

PLANTING Plant nursery-grown cheddar pink dianthus in early spring or summer in full to part sun in well-drained organically rich beds. Prior to planting, incorporate 3–4 inches of compost or humus with 2 pounds of a slow-release 12-6-6 fertilizer per 100 square feet. Space the plants 12–18 inches apart and within two seasons see a handsome groundcover of gray-green foliage, 4–6 inches high.

GROWING The cheddar pink dianthus is beautiful as a landscape plant and requires little maintenance. Fertilize plants after flowering and 2–3 times during the growing season with light applications of fertilizer. Divide and thin plants in the fall when they become too thick and dense or spread beyond the area desired.

LANDSCAPE USE If you are looking for a groundcover, and especially one that blooms, the cheddar pink dianthus is the one for you. For a natural look, plant in a border and grow old garden roses in various shades of pink or white. Other good companions are ox-eye daisies, irises, and azaleas.

VARIETIES The Georgia Gold Medal winner 'Bath's Pink' is the standard by which others are judged. Some believe 'Mountain Mist' is now the best, but it requires colder temperatures to bloom in more southern locations. 'Firewitch' is very attractive but is more mounded and does not spread like 'Bath's Pink.' 'Bewitched' is also outstanding.

Echinacea (ek-in-AY-sea) purpurea

Purple Coneflower

FAMILY: *Asteraceae*
ORIGIN: Eastern United States
RELATIVES: Rudbeckia,
Shasta Daisy
PROPAGATION: Division, seed
ZONE: 3–8
LIGHT: Sun to part shade
WATER: Less than average
SIZE: 3–5 feet
COLOR: Light purple, pink, rose,
white

list of virtues, the ability to withstand soggy conditions is not one of them. While high fertility is not necessary the soil needs to be well drained. Accomplish this by adding organic matter like compost or humus and tilling in to a depth of 8–10 inches. Select healthy transplants, without buds, and plant at the same depth as in the container. Space plants 2–3 feet apart. Purple coneflowers can also be grown from seed by planting in the fall.

GROWING Feed established plantings in early spring with a light application of a slow-release 12-6-6 fertilizer and again in midsummer. Keep the flowers deadheaded for increased bloom. Sprinkle the seeds from dried cones in August through October to increase size of planting or to develop a wildflower meadow look. Divide clumps in the fall every 3–5 years or as needed.

LANDSCAPE USE Purple coneflowers are ideally planted in large informal drifts in perennial gardens, with companions like liatris, Shasta daisy, rudbeckia, salvia, and Russian sage. They look terrific with dwarf fountain grass 'Hameln' or purple fountain grass.

Purple coneflowers are native to the eastern United States and will be at home in your garden too.

TOUGHNESS This native of the United States produces some of the most beautiful pink to purple fragrant flowers in the garden. Withstanding heat, high humidity, drought, partial shade, and extreme cold, this plant comes back every year too. Why then is its name echinacea, meaning hedgehog or sea urchin?

PLANTING Though this plant has a long

VARIETIES Despite being sold generically, there are a number of selections to argue over. 'Magnus,' with a slightly more horizontal angle to the petals, was a recent Perennial Plant of the Year. My favorite is 'Bravado.' I fell in love with its particularly strong morning fragrance. Other choice varieties are 'Bright Star' and 'Robert Bloom.' 'White Swan' is the leading white variety.

Echinops (EK-in-ops) ritro

Globe Thistle

FAMILY: *Asteraceae*
ORIGIN: Central and Eastern
Europe, Asia
RELATIVES: Rudbeckia
PROPAGATION: Division, seed,
root cutting
ZONE: 3–8
LIGHT: Sun
WATER: Average
SIZE: 3–5 feet
COLOR: Blue, lavender-blue

Globe thistle is highly ornamental in the perennial garden.

TOUGHNESS The globe thistle produces an abundance of blue flowers slightly larger than golf balls that are great for cutting or drying. The flowers produced from late summer through fall prove to entice both butterflies and bees, making it ideal for the wildlife habitat. The globe thistle is drought-tolerant and returns easily from extreme winter temperatures. The dark gray-green leaves are deeply cut, giving added garden interest.

PLANTING If you were to go to your local garden center and mention thistle, you most likely would get directions to the herbicide aisle. The globe thistle is an asset to the garden and not a weed. This, however, points out a problem with locating the plants. The solution to this problem is to buy seeds and start in a seed flat or small pots for transplanting. Sow these seedlings in the early spring. The globe thistle doesn't need high fertility or copious quantities of organic matter, just sun and well-drained soil. Well-drained soil is essential for surviving the winter. Plant transplants 24–36 inches apart, planting at the same depth as in the container.

GROWING Water to get the plants established but then sparingly. A light application of a slow-release, balanced fertilizer a month after transplanting should be sufficient for bountiful bouquets. If harvesting for drying, cut just prior to opening and hang upside down in a well-ventilated room. Once the bloom cycle is complete, cut back to the ground for new growth and another bloom. Divide clumps in early spring if desired.

LANDSCAPE USE The globe thistle may remind you faintly of a prairie weed. After combining it with rudbeckias or 'New Gold' lantana, however, you will have a new and lasting opinion. Use with ornamental grasses, purple coneflowers, or the sea holly.

VARIETIES 'Taplow Blue' (3 feet), is the easiest to find, but look for 'Taplow Purple' (lavender blue, 3 feet), 'Blue Cloud' (4 feet), 'Blue Glow' (3 feet), and 'Veitch's Blue' (2–3 feet). Try also *E. bannaticus* 'Blue Ball' (3 feet).

Eryngium (e-RINJ-ium) species

Sea Holly

FAMILY: *Apiaceae*
ORIGIN: Europe,
United States
RELATIVES: Celery, Coriander
PROPAGATION: Root cutting,
division, seed
ZONE: 4–9
LIGHT: Sun
WATER: Less than average
SIZE: 2–4 feet
COLOR: Blue and silver shades

TOUGHNESS British garden journalist William Robinson was so enthralled with the sea holly he declared this perennial to be "not surpassed" in beauty by any plant. Unfortunately it has been passed over by—or, better stated, not offered to—gardeners in the south. It is found blooming in spring and early summer in trial gardens, attracting the gaze of visitors and the feasting of bees. The sea holly with its thistlelike blue-to-amethyst flowers is rugged and persevering, withstanding cold winters, heat, and drought. The plants are spiny, adding a degree of toughness of a differing nature.

PLANTING The sea holly is not easily found at garden centers. There are several commercial producers of sea holly, so ask your local garden center to make these great plants available. Another option to explore is specialty catalogs or ordering via the Internet. This trooper doesn't require high fertility or great quantities of organic matter, just sun and well-drained soil. Well-drained soil is essential for winter survival, and sun is needed for best coloration. Plant 18–36 inches apart, depending on variety, planting at the same depth as in the container.

GROWING Water to get the plants established but then sparingly. A light application of a slow-release balanced fertilizer a month after transplanting should be sufficient for vigorous growth. Separating plantlets that have formed at the base may be the easiest method of propagation. Many self-sow for easy thinning and transplanting. The sea holly is excellent as a cut flower. Handle with care: the spines will stick!

LANDSCAPE USE The blue, amethyst, or silver bracts allow the sea holly to work well with other plants requiring similar surroundings. Lantana, goldenrod, gomphrena, purple coneflower, and rudbeckia are all great companion plants. For a superior look, add ornamental grasses.

VARIETIES *E. alpinum* and hybrids 'Amethyst,' 'Blue Star,' 'Opal,' and 'Sapphire Blue' are among the easiest to locate. Look also for *E. giganteum* variety 'Silver Ghost' and *E. planum* varieties 'Blue Cap,' 'Blue Diamond,' 'Blue Ribbon,' and 'Roseum.'

The sea holly is an excellent cut flower.

Eupatorium (yew-pat-OR-ium)
coelestinum

Wild Ageratum

FAMILY: *Asteraceae*
ORIGIN: Eastern United States
RELATIVES: Purple Coneflower
PROPAGATION: Division,
cutting, seed
ZONE: 6–10
LIGHT: Sun to part shade
WATER: Average
SIZE: 2–4 feet
COLOR: Blue, white

Wild ageratum and swamp sunflower are spectacular along the roadside and will be the same in the garden.

TOUGHNESS Every year in late summer and fall when the gardens of the region look tired and at their worst, our Creator brings forth a colorful show along the roadside, causing people to stare and utter words like, "Why aren't those flowers in my garden?" The wild ageratum, with unbelievable blue flowers is one such plant. The garden ageratum fell prey to either heat or spider mites weeks ago, but the native puts on a show that is unrivaled. These flowers are borne on tall plants and are often grown next to goldenrod, teaching us also about color combinations.

PLANTING Before planting, let's admit this wild ageratum is a happy plant that can spread. It is not available at the run-of-the-mill garden center but from specialty nurseries that sell natives or as a pass-along. Check the ditch in front of the house. The wild ageratum likes sun, fertile soil, and moisture. Supply these and then stand back.

GROWING The wild ageratum can develop a lanky growth. Pinch a couple of times, like growers do for chrysanthemums, and you'll develop a bushier plant. Do monitor the spread and remove sections you do not want. These unwanted volunteers are usually the first ones snatched at plant swaps. Divide or thin in the spring, every 3–4 years.

LANDSCAPE USE Most selections are tall and will look best in the middle or back of the border. Plant similarly to what you see along the roadside, not lined up like soldiers but in informal drifts. Use with goldenrods, rudbeckias, lantanas, ironweed, zebra grass, or old-fashioned 'Country Girl' chrysanthemums.

VARIETIES The scientific name for wild ageratum has recently been changed and so may be listed elsewhere as *Conoclinium (con-o-KLEN-ium) coelestinum*. The door is open for you to make a selection, name it, and spread it around. 'Wayside' (compact, 15 inches), 'Album' (white), and 'Cori' (better blue) are out there somewhere.

Eupatorium (yew-pat-OR-ium) purpureum and *E. maculatum*

Joe Pye Weed

FAMILY: *Asteraceae*
ORIGIN: Eastern United States
RELATIVES: Chrysanthemums
PROPAGATION: Division, seed
ZONE: 4–9
LIGHT: Sun
WATER: Average
SIZE: 3–8 feet
COLOR: Rose-pink

'Gateway' is a standout selection of Joe Pye weed.

TOUGHNESS The Joe Pye is roadside tough, which is where you will mostly find it. Grown in gardens in Europe and the northern U.S., it is still rare in the southern garden, although native to the region. Is it because someone stuck the word "weed" on it? Deep rose-pink blooms emerge in late summer and fall to the delight of swallowtail butterflies, which find them irresistible.

PLANTING Thankfully these plants are finding their way to garden centers but still short of the demand. Select a site in fertile, loamy, well-drained soil. Plant at the same depth as in the container. Space the plants 3 feet apart. Put to the back of the border as the shorter varieties get 5 feet tall. Provide supplemental water during prolonged dry periods and keep mulched.

GROWING The growth pattern will inevitably be larger than you think, so pinch a couple of times to encourage branching. The plant will still get enormous but a little bushier. Watch for the spread of volunteers and seedlings and remove the unwanted plants. The best guess is someone in a garden club in your community would love for you to share. Plants will need dividing or thinning in the spring every 3–4 years.

LANDSCAPE USE The Joe Pye weed is wonderful in the butterfly or perennial garden. Use with buddleia or butterfly bush, blue anise sage *Salvia guaranitica,* purple fountain grass, 'Hameln' dwarf fountain grass, goldenrod, and tall forms of gomphrena.

VARIETIES 'Big Umbrella' has been the leading named variety, but 'Gateway' is now causing the most attention. It is a compact, 4–5-foot form and is believed to be *E. maculatum.* 'Chocolate,' a bronzed-leaf form of *E. rugosum,* is very striking and much shorter.

Gaura (GAW-ra) lindheimeri

Gaura

FAMILY: *Onagraceae*

ORIGIN: Texas, Louisiana

RELATIVES: Evening Primrose, Fuchsia

PROPAGATION: Seed, root division

ZONE: 5–10

LIGHT: Sun

WATER: Less than average

SIZE: 2½–4 feet

COLOR: White, pink, deep rose

Gaura is very drought-tolerant.

TOUGHNESS Gaura comes from the Greek word *gauros,* meaning superb, and this is precisely how gardeners feel about this new plant. It is cold-hardy to zone 5 yet thrives to the coast. It gives a unique texture in the garden with butterfly-like flowers that are white, pink, or deep rose and are borne at the top of tall, airy spikes. The gaura tolerates our heat and humidity and blooms from spring through frost.

PLANTING Gaura is very drought-tolerant, forming a long taproot. This taproot will form best in well-drained soil with full sun. Gaura does not need copious quantities of organic matter or frequent applications of fertilizer to put on a good performance. Nurseries are stocking not only good quantities but also choices in varieties in gallon and larger sizes. Set out transplants in the spring after the soil has warmed, and plant at the same depth as in the container.

GROWING Deadheading flower stalks will reduce the amount of reseeding. Although a perennial, gaura won't need dividing. If interested in additional plants, save seeds to plant later. Germination takes place in 14–21 days. You can also let the plants reseed by themselves, pluck the

ones you do not want, and transplant the others. Softwood to semi-hardwood cuttings can be rooted in spring in a well-drained potting mix. A rooting hormone will help increase your percentages.

LANDSCAPE USE The gaura is ideally suited to the new southern cottage garden look and combines well with salvias, Shasta daises, liatris, and purple coneflowers. Society garlic and angelonias also work very well with gaura.

VARIETIES 'Siskiyou Pink' (pink), 'Whirling Butterflies' (white dwarf, 18–24 inches), 'Sunny Butterflies' (white), 'Crimson Butterflies' (deep pink), 'Blushing Butterflies' (white blush-pink), 'Corries' Gold' (white, variegated foliage), 'Walberton Pink' (white-pink blush), 'Walberton White' (white), 'Pink Fountain' (deep rose pink), 'Perky Pink' (red foliage, pink flowers, dwarf, 16 inches), 'Ballerina Blush' (pink dwarf, 12–18 inches), and 'Ballerina Rose' (dark rose pink dwarf, 12–18 inches).

Heuchera (hew-KER-a) hybrids

Coral Bells

FAMILY: *Saxifragaceae*
ORIGIN: North America
RELATIVES: Astilbe, Tiarella
PROPAGATION: Division, seed
ZONE: 4–10
LIGHT: Part shade
WATER: Average
SIZE: 2–5 feet
COLOR: Grown for foliage, some
with variegation; flowers—pink, coral,
red, white

'Amber Waves' *Heuchera* is known for its striking foliage.

TOUGHNESS *Heuchera* is native to the United States and thrives from north to south and east to west. This plant will tolerate extremes in temperatures. It produces tall, airy flowers in pink, coral, red, or white. Many have foliage so colorful and ornately shaped that it will cause you to stop dead in your tracks, and you could care less if they ever bloomed. Coral bells are rarely found in the landscape, as gardeners usually choose other materials. A great plant, coral bells deserve a place in the part-shade garden.

PLANTING A well-drained, organically rich bed in part shade will provide a good environment for coral bells. Amend tight clay soils with 3–4 inches of organic matter and till to a depth of 6–8 inches. Incorporate 2 pounds of a slow-release fertilizer such as a 12-6-6 per 100 square feet. Plant nursery-grown transplants in the spring at the same depth as in the container. Space the plants 9–15 inches apart. Coral bells can also be planted by seed. Germination takes about 3 weeks.

GROWING In the spring feed with a light application of a 5-10-5 or 12-6-6 fertilizer. Keep the coral bells watered and mulched through the growing season. Remove spent flowers to increase bloom production. Divide mature clumps every 3–4 years in the fall or with the emergence of spring growth. Replant the young vigorous divisions, disposing of the old woody stems.

LANDSCAPE USE A question often asked is what to plant in the shade. The answer is *Heuchera,* or coral bells. Plant along woodland trails, in front of shrubs or roses. Great combinations can be made with wood fern or autumn fern. Let your artistic nature shine and use with hostas. It sounds gaudy but the turnout will surprise you.

VARIETIES *Heuchera* hybrids that are causing excitement in the industry for their foliage are 'Amber Waves' (ruffled amber-gold foliage, rose flowers), 'Amethyst Myst' (burgundy foliage with amethyst overtone), and 'Green Spice' (dark-gray-edged silver leaves with purple venation), and 'Velvet Night' (dark purple and pink with even darker veins). *Heuchera micrantha* hybrid 'Palace Purple' with maple-shaped leaves and white flowers is very popular. *Heuchera sanguinea* selections have more green leaves but perhaps the showiest blooms. Some of the better choices are 'Fireglow,' 'Hunstman,' and 'Raspberry Regal.'

Hibiscus (hy-BISK-us) coccineus

Swamp Mallow, Scarlet Mallow

FAMILY: *Malvaceae*
ORIGIN: Georgia, Florida
RELATIVES: French Hollyhock
PROPAGATION: Cutting, division, seed
ZONE: 5–10
LIGHT: Sun
WATER: Average
SIZE: 6–8 feet
COLOR: Red, dark pink

Scarlet mallow is perfect in the cottage garden for those desiring the tropical look.

TOUGHNESS Brilliant red, star-shaped flowers with maplelike leaves are borne from early summer through frost. These flowers are produced on giant plants that are exotic-looking and native and exhibit unbelievable cold hardiness. The flowers stop visitors in their tracks, and the ruby-throated hummingbirds find them delectable.

PLANTING Select a site in full sun for best blooming. The swamp mallow performs in all types of soils, preferring slightly acidic. Well-prepared, fertile, well-drained but moisture-retentive beds yield the most spectacular plants. Set nursery-grown transplants at least 3 feet apart and apply a layer of mulch.

GROWING Cut frozen stalks back to the ground. If stalks survive the winter, prune back by 75 percent to encourage lateral branching and bushiness. Feed in early spring with a light application of a slow-release 12-6-6 fertilizer as growth is resuming. Give supplemental water during prolonged droughts.

LANDSCAPE USE The swamp mallow flower and leaf texture allow it to be used in the tropical landscape or the old-fashioned cottage garden. Plant to the back of the border so their birdlike legs will not be noticed. In the tropical garden use with bananas, upright elephant ears *Alocasia macrorrhiza,* bush allamanda, candle-stick plants, and dwarf cannas. In the cottage garden or hummingbird garden use with white butterfly bush, blue anise sage, forsythia sage, and 'Goldsturm' rudbeckia.

VARIETIES There are no named selections, but the industry has almost universally adopted the name 'Texas Star.'

Hibiscus (hy-BISK-us) moscheutos

Perennial Hibiscus, Rose Mallow

FAMILY: *Malvaceae*
ORIGIN: Southern United States
RELATIVES: Chinese Hibiscus
PROPAGATION: Cutting,
division, seed
ZONE: 5–10
LIGHT: Sun
WATER: Average
SIZE: 3–6 feet
COLOR: Red, burgundy, pink, white,
blends

The perennial hibiscus is as showy as its tropical cousin.

TOUGHNESS The rose mallow or perennial hibiscus has the look of the tropics but the cold-hardiness that allows it to be grown in much of the United States as a perennial. The flowers are large, many approaching 12 inches, and as showy as any perennial in existence. Like other hibiscus, the flowers are favorite feeding sites for butterflies and hummingbirds.

PLANTING Thankfully almost every garden center offers these each spring. Plant in full sun, although part shade is tolerated very well. The soil should be well drained, containing plenty of organic matter and nutrients. Loosen tightly compacted clay soils by incorporating 3–4 inches of organic matter, including a preplant slow-release fertilizer. These are shrublike plants. Dig the planting hole twice as large as the root ball and plant at the same depth as in the container.

GROWING Remove frozen stalks in the fall and add a layer of mulch. Feed established plantings with a light application of a slow-release fertilizer like a 12-6-6 in the spring with the resuming of growth and every 6–8 weeks through the growing season. Keep well watered during dry periods to keep the plant growing. Remove spent flowers or seedpods to keep the plant blooming.

LANDSCAPE USE The rose mallow is well suited to the perennial border, the tropical garden, or the garden dedicated to hummingbirds and butterflies. In the tropical garden, plant around palms or in front of a picket fence draped with coral vine *Antigonon leptopus*. Grow in the cottage garden with antique roses and salvias of all types.

VARIETIES Three *H. mosheutos* hybrids have been awarded Texas Superstar status. 'Moy Grande' features the largest open-faced hibiscus in the world. Each rose-pink bloom measures 12 inches across. 'Flare' is one of the prettiest available. The leaves are dark apple green and the flowers are large and iridescent fuchsia in color. The last and perhaps best known is 'Lord Baltimore.' The foliage is semiglossy, reminiscent of the tropical hibiscus, with 10-inch red flowers. Look also for 'Disco Belle,' 'Rio Carnival,' and 'Frisbee.'

Hylotelephium (Hi-LO-te-LEF-ee-um)
species and hybrids

Stonecrop, Sedum

FAMILY: *Crassulaceae*
ORIGIN: China, Japan, Korea,
Eastern Europe
RELATIVES: Sedum
PROPAGATION: Division, seed
ZONE: 3–8
LIGHT: Sun to part shade
WATER: Less than average
SIZE: 2–3 feet
COLOR: Pink, rose-red

Overseas, sedum is known as "live-forever plant."

TOUGHNESS If everyone knows a plant, it must be time to change the name. Just kidding, but if you look above you will see the new name of the plant we call sedum. Is it tough? One of the common names overseas is "live-forever plant." Sedum is indeed a tenacious plant even if it might not be everlasting. Beautiful clusters of pink, rose, or maroon flowers appear from succulent-looking foliage that is equally striking in colors from gray-green to burgundy. Butterflies adore the plants as much as gardeners.

PLANTING Select a site in full sun to part shade, with fertile, freely draining soil. Amend the soil with 3–4 inches of organic matter, tilling to a depth of 6–8 inches. Set out nursery-grown plants at the same depth as in the container, spacing 12–16 inches apart depending on variety. Apply a good layer of mulch after planting.

GROWING Water to get the plants established but then sparingly. A light application of a slow-release, balanced fertilizer a month after transplanting should be sufficient for an abundance of blooms. Feed established plants with a light application of fertilizer with the emergence of spring growth. Once the bloom cycle is complete, the flowers turn a russet brown. Some gardeners leave them. I like to cut them back to the ground and side-dress with a little fertilizer for new growth and blooms in the fall. Divide in the spring or fall when needed. The sedum is easily propagated from cuttings.

LANDSCAPE USE The sedum can be used effectively as a border or in informal drifts. Combine sedums like 'Autumn Joy' or 'Ruby Glow' with grasses like purple fountain, 'Hameln' dwarf fountain, and purple muhly. Use also underneath Joe Pye weed varieties 'Gateway' and 'Chocolate.' Try growing sedums like 'Sunset Cloud' or 'Strawberries and Cream,' with sun coleus varieties like 'Pink Parfait,' 'Burgundy Sun,' or 'Mississippi Summer.'

VARIETIES 'Autumn Joy' (*H. telephium x H. spectabile*, pink flowers, darker with age), 'Ruby Glow' (*H. cauticolon x H. telephium,* ruby red flowers), 'Sunset Cloud' (*H. telephium x Atropurpureum x* 'Ruby Glow,' rose-red flowers), and 'Strawberries and Cream' *(H. telephium munstead,* lavender and rose) are just a sampling of many that need to be grown. The goldmoss sedum that kept its old botanical name *(Sedum acre)* is perfect for tucking in among rocks along paths.

Kniphofia (ny-FO-fia) uvaria
and hybrids

Red-Hot Poker, Torch Lily

FAMILY: *Liliaceae*
ORIGIN: South Africa
RELATIVES: Daylily, Liriope
PROPAGATION: Division, seed
ZONE: 5–8
LIGHT: Sun to part shade
WATER: Less than average
SIZE: 2–6 feet
COLOR: Orange, cream, red, yellow

'Flamenco' was a 1999 All America Selections winner.

TOUGHNESS It is hard to find a more striking garden flower than the red-hot poker. The tall flower stalks made of clusters of brightly colored blooms tower above the plant in spring and summer. The ruby-throated hummingbird is passionate about them. The showy red-hot poker flowers stand out when cut and used in a vase. They are much easier to grow than gardeners realize and are able to withstand the temperature extremes in the south.

PLANTING Select a site with plenty of sun, though a little midafternoon shade is certainly tolerated. Well-drained, loose soil is an absolute must if gardeners are to be happy with the red-hot poker. Amend tight clay and poorly drained soil with 3–4 inches of compost or humus and till to a depth of 8–10 inches. While preparing the soil, incorporate 2 pounds of a slow release 12-6-6 fertilizer per 100 square feet of bed space. Set out nursery-grown transplants at the same depth as in the container. Seeds can also be sown in a flat or at the site. Germination takes about 3 weeks. Space plants 16–24 inches apart, depending on variety.

GROWING Feed plants lightly with fertilizer every 4–6 weeks through the growing season. Water the plants infrequently but deeply when needed. Remove faded flower spikes to keep tidy and to encourage further blooming. Once cold weather arrives cut the foliage back to ground level and apply an added layer of mulch. In colder areas tie the foliage together, covering the crown, to prevent gathering rain and subsequent freezing. If you are tying, cut the foliage back to near the ground just prior to spring growth. Dividing will not need to be done for several years.

LANDSCAPE USE The bright red-orange and yellow selections combine wonderfully with the blue globe thistle, Jerusalem sage, dark blue and violet buddleia, and Brazilian sage. Use also with perennial verbenas like 'Homestead Purple' and 'Biloxi Blue.' The red-hot poker blooms in the same season as many daylilies, making interesting companions.

VARIETIES The red-hot poker has become popular in recent years with the naming of 'Flamenco' as an All America Selections winner in 1999. The blossoms reach 30 inches and are produced in orange, cream, yellow, and red, all on the same plant. Other good multicolored choices are 'Border Ballet,' 'Bressingham Comet,' and 'Atlantia.' Choice yellow selections are 'Primrose Beauty,' 'Shining Scepter,' and 'Sunningdale Yellow.' Look also for orange selections such as 'Catherine's Orange' and 'Kingston Flame.'

Lantana (lan-TAN-a) camara
and hybrids

Lantana

FAMILY: *Verbenaceae*
ORIGIN: Tropical America
RELATIVES: Verbena
PROPAGATION: Cutting, layering
ZONE: (7) 8–10
LIGHT: Sun
WATER: Less than average
SIZE: 2–6 feet
COLOR: All shades and blends
except blue

'Sonset' lantana

TOUGHNESS In August, when the family has the thermostat turned to 67 degrees, few plants are showing off in the garden. The lantana is, and remarkably it has been doing so since the first blooms of spring. The lantana is the South's toughest flower and now comes in a range of brilliant colors in which at least one should be acceptable to your color palette. Not only do hummingbirds feast on the nectar, the flowers are also virtual butterfly magnets.

PLANTING Select a site in full sun with soil that is fertile and well drained. Good drainage is most important from the standpoint of overwintering. Many years it will not be the cold that

prevents them from returning in zone 7 but the combination of cold and soggy conditions. Amend the soil with 3–4 inches of organic matter and till to a depth of 6–8 inches. While preparing the soil incorporate 2 pounds of a slow-release 12-6-6 fertilizer containing minor nutrients. Plant the lantana at the same depth it is growing in the container and space as recommended for your variety. Keep in mind that many spread 36 inches. Mulch them well after planting.

GROWING Don't be afraid to cut back or prune at any time to control size, shape, or spread. If blooms have ceased, prune by a third. New growth will be generated as well as blooms. Feed a month after transplanting and again in midsummer with a light application of fertilizer. Even though the lantana is very drought-tolerant give supplemental water during long dry periods. Once the plant has sustained significant frost damage cut back and apply extra mulch. This is also a good time to plant 6-inch dianthus or pansies in between the crowns of lantana.

LANDSCAPE USE The bright, bold colors show up even better with a backdrop of evergreen shrubs. Combine with buddleias, castor bean, Brazilian sage, and bananas for the look of the islands. Use with other indestructible plants like purple heart *(Tradescantia pallida)*, 'New Wonder' scaevola, and Brazilian verbena *(Verbena bonariensis)*.

VARIETIES Lantana as a genus was selected as a Louisiana Select winner. 'New Gold' lanatana (gold, 18-inch spreading) received the Mississippi Medallion award, Georgia Gold Medal, and Texas Superstar designation. 'Sonset' (yellow-orange-red-magenta, 3–4 feet) has also received the Mississippi Medallion award. 'Miss Huff' (orange and yellow, 5–6 feet) and 'Athens Rose' (rose and yellow, 3–4 feet) are known for extra cold-hardiness. 'Samson' (orange and yellow, 3–4 feet) and 'Sonrise' (yellow, orange, pink, 3–4 feet) are known for cold-hardiness and outstanding bloom in Mississippi trials.

Leucanthemum (lew-CANTH-e-mum)
x superbum

Shasta Daisy

FAMILY: *Asteraceae*
ORIGIN: Portugal, Pyrenees
RELATIVES: Purple Coneflower,
Rudbeckia
PROPAGATION: Division, seed
ZONE: 4–9
LIGHT: Sun to part shade
WATER: Average
SIZE: 10–36 inches
COLOR: White

'Becky' is one of the toughest Shasta daisies for the Deep South.

TOUGHNESS The old-fashioned Shasta daisy is still one of the most loved plants in the South. Sure, some varieties fall apart, but others are rock solid. Pristine, glistening white flowers light up the spring and early summer like no other plant. This is the flower that little girls and young ladies alike find most enchanting.

PLANTING The Shasta daisy has the potential of being around your home for a while if you select the right varieties and do proper bed prepa-ration. Choose a site with 6 hours of sun and a little afternoon shade protection. The soil must be fertile, organically rich, moist, and very well drained. If plagued by tight, heavy soil that doesn't drain, then amend with 3–4 inches of organic matter and till to a depth of 6–8 inches. While tilling incorporate 2 pounds of a slow-release fertilizer per 100 square feet of bed space. A 12-6-6 or balanced 8-8-8 blend with minor nutrients included is a good choice. Space plants 12–15 inches apart. Plant at the same depth as in the container. Apply a layer of mulch after planting.

GROWING Maintain moisture through the long, hot summer and feed with a light application of fertilizer every 4–6 weeks. Keep the flowers deadheaded for both a tidy look and increased flower production. Vigorous varieties will often repeat. Divide in the fall, spacing as recommended. This will be a yearly event if you want the best blooms and healthiest plants.

LANDSCAPE USE Shasta daisies should be grown boldly, in sweeping drifts of color. They combine wonderfully with the blazing star *(Liatris spicata)*, purple coneflower, 'Victoria' blue salvia, indigo spires salvia, and Japanese iris.

VARIETIES 'Becky' (30 inches) is one of the toughest in the Deep South. 'Snowcap' (18 inches) also has good heat-tolerance. Dwarf varieties 'Silver Princess' and 'Little Miss Muffet' have a good track record for longer blooming. 'Snow Lady,' also a dwarf, won the All America Selections award in 1991. 'Alaska' (36 inches) is still a favorite and has excellent cold-tolerance. Two of the newest promising selections are 'Darling Daisy' (15 inches) and 'Angel Daisy' (18–24 inches, shaped like a coneflower).

*Leucanthemum
(lew-CANTH-e-mum) vulgare*

Ox-eye Daisy

FAMILY: *Asteraceae*
ORIGIN: Eurasia
RELATIVES: Purple Coneflower,
Rudbeckia
PROPAGATION: Division, seed
ZONE: 3–9
LIGHT: Sun to part shade
WATER: Average
SIZE: 10–36 inches
COLOR: White

Ox-eye daisy yields pristine white spring flowers and returns faithfully.

TOUGHNESS When you see a plant growing in the highway medians you've got to figure it is tough. This is precisely what has happened with the ox-eye daisy. The brilliant white blossoms adorn this good perennial. While the Shasta daisies are gearing up for their display, the ox-eye is already putting on a show. It's not a repeat bloomer but it will be back next year. The ox-eye daisy does have a slight wildflower look and habit,

and some gardeners consider it on the aggressive side.

PLANTING Plant in full sun or with at least 6 hours of morning sun. The soil must be fertile and very well drained. If plagued by tight, heavy soil that doesn't drain, then amend with 3–4 inches of organic matter and till to a depth of 6–8 inches. While tilling incorporate 2 pounds of a slow-release fertilizer per 100 square feet of bed space. A 12-6-6 or balanced 8-8-8 blend with minor nutrients included is a good choice. Space plants 12–15 inches apart. Plant at the same depth as in the container. Apply a layer of mulch after planting.

GROWING Maintain moisture while in bloom. Keep the flowers deadheaded for a tidy look. Feed with a light application of fertilizer with the emergence of growth in the spring. The ox-eye daisy spreads by underground rhizomes and has been declared a noxious weed in some states. Make thinning or managing the spread part of your routine if you grow the ox-eye daisy. Cut plants back after the bloom. Divide in the fall if necessary.

LANDSCAPE USE The ox-eye daisy is the perfect seasonal match with larkspurs *(Consolida ambigua)*, yarrow, verbena, and hollyhocks. Use with Shasta daisies. The Shasta will not be blooming until the ox-eye is finishing, but your neighbors will swear your daisies bloomed for months and months. Grow in informal drifts with 'Early Sunrise' coreopsis.

VARIETIES The ox-eye is usually sold generically if at all. 'May Queen' is a named selection.

Liatris (ly-AY-tris) spicata

Blazing Star

FAMILY: *Asteraceae*
ORIGIN: Midwest and
Eastern United States
RELATIVES: Rudbeckia
PROPAGATION: Division, seed
ZONE: 3–9
LIGHT: Sun
WATER: Average
SIZE: 2–5 feet
COLOR: Blue, lilac, white

Blazing star is great in the garden and the vase.

TOUGHNESS When you search for tough plants those that are native usually make good choices, and the liatris is one of the best. Liatris or blazing star sends up tall spikes of purple, lavender, or white flowers on stiff stems that need no staking and are weather-tough. A strange horticultural phenomenon occurs on the liatris as blossoms open from top down in sequence. The blazing star ranks as one of the best cut flowers and is loved by butterflies.

PLANTING Select a site in full sun with fertile, well-drained soil. Well-drained soil is essential for a spring return. Amend with 3–4 inches of organic matter if necessary. While preparing the soil incorporate 2 pounds of a slow-release 12-6-6 fertilizer per 100 square feet of planting area. Plant nursery-grown transplants at the same depth as in the container. Space the plants 12–18 inches apart. Apply a good layer of mulch after planting. The liatris can also be grown from seed by sowing in September and October.

GROWING When growth resumes in the spring, feed with a light application of the fertilizer. Thin the seedlings or volunteers to the proper spacing. Deadhead flower stalks once the bloom

has finished. When the clump gets crowded, lift and divide in the spring. Discard older woody material, dust with a fungicide, and plant. Harvest flowers for cutting when the stems are one-third open and condition in warm water.

LANDSCAPE USE Plant the liatris boldly in informal drifts versus spot planting. Grow with Shasta daisies, 'Goldsturm' rudbeckia, and purple coneflowers. Use also with 'New Gold' lantana, melampodium, and 'Sunningdale Yellow' *Kniphofia uvaria*.

VARIETIES 'Kobold' (lilac) is still the leading variety. 'Floristan Violet' and 'Floristan White' are considered among the best. 'Blue Bird' (blue) is unique in color but hard to find. Try also *L. microcephala* that is rose-purple and dwarf.

Lysimachia (ly-sim-AK-ia) congestiflora

Golden Globes

FAMILY: *Primulaceae*
ORIGIN: China
RELATIVES: Primula
PROPAGATION: Division
ZONE: 7–10
LIGHT: Sun to part shade
WATER: Less than average
SIZE: 3–4 inches and spreading
COLOR: Golden yellow, some with variegated foliage

TOUGHNESS The lysimachia has been a much-loved plant, but this relatively new species from China is not even mentioned in most reference books. It has, however, skyrocketed in popularity. The golden globes is an outstanding deciduous groundcover with attractive foliage and yellow, bell-shaped flowers produced from spring through summer. It thrives in the heat.

PLANTING Select a site with morning sun and afternoon shade and fertile, well-drained soil. Amend tight, heavy soil with 3–4 inches of organic matter and till to a depth of 6-8 inches. Incorporate 2 pounds of a slow-release 12-6-6 fertilizer per 100 square feet of planting area. Plant at the same depth as in the container, spacing 12–18 inches apart.

GROWING Water to get the plants established but then sparingly. A light application of a slow-release, balanced fertilizer a month after transplanting should be sufficient for vigorous growth. Pinch or prune as needed to keep confined. In colder areas apply an added layer of mulch for winter protection. Feed established plants with a light application of fertilizer as growth resumes in the spring. Divide in early spring when needed.

LANDSCAPE USE Grow the golden globes as a groundcover with other drought-tolerant plants like 'New Wonder' scaevola and purple heart and gomphrena. Use in hanging baskets and as cascading plants in mixed containers. Petunias like 'Purple Wave' and 'Blue Wave' make nice companion plants.

VARIETIES 'Outback Sunset' with gold and green variegation in addition to the yellow blossoms has become the most popular selection. 'Eco Dark Satin' green foliage and yellow flowers with reddish-brown centers was the first selection and is also a very good choice. *L. japonica,* known as miniature moneywort, and *L. nummularia* creeping Jenny are other good groundcover species.

'Outback Sunset' lysimachia and purple heart make a striking groundcover of complementary colors.

Lythrum (LY-thrum) virgatum

Purple Loosestrife

FAMILY: *Lythraceae*
ORIGIN: Europe, Asia
RELATIVES: Crape myrtle
PROPAGATION: Division, cutting
ZONE: 3–9
LIGHT: Sun
WATER: Average
SIZE: 3–4 feet
COLOR: Rose, pink, purple

TOUGHNESS Gardeners everywhere love the purple loosestrife with its tall, spiky blossoms in purple, pink, and rose, but it comes with a CAUTION label. Loosestrife, and particularly *L. salicaria,* has escaped. Though it is beautiful it has become kudzulike and has been declared a noxious weed in many states. The *L. virgatum* hybrids 'Morden's Gleam,' 'Morden's Pink,' and 'Morden's Rose' are sterile and will not spread— if there are none of the invasive species in close

proximity. The Morden varieties have performed very well and with no spread in these situations. Check before you buy to see if it is illegal or if there is any naturalization occurring in your area. If you have never seen this plant in full bloom it almost takes your breath away with its beauty. Blooming lasts for weeks.

GROWING Select a site in full sun with well-drained organically rich soil. Amend tight, poorly drained soil with the addition of 3–4 inches of compost or humus and till to a depth of 6–8 inches. Set transplants at the same depth as in the container, spacing 24–36 inches apart. Apply a good layer of mulch after planting.

LANDSCAPE USE The purple loosestrife is as at home against a white picket fence as a palm tree is in Florida. Grow with daylilies, rudbeckias, salvias, or English roses for a cottage garden look. Use also with purple gomphrena. Burgundy-leafed varieties of coleus also look stunning as companion plants.

VARIETIES 'Morden's Gleam' (rose), 'Morden's Pink' (pink), 'Morden's Rose' (compact rose red), and 'Dropmore Purple' (purple-pink) are some of the best varieties.

The tall, spiky flowers of the loosestrife are among the most beautiful in the garden.

Malva (MAL-va) sylvestris

French Hollyhock

FAMILY: *Malvaceae*
ORIGIN: Europe, North Africa
RELATIVES: Hibiscus, Hollyhocks
PROPAGATION: Division, seed
ZONE: 4–9
LIGHT: Sun to part shade
WATER: Average
SIZE: 2–4 feet
COLOR: Lavender-pink, rose, light blue, most with purple stripes

The French hollyhock is an heirloom plant that is still loved by gardeners everywhere.

TOUGHNESS The French hollyhock is an old southern cottage garden plant that is easy to grow. Though considered a short-lived perennial or biennial, it will give a perennial-like performance by reseeding. The flowers are smaller than a hollyhock but are nonetheless beautiful. The light mauve flowers with purple stripes were much admired in the garden of Thomas Jefferson and will be loved in yours too.

PLANTING Select a site in full sun. The soil need not be overly rich but must be well drained. Plant nursery-grown transplants in the spring after the soil has warmed. Seeds can be planted in the fall or early spring and will bloom in the first year. Space plants or thin the seedlings to 2 feet apart.

GROWING Enjoy the natural growth pattern of the French hollyhock. Don't apply mulch too deeply during the growing season because you will want the seeds to find good soil. Do remove frost-damaged foliage in the fall and ad a layer of pine straw. With the emergence of spring growth, thin the seedlings to proper spacing. Give some to friends.

LANDSCAPE USE This French hollyhock is natural in gardens with picket fences, gazebos, or white lattice. They are ideally suited to the middle or back of the border, reaching about 4 feet in height. Plant them in an old-fashioned garden with antique roses, larkspurs, yarrow, daisies, and verbenas.

VARIETIES They are most often sold as *M. sylvestris* var. 'Zebrina' but are also still marketed under old nomenclature *Alcea zebrina* and *Althea zebrina* (lavender-pink with purple stripes). 'Brave Heart' (rose-pink with purple eye), 'Mauritiana' (rose with purple stripes), and 'Primley Blue' (light blue with darker veins) are improved selections but harder to find.

Malvaviscus (mal-va-VIS-kus) arboreus

Turk's Cap, Wax Mallow

FAMILY: *Malvaceae*
ORIGIN: Mexico, Peru, Brazil
RELATIVES: Hibiscus
PROPAGATION: Cutting, seed
ZONE: (7) 8–11
LIGHT: Sun to part shade
WATER: Average to less than average
SIZE: 5–6 feet
COLOR: Scarlet red

Turk's cap hibiscus is rugged, tough, and one of the best for the hummingbird garden.

TOUGHNESS It's funny to see gardeners act nonchalant about this plant because it appears as if the hibiscus flowers failed to open. Then as they watch the ruby-throated hummingbirds come in to feast on the scarlet red blossoms it becomes one of the world's greatest plants. The Turk's cap thrives with little care, sun to part shade, water or drought, it just keeps blooming from early summer through fall.

PLANTING Even though it is a great plant it may take a search to find yours. Plant it in fertile, well-drained soil with plenty of sunlight. Good drainage improves the chances of a spring return in colder areas. Dig the planting hole 2–3 times as wide as the root ball but no deeper and plant at the same depth it is growing in the container. Do remember the plants get large, so place to the middle or back of the border.

GROWING In northern zone 8 or 7 prune frost-damaged limbs in the fall and give an added layer of mulch. In southern zone 8 and 9 cut back damaged limbs in the early spring to tidy up. Feed with a light application of a slow-release 12-6-6 fertilizer as growth resumes in the spring and again in midsummer. Supplemental water during the summer rewards the gardener with a showier specimen.

LANDSCAPE USE The Turk's cap hibiscus is at home in the tropical or perennial cottage garden. Combine with other hummingbird plants. Use in front of bananas, tall cannas, and with 'Sungold' buddleia *(Buddleia weyeriana)*. Try low-growing lantanas in front of the Turk's cap.

VARIETIES *M. arboreus* var. *drummondii* (compact) and *M. arboreus* var. *Mexicana* (leaves lanceolate) are possible selections.

Mirabilis (my-RAB-il-is) jalapa

Four-O'-Clock, Marvel of Peru

FAMILY: *Nyctaginaceae*

ORIGIN: Peru

RELATIVES: Tobacco

PROPAGATION: Seed

ZONE: 7–11

LIGHT: Sun

WATER: Less than average

SIZE: 4–6 feet

COLOR: Red, yellow, white, pink, multicolored blends

Four-o'-clock offers a durable performance and a delightful fragrance.

TOUGHNESS If you were raised in the South you no doubt have experienced the four-o'-clock. The red, yellow, white, or multicolored flowers open in the afternoon at 4 o'clock, give or take an hour. The blossoms emit a tantalizing fragrance that makes the family want to sit on the porch, talk a while, but mostly cherish the botanical experience. This performance, which lasts all night, runs from summer through fall.

PLANTING This plant that all southerners have experienced and loved is harder to find than a four-leafed clover. Four-o'-clock is an easy-to-grow plant, but most likely you will be getting yours from the neighbor or Aunt Grace. Once you get your start, plant it in full sun in well-drained fertile soil. This is a large, shrublike plant reaching 4 feet in height and width, so place it accordingly.

GROWING Remove frozen foliage in the fall and add a layer of mulch in colder regions. The four-o'-clock reseeds with vigor so each spring make it a point to remove the ones you do not want. A little supplemental water during prolonged dry periods keeps the plant looking crisp, though it is very drought-tolerant.

LANDSCAPE USE The leaf texture and tubular flower form allows it to fit into the tropical landscape as easily as the cottage garden. Grow in front of bananas and with hibiscus in the tropical garden. In the cottage garden grow with other drought-tolerant plants like lantana, melampodium, and 'Goldsturm' rudbeckia. The most important consideration is location: place the four-o'-clock close to the porch, patio, or deck so the family can enjoy its enticing fragrance.

VARIETIES The four-o'-clock is rare at the garden center. Although commercially produced, it is still considered generic.

Nepeta (NEP-et-a) x faassenii

Catmint

FAMILY: *Lamiaceae*
ORIGIN: North Africa
RELATIVES: Salvia, Coleus
PROPAGATION: Division, cutting
ZONE: 5–9
LIGHT: Sun to part shade
WATER: Less than average
SIZE: 1–3 feet
COLOR: Blue, lavender, violet

Catmints are choice selections for the herb or perennial garden, yielding blue flowers and gray foliage.

TOUGHNESS The catmint is a drought-tolerant, durable plant for the perennial or herb garden. It produces an abundance of beautiful lavender-blue flowers in spring and summer that give the appearance of a rolling sea in the wind. The aromatic gray-green leaves give added interest to the garden as well as the strolling pet cat that may just have to go and nibble from time to time.

PLANTING The ideal site is morning sun and afternoon shade. More sun is tolerated in zones 6 and 7. The plants need well-drained beds, so anything less requires soil preparation. Incorporate 3–4 inches organic matter like fine pine bark or compost with 1 pound of a slow-release 5-10-5 fertilizer containing minor nutrients. Set out transplants 1–2 feet apart and plant at the same depth as in the container. Water and mulch after planting, and the plants will develop into a perennial groundcover.

GROWING Shear back after blooming and feed with a water-soluble fertilizer, or side-dress with time-released granules. A new flush of growth and blossoms often appear. The catmints can be vigorous and spreading, but don't be afraid to thin as necessary to keep contained.

LANDSCAPE USE The catmint makes a good groundcover. Plant in front of fountain grass, maiden grass, or the relatively new Mexican feather grass. The movement of the grasses and the catmint will work in harmony. 'Profusion Orange' zinnia and 'Samson' lantana make especially nice companions.

VARIETIES The most common variety, and many think the prettiest, is the 'Six Hills Giant' (dark violet, 2–3 feet). 'Dropmore' (deep lavender, 2 feet), and 'Porcelain' or 'Porzellan' (soft blue, 2 feet) are other good choices.

Oenothera (ee-no-THEE-ra) fruticosa

Sundrops, Evening Primrose

FAMILY: *Onagraceae*
ORIGIN: Eastern United States
RELATIVES: Gaura
PROPAGATION: Division, cutting
ZONE: 4–8
LIGHT: Sun to part shade
WATER: Less than average
SIZE: 2 feet
COLOR: Yellow

The sundrops are a stalwart performer in the southern cottage garden.

TOUGHNESS The sundrops or evening primrose is a staple in both the old and new southern cottage garden. The yellow blossoms are almost iridescent and bloom in late spring and summer. Although vigorous, this native U.S. plant isn't at all wild looking and is well suited to the flower border. The sundrops return from frigid winters, perform in torrid summers, and are drought-tolerant.

PLANTING Select a site in full to part sun with fertile, well-drained soil. If this doesn't describe your location, amend with 3–4 inches of compost or humus. While preparing the bed incorporate 2 pounds of a balanced 8-8-8 fertilizer per 100 square feet of planted area and till to a depth of 6–8 inches. Set out plants 12–18 inches apart and plant at the same depth as in the container. Apply a layer of mulch after planting.

GROWING Water to get the plants established but then sparingly. A light application of a slow-release, balanced fertilizer a month after transplanting should be sufficient for vigorous growth. Plants can be divided in the spring or summer as needed. Although they are not horribly aggressive, prune to maintain size and shape.

LANDSCAPE USE The sundrops are ideal for the cottage garden or perennial garden and combine wonderfully with 'Blue Daze' *Evolvulus,* which has icy blue flowers and gray-green foliage. Placing them in front of tall 'Becky' Shasta daisies demands a photograph. Other outstanding choice companions are violet to blue salvias like 'Victoria,' 'Black and Blue' *Salvia guaranitica,* and the 'Navajo' *Salvia greggi.* Try also in front of liatris or purple coneflower. The sundrops also look at home with petunias that are purple, blue, pink, or white.

VARIETIES Still offered generically, but look for 'Yellow River' (attractive reddish-brown fall foliage), 'Fireworks' (red stems and buds open to yellow), 'Sonnenwende' (pink buds open to yellow), and 'Summer Solstice' (reddish-purple fall foliage).

Penstemon (pen-STEE-mon) digitalis

'Husker Red,' Beard Tongue

FAMILY: *Scrophulariaceae*
ORIGIN: South Dakota to Maine, Texas, Alabama, Virginia
RELATIVES: Snapdragon
PROPAGATION: Divison
ZONE: 3–8
LIGHT: Sun to part shade
WATER: Less than average
SIZE: 2½–3 feet
COLOR: White with burgundy-red foliage

The white-flowered 'Husker Red' is complemented by its burgundy-red foliage.

TOUGHNESS 'Husker Red' penstemon released from the University of Nebraska was recognized as Perennial Plant of the Year due to its long-season, ornamental effect and adaptability to most areas of North America. It has as many as 50 white flowers on each airy flower stalk. The foliage is a rich bronze-red that provides striking contrast with its masses of white flowers and is equally showy. It is a versatile garden perennial, is valuable as a specimen or cut flower, and is loved by hummingbirds.

PLANTING 'Husker Red' prefers a slightly acidic, well-drained soil. Well-drained soil is especially crucial during the winter. Cold conditions coupled with wet feet will prevent the penstemon from returning in the spring. Plant nursery-grown transplants in full sun to light shade at the same depth as in the container.

GROWING This plant is drought-tolerant once established. Do provide supplemental water during prolonged summer dry periods and keep mulched. Plants should be cut back hard after flowering. For established gardens, sprinkle 1 pound of a slow-release 12-6-6 or similar garden fertilizer per 100 square feet of soil in early spring when new growth begins. Divide in the spring every 3 years. 'Husker Red' can be propagated by division or from cuttings. Basal or shoot tip cuttings taken from new growth before flowering will root within 15 days.

LANDSCAPE USE Keep in mind that 'Husker Red' reaches 30 inches in height, so place accordingly in the perennial garden. 'Husker Red' can be massed at the back of the perennial border or used as a specimen plant. The white flowers and bronze-red foliage can be easily combined with almost any other perennial. Coreopsis, purple coneflowers, rudbeckias, Shasta daisies, and yarrow all work nicely.

VARIETIES In addition to *Penstemon digitalis* 'Husker Red,' try *also P. barbatus* Beardlip Penstemon, *P. havardii* Harvard Penstemon, *P. smallii* Smalls Penstemon, and *P. tenuis* Gulf Coast Penstemon.

Perovskia (pe-ROF-skee-a) atripilicifolia

Russian Sage

FAMILY: *Lamiaceae*

ORIGIN: Afghanistan, Pakistan

RELATIVES: Coleus, Agastache

PROPAGATION: Division, cutting, seed

ZONE: 5–9

LIGHT: Sun to part shade

WATER: Average

SIZE: 4–5 feet

COLOR: Blue, violet

TOUGHNESS This plant is one of the anomalies in the horticultural world in that it is called Russian sage but is not from Russia. Russian sage, however, was the Perennial Plant of the Year in 1995 and is one that does well over much of the country. The plant is one of the most versatile perennials, having cold-hardiness over a huge area and offering unique flowers in shades of blue and olive gray-green foliage that is equally striking. The bloom period is over 3 months, making this plant a must for the garden.

PLANTING Select a site in full sun. The soil should be very well drained. Plant on raised beds or amend heavy soils with the addition of compost or humus. Well-drained soil may encourage it to return further north than expected. While preparing the soil incorporate 2 pounds of a slow-release 12-6-6 fertilizer per 100 square feet of bed space. Space the plants 24–36 inches apart, planting at the same depth as in the container.

GROWING Give supplemental water during long dry periods. In the fall once the plant has received significant frost damage, prune to 12 inches and add a layer of mulch for winter protection. Feed in the spring with a light application of fertilizer with the emergence of growth and every 6–8 weeks through September. Pinch in late spring to improve branching. Divide offshoots with the emergence of spring growth.

LANDSCAPE USE Russian sage is large but works well in large drifts with gold yarrow and 'Stella d'Oro' daylily or used in the cottage garden in front of a white picket fence draped by a David Austin English rose like 'Graham Thomas.' Plant it also with 'Moonbeam' coreopsis.

VARIETIES Russian sage is often sold generically, but look for 'Blue Spire' or 'Longin' with violet flowers. 'Filagran' has filigreed foliage and pale blue flowers.

Tall blue Russian sage combines effectively with the white yarrow.

Phlomis (FLO-mis) fruticosa

Jerusalem Sage

FAMILY: *Lamiaceae*
ORIGIN: Mediterranean
RELATIVES: Salvias
PROPAGATION: Division,
cutting, seed
ZONE: 6–9
LIGHT: Sun to part shade
WATER: Average
SIZE: 4 feet
COLOR: Yellow

TOUGHNESS The Jerusalem sage is just now making its way to southern gardens, and those that have it are ecstatic with its performance. The gardeners who have seen it but don't have it are searching for it. Why all the fuss, you might ask? The answer lies in the bright, cheerful, yellow blossoms that open in whorls along the upright stems. The flowers are accompanied by foliage that is hairy and silvery green, making it an asset to the garden even if it never bloomed.

The flowers give way to 3-sided fruit that also adds garden interest.

PLANTING This Mediterranean plant will perform admirably in the hot, humid South and is not fussy about soil fertility if it is well drained. If it is not well drained add 3–4 inches of organic matter and till in 6–8 inches deep. The Jerusalem sage needs plenty of sunlight to bloom best but is tolerant of a little afternoon shade. Amend the planting area with a cup of a 5-10-5 fertilizer prior to planting. Dig the planting hole 2–3 times as wide as the root ball but no deeper. Plant at the same depth it is growing in the container.

GROWING The Jerusalem sage is drought-tolerant but will perform better with supplemental water during the summer. Removing old flower stems will encourage successive blooms. This plant is considered a sub shrub and gets woody. Cutting back hard in early spring every 2–3 years will be similar to a rejuvenation-type pruning.

LANDSCAPE USE The handsome woolly gray foliage is evergreen and stands out in the garden against traditional deep green foliage. Both the foliage and flower combine wonderfully with buddleia like 'Nanho Purple.' Use with salvias like the Brazilian sage or indigo spires. Grow with the Russian sage *Perovskia atriplicifolia.* Try 'Blue Daze' *Evolvulus* around the base of the plant for a nice companion planting of flower colors and foliage.

VARIETIES The Jerusalem sage is sold generically. Also sold as Jerusalem sage is *P. lanata.* 'Edward Bowles' is a hybrid *P. fruticosa x P. russeliana* with bicolored dark and light yellow blossoms.

Jerusalem sage is a garden asset with yellow flowers and olive gray foliage.

Phlox (flox) divaricata

Woodland Phlox, Louisiana Phlox,

FAMILY: *Polemoniaceae*
ORIGIN: United States, Canada
RELATIVES: Jacob's Ladder
PROPAGATION: Cutting, division, seed
ZONE: 4–9
LIGHT: Part shade to shade
WATER: Average
SIZE: 12–15 inches
COLOR: Blue, lavender, purple, pink

Woodland phlox provides welcome blue springtime colors.

TOUGHNESS This native covers a huge area of the United States from east Texas to Alaska, the Dakotas, Quebec, and then over the entire Southeast. This means woodland phlox is well adapted. It is a tried-and-true perennial that offers fragrant flowers in bright blues, lavenders, and pinks that bloom underneath dogwoods and redbuds for a spectacular spring display.

PLANTING Select a site with morning sun and afternoon shade or high filtered light. The bed should be fertile, organically rich, and well drained. Add 3–4 inches of compost or humus along with 2 pounds of a preplant fertilizer per 100 square feet of bed space. Use a blend like a slow-release 12-6-6 with minor nutrients. Till the soil and amendments 6–8 inches deep. Plant nursery-grown transplants 10–12 inches apart, planting at the same depth as in the container. Apply a layer of mulch after planting.

GROWING Once woodland phlox has finished blooming, cut the foliage back by half. This will encourage new growth. Stick the cuttings in moist sand or peat to start more plants. Since the foliage serves no landscape purpose from this point on until next season, consider dropping in caladium bulbs between plants. These will offer landscape beauty and will be gone when the phlox leafs out in the early spring. When new growth resumes in the spring, side-dress with a light application of fertilizer. Clumps can be divided in early spring to add to the landscape.

LANDSCAPE USE The woodland phlox blooms at the most wonderful time of the year in the South. Use along woodland trails with dogwoods, redbuds, azaleas, and daffodils. Use with Japanese maples like the 'Bloodgood.'

VARIETIES The woodland phlox is often sold generically despite several well-known varieties. 'Louisiana Blue' (blue-purple with magenta eye), 'May Breeze' (lavender-blue), 'London Grove' Blue (deep blue), and 'Chattahooche' (light purple, dark eye, hybrid *P divaricata x P. pilosa*)

Phlox (flox) paniculata

Perennial Phlox, Summer Phlox

FAMILY: *Polemoniaceae*
ORIGIN: Eastern United States
RELATIVES: Woodland Phlox
PROPAGATION: Cutting,
division, seed
ZONE: 4–9
LIGHT: Part shade to shade
WATER: Average
SIZE: 3–5 inches
COLOR: Pink, white, magenta, blue,
red

Pink phlox and melampodium brighten the summer garden.

TOUGHNESS This is an old-fashioned heirloom plant that you see returning to cottage gardens everywhere in the southeastern United States. There are stories of plants plagued by powdery mildew, but the old magenta-colored phlox is rock-solid, as are several others. Tall, fragrant flowers are borne during the scorching time of the summer from June through August.

PLANTING The ideal site would be morning sunlight followed by a little midafternoon sun protection. The bed should be fertile, organically rich, and well drained. Add 3–4 inches of compost or humus along with 2 pounds of a preplant fertilizer per 100 square feet of bed space. Use a blend like a slow-release 12-6-6 with minor nutrients. Till the soil and amendments, 6–8 inches deep. Plant nursery-grown transplants 12–18-inches apart, planting at the same depth as in the container. Apply a layer of mulch after planting.

GROWING Feed the phlox with a light application of fertilizer once growth resumes in the spring and again in midsummer. Keeping flowers deadheaded and the plants watered encourages repeat blooms through the summer and often into the fall. Staking may be required since the plants do get tall. Another option is to grow stiff clumping flowers in front, such as the 'Goldsturm' rudbeckia. Keeping the plants well spaced and thinned helps in the prevention of powdery mildew, as does watering from the bottom of the plant versus overhead irrigation. Choose varieties known to be resistant.

LANDSCAPE USE The summer phlox is a staple of the old-fashioned cottage garden and was made for planting against the picket fence. Plant boldly, grouping several plants, versus spot planting. Use with the black-eyed Susan, 'Stella d'Oro' daylily, or melampodium. Try with angelonias, to give a spiky snapdragon look.

VARIETIES Some of the best for resistance to powdery mildew are 'David' (white Perennial Plant of the Year), 'Katherine' (lavender, white eye), 'Robert Poore' (red-purple), 'Laura' (purple-violet, white-blushed eye), and 'Eva McCullum' (pink with red eye)

Phlox (flox) subulata

Moss Pink, Creeping Phlox

FAMILY: *Polemoniaceae*
ORIGIN: New York, Maryland, Michigan
RELATIVES: Jacob's Ladder
PROPAGATION: Division, cutting, seed
ZONE: 3–9
LIGHT: Part shade to shade
WATER: Average
SIZE: 6 inches, spreading
COLOR: Blue, pink, red, white

TOUGHNESS Horticulturists are always looking for plants that are sometimes referred to as "sixty-mile-per-hour plants." This means that while zipping down the highway, your attention is diverted to the pretty flowers in some landscape. This is exactly what the moss pink can do. Most of the year it is an attractive groundcover; then in the spring it is shocking pink, blue, or red in iri-descent color. The moss pink is more drought-tolerant and sun-tolerant than other phlox.

PLANTING The ideal site is morning sun-light followed by afternoon sun protection. The bed should be fertile, organically rich, and well drained. Add 3–4 inches of compost or humus along with 2 pounds of a preplant fertilizer per 100 square feet of bed space. Use a blend such as a slow-release 12-6-6 with minor nutrients. Till the soil and amendments, 6–8 inches deep. Plant nursery-grown transplants 12–18 inches apart, planting at the same depth as in the container. Apply a layer of mulch after planting.

GROWING Feed with a light application of fertilizer, once growth resumes in the spring. After the bloom cycle, shear back by half, removing spent flowers and lightly pruning the foliage. Feed with another light application of fertilizer. Shear as needed to maintain a nice carpet of foliage. Give supplemental water during dry periods to maintain vigor. Propagation is best done by division or by cuttings taken in the fall.

VARIETIES Blue types are the most popular. Look for 'Emerald Blue,' 'Blue Hills,' and 'Emerald Cushion Blue.' 'Emerald Cushion Pink,' 'Apple Blossom,' and 'Perfection' are choice pink selections. 'Cracker Jack' and 'Scarlet Flame' are leading red varieties. For white, try 'Snowflake' or 'White Delight.' Also try *Phlox stolonifera* creeping phlox.

Moss pink is an attractive blooming groundcover.

Rudbeckia (rood-BEK-ia) fulgida

Orange Coneflower, Perennial Black-eyed Susan

FAMILY: *Asteraceae*
ORIGIN: Southeast United States
RELATIVES: Asters
PROPAGATION: Division, seed, cutting
ZONE: 3–8
LIGHT: Sun to part shade
WATER: Average
SIZE: 2–3 feet
COLOR: Orange-gold

'Goldsturm' rudbeckia is one of the most reliable perennials.

TOUGHNESS The variety 'Goldsturm' is one of the most celebrated plants in the Southeast. This Perennial Plant of the Year and Louisiana Select winner may be the perfect perennial. Golden yellow black-eyed Susan flowers adorn the plant from late spring through frost. A 4-inch container transplanted in the spring yields enough growth for a half-dozen plants a year later.

PLANTING This is a long-lived perennial spreading with vigor but only when planted in well-drained soil. If plagued by tight, heavy soil that doesn't drain, amend with 3–4 inches of organic matter and till to a depth of 6–8 inches. While tilling incorporate 2 pounds of a slow-release fertilizer per 100 square feet of bed space. A 12-6-6 or balanced 8-8-8 blend with minor nutrients included is a good choice. Full sun gives the most spectacular bloom. Space plants 12–15 inches apart. Plant at the same depth as in the container. Apply a layer of mulch after planting.

GROWING Maintain moisture through the long hot summer and feed with a light application of fertilizer every 4–6 weeks. Keep the flowers deadheaded for both a tidy look and increased flower production. It is not uncommon for blooms to be sparse by August. If this occurs prune all flower stalks, and larger ones will develop for a good fall display. Divide plants in the early spring as growth starts to resume.

LANDSCAPE USE 'Goldsturm' is perhaps the most popular perennial in the United States. It combines wonderfully with blue or violet flowers from salvias or verbenas. It is quite at home with purple coneflowers, Shasta daisies, and all kinds of ornamental grasses from purple fountain, the best, to Japanese silver. Try a blue gazing globe in the middle of the 'Goldsturm' clump.

VARIETIES The award-winning 'Goldsturm' is basically the name everything is sold by. References suggest that *R. fulgida* var. *deamii*, *R. fulgida* var. *speciosa*, and *R. fulgida* var. *sullivantii* all have slight differences.

Rudbeckia (rood-BEK-ia) lanciniata

Cutleaf Coneflower

FAMILY: *Asteraceae*
ORIGIN: North America, Manitoba to Arizona, Texas, Florida
RELATIVES: Yarrow
PROPAGATION: Seed, division, cutting
ZONE: 3–9
LIGHT: Sun to part shade
WATER: Average
SIZE: 4–7 feet
COLOR: Yellow-gold

Cutleaf coneflower is a giant in the garden and worth the effort.

TOUGHNESS Gardeners who have never seen the giant varieties of this plant often stand and stare in disbelief at this 7-foot-tall plant with scores of yellow black-eyed-Susan-like flowers. This is a rough, tough perennial, able to withstand the extremes of winter and torrid summers as well.

PLANTING This is a long-lived perennial when planted in well-drained soil. If plagued by tight, heavy soil that doesn't drain, amend with 3–4 inches of organic matter and till to a depth of 6–8 inches. While tilling, incorporate 2 pounds of a slow-release fertilizer per 100 square feet of bed space. A 12-6-6 or balanced 8-8-8 blend with minor nutrients included is a good choice. Full sun with protection from wind yields the best-looking plants, with a bloom that might be considered a spectacle. Space plants 36 inches apart. Plant toward the back of the border at the same depth as in the container. Apply a layer of mulch after planting.

GROWING If grown in windy conditions or partial shade, staking or tying for support is necessary. Deadheading after the first flush of blooms will generate another round of blooms for fall. Keep watered and fed with light applications of fertilizer every 4–6 weeks. Divide in the early spring if needed, when growth has resumed.

LANDSCAPE USE Not only is this plant well suited to the back of the border, it can also serve well in the middle of a long border by acting as a foil or screen to keep you from seeing what is next. By all means plant in front or around the flower, particularly if staking or tying is required. Russian sage, Brazilian sage, 'Nanho Purple' buddleia, and Joe Pye weed are good choices.

VARIETIES 'Golden Glow' (3–5 feet), 'Gold-quelle' (double yellow, 4 feet), and 'Herbstonne,' also called 'Autumn Sun' (*R. lanciniata x R. nitida* hybrid, 7 feet), are the favorites.

Rudbeckia (rood-BEK-ia) maxima

Giant Coneflower

FAMILY: *Asteraceae*
ORIGIN: Central and
Southern United States
RELATIVES: Purple Coneflower
PROPAGATION: Root cutting
ZONE: 5–9
LIGHT: Sun to part shade
WATER: Average
SIZE: 5–8 feet
COLOR: Yellow, gold

The giant coneflower offers beauty in foliage and flower.

TOUGHNESS The giant coneflower is indeed monolithic. The attractive, unique, blue-green leaves may be 2 feet long and 8 inches wide and are borne on plants that may indeed get 8 feet tall. Incredibly, if grown in full sun, it will not need staking. The yellow-gold flowers are at least 3 inches wide, and the brown-black cone is longer, reaching 2 inches.

PLANTING Trials have shown this to be a long-lived perennial in the South when planted in well-drained soil. If plagued by tight, heavy soil that doesn't drain well, amend with 3–4 inches of organic matter and till to a depth of 6–8 inches. While tilling incorporate 2 pounds of a slow-release fertilizer per 100 square feet of bed space. A 12-6-6 or balanced 8-8-8 blend with minor nutrients included is a good choice. Although this is a tall plant, it is sturdy and will not need support if grown in full sun. Space plants 36 inches apart, toward the back of the border, at the same depth as in the container. Apply a layer of mulch after planting.

GROWING Maintain moisture during the long hot summer and feed with a light application of fertilizer, every 4–6 weeks. Keep the flowers deadheaded for both a tidy look and increased flower production. Leave a few flowers for seed development. Divide plants in the early spring as growth starts to resume. Look around and you may also find some seedlings. Thin as needed or transplant to other areas of the garden.

LANDSCAPE USE The large blue-green foliage is almost as much a landscape asset as the flower. Use to the back of the border. The dark purple buddleia would excel in front. Use with red cannas for an exceptional look. The 'Costa Rica Blue' variety of Brazilian sage combines well.

VARIETIES The *R. maxima* is sold generically.

Rudbeckia (rood-BEK-ia) triloba

Three-lobed Coneflower

FAMILY: *Asteraceae*
ORIGIN: Central Eastern United States
RELATIVES: Shasta Daisy
PROPAGATION: Division, seed, cutting
ZONE: 5–9
LIGHT: Sun to part shade
WATER: Average
SIZE: 2–4 feet
COLOR: Yellow-orange

The three-lobed coneflower is a Georgia Gold Medal winner.

TOUGHNESS This genus was recognized as a Georgia Gold Medal winner and would qualify just about everywhere in the South. It can be grown in many different soils, making it Amer-ica's plant. The black-eyed-Susan-like flowers are yellow-orange and produced in abundance all summer long from attractive 3-lobed leaves.

PLANTING Some references suggest that this plant is biennial or a short-lived perennial; others say, perennial that reseeds too. One thing is for sure. You will have it around, one way or another, for a long time if you plant in fertile, well-drained soil in full sun. If plagued by tight, heavy soil that doesn't drain well, amend with 3–4 inches of organic matter and till to a depth of 6–8 inches. While tilling, incorporate 2 pounds of a slow-release fertilizer per 100 square feet of bed space. A 12-6-6 or balanced 8-8-8 blend with minor nutrients included is a good choice. Space plants 24–36 inches apart toward the middle or back of the border. Plant at the same depth as in the container. These are easy to grow from seed and will flower the first year. Apply a layer of mulch after planting or when the seedlings have reached 6–8 inches.

GROWING Watering during periods of drought keeps the plant at full speed with growth and blooms. Feed with a light application of fertilizer every 4–6 weeks. Keeping the flowers deadheaded increases flower production. Leave a few flowers for seed development. Divide plants in the early spring as growth starts to resume. Look around because you will also find some seedlings. Thin as needed or transplant to other areas of the garden.

LANDSCAPE USE Those desiring a wildflower meadow look will like this species. Use in bold informal drifts with other meadow-looking plants such as the purple coneflower or red autumn sage. The perennial border with blue salvias and Shasta daisies will welcome the yellow-orange triloba. Use also with ornamental grasses.

VARIETIES The *R. triloba* is sold generically, although a dwarf form *R. triloba* var. *nana* has been selected.

Ruellia (roo-ELL-ia) brittoniana

Ruellia, Mexican Petunia

FAMILY: *Acanthaceae*
ORIGIN: Mexico
RELATIVES: Shrimp Plant, Thunbergia
PROPAGATION: Divison, cutting, seed
ZONE: 7–10
LIGHT: Sun to part shade
WATER: Average
SIZE: 8–48 inches
COLOR: Blue-purple, pink, white

Mexican petunias offer bluish-purple flowers that are almost iridescent.

TOUGHNESS Few plants are as tough and as deserving of a place in the southern flower border as the ruellia. It not only endures our high heat but also thrives in it. The 2-inch tubular bluish-purple or pink flowers are almost iridescent and borne in clusters on forked branches. Flowers radiate from the plant from summer through fall. The deep green foliage on stems of burgundy to purple gives a special texture in the garden. Although called the Mexican petunia, ruellia is not related to petunias.

PLANTING The Mexican petunia thrives in moist, well-drained, organically rich soils and performs well in poorer soils too. A word of warning: in the highly rich soils, it can spread if you don't pay close attention. Protection from midafternoon sun allows for a lush appearance. Tight, heavy soil prevents the ruellia from reaching its potential. Amend the soil with organic matter if necessary.

GROWING Remove frozen foliage to keep tidy. Pay attention to volunteers and keep under control. Supplemental water during the long hot summer will keep the plant looking its best. In colder areas protect with added mulch going into winter.

LANDSCAPE USE Ruellias look good massplanted or spot-planted in the perennial border. Purple varieties are exceptional with lantanas like 'New Gold,' 'Samson,' and 'Silver Mound.' Other good companions are purple coneflowers, oldfashioned summer phlox, pentas, and pink verbenas.

VARIETIES The taller purple-flowered selections are often sold generically. Other good choices are 'Chi-Chi' (pink, 36–48 inches), 'Katie's Dwarf' (purple, 8–12 inches), 'Colobe Pink' (pink, 8 inches), and 'Alba' (white, 30–36 inches). Look also for *Ruellia elegans,* elegant ruellia, (scarletred, 12 inches, and spreading).

Salvia (SAL-via) coccinea

Texas Sage

FAMILY: *Lamiaceae*
ORIGIN: Tropical South America
RELATIVES: Coleus, Agastache
PROPAGATION: Division,
cutting, seed
ZONE: 9–10, reseeding
annual elsewhere
LIGHT: Sun to part shade
WATER: Average
SIZE: 2–3 feet
COLOR: Red, coral, pink, white

TOUGHNESS Although perennial in zone 9 and further south, the 'Lady in Red' variety has been designated as both Louisiana Select and Arkansas Select winners and an All America Selections winner. If red isn't your color there is coral, pink, and white too. The flowers are prolific from spring through frost. The Texas sage gives a perennial-like performance by reseeding.

PLANTING The ideal site is morning sun and afternoon shade. The soil should be very well drained, as this plant is native to the west. Plant on raised beds or amend heavy soils with the addition of compost or humus. Well-drained soil may encourage returning further north than expected, although reseeding is normal. While preparing the soil incorporate 2 pounds of a slow-release 12-6-6 fertilizer per 100 square feet of bed space. Space the plants 12 inches apart, planting at the same depth as in the container.

GROWING Although drought-tolerant, the Texas sage performs best if given supplemental water during long dry periods. In the fall, when the plant has received significant frost damage, prune to ground level and add a layer of mulch for winter protection. Feed in the spring with a light application of fertilizer with the emergence of growth or when seedlings are 8 inches tall and every 6–8 weeks through September. Thin the seedlings to proper spacing. Deadhead spent flowers and occasionally prune to maintain bushiness.

LANDSCAPE USE 'Lady in Red' is wonderful with yellow flowers like rudbeckia, lantana, or melampodium, while very effective displays can be created using 'Coral Nymph' or 'White Nymph' with purple heart, 'Blackie' sweet potato, or 'Purple Palace' *Heuchera*.

VARIETIES 'Lady in Red' (red) is the big award winner; look also for 'Coral Nymph' (coral-pink) and 'White Nymph' (white).

'Lady in Red' *Salvia coccinea* has won awards in several states.

Salvia (SAL-via) elegans

Pineapple Sage

FAMILY: *Lamiaceae*
ORIGIN: Tropical Mexico, Guatemala
RELATIVES: Coleus, Lamium
PROPAGATION: Division, cutting, seed
ZONE: (7)–10
LIGHT: Sun to part shade
WATER: Average
SIZE: 2–5 feet
COLOR: Red

Pineapple sage yields tasty leaves for the table and scarlet red flowers for hummingbirds.

TOUGHNESS The pineapple sage is useful from spring through frost, wherever it is grown. The flowers appear in late summer, and the leaves give the aroma and flavor of opening a can of crushed pineapple. Hummingbirds relish the scarlet flowers, while the chef of the house will love using the leaves to flavor drinks and cream cheese.

PLANTING The ideal site would be morning sun and afternoon shade. The soil should be very well drained. Plant on raised beds or amend heavy soils with the addition of compost or humus. Well-drained soil may encourage a return further north than expected. While preparing the soil incorporate 2 pounds of a slow-release 12-6-6 fertilizer per 100 square feet of bed space. Space the plants 24 inches apart, planting at the same depth as in the container. Note: do not plant under streetlights or floodlights, as these plants bloom in response to number of dark hours.

GROWING Give supplemental water during long dry periods. In the fall, once the plant has received significant frost damage, prune to ground level and add a layer of mulch for winter protection. Feed in the spring with a light application of fertilizer with the emergence of growth and every 6–8 weeks through September. Pinch a couple of times to maintain bushiness. Harvest young tender leaves in the morning for use in flavoring.

LANDSCAPE USE The pineapple sage is well suited to the herb, perennial, or tropical garden. Use with other fall-blooming salvias in the perennial garden. In the tropical garden, combine with yellow shrimp plant or bush allamanda. Plant in front of large bananas or *Alocasia* elephant ears.

VARIETIES The pineapple sage is sold generically.

Salvia (SAL-via) farinacea

Mealy-Cup Sage

FAMILY: *Lamiaceae*

ORIGIN: Texas, Mexico

RELATIVES: Coleus, Mint

PROPAGATION: Division,
cutting, seed

ZONE: 7–10

LIGHT: Sun to part shade

WATER: Average

SIZE: 2–3 feet

COLOR: Blue, white, blends

'Victoria' blue salvia was selected as a Mississippi Medallion winner for its long blooming season.

TOUGHNESS The 'Victoria' blue variety of the mealy-cup sage was chosen as a Mississippi Medallion winner. The deep blue flowers arise above the plant, attracting bees and butterflies. The spiky texture and blue blossoms are most welcome in the world of round flowers. The flowers produce from spring through frost.

PLANTING Select a site in full sun, although some afternoon shade is tolerated. The soil should be very well drained, as this plant is native to the Southwest. Plant on raised beds or amend heavy soils with the addition of compost or humus. Well-drained soil may encourage a return further north than expected. While preparing the soil incorporate 2 pounds of a slow-release 12-6-6 fertilizer per 100 square feet of bed space. Space the plants 12 inches apart, planting at the same depth as in the container.

GROWING Water your mealy-cup sage during long dry periods. In the fall, after significant frost damage, prune plant to ground level and add a layer of mulch for winter protection. Feed in the spring with a light application of fertilizer with the emergence of growth and every 6–8 weeks through September. Keep the plant deadheaded to increase flower production. The mealy-cup sage responds well to hard pruning in August for an extra-special fall display.

LANDSCAPE USE The mealy-cup sage looks like the poster plant for cottage gardening. Combine with white picket fences and antique roses. Use with companions like purple coneflower, Shasta daisies, yarrow, or its complementary color coming from the 'Goldsturm' rudbeckia.

VARIETIES 'Victoria,' the Mississippi Medallion award winner, 'Argent' (silver and white), 'Reference' (blue and white), and the All America Selections winner 'Strata' (white and blue) are leading selections.

Salvia (SAL-via) greggii

Autumn Sage

FAMILY: *Lamiaceae*
ORIGIN: Texas, Mexico
RELATIVES: Coleus, Lavender
PROPAGATION: Cutting, seed
ZONE: 7–10
LIGHT: Sun to part shade
WATER: Less than average
SIZE: 3–4 feet
COLOR: Red, pink, white, rose,
salmon, cream

If you are plagued by deer try Autumn sage. Deer reportedly hate them.

TOUGHNESS Although called autumn sage, the flowers are nonstop from spring through frost and come in a nice range of colors. The flowers are striking in the garden and attractive to hummingbirds. The best feature of the plants could be that deer detest them. Many gardeners mix these plants in with others that the deer consider delicacies.

PLANTING The ideal site is full sun, but some shade is certainly tolerated. The soil should be very well drained, as this plant is native to the arid West. Plant on raised beds or loosen heavy soils with the addition of compost or humus. Well-drained soil may encourage a return further north than expected. While preparing the soil incorporate 2 pounds of a slow-release 12-6-6 fertilizer per 100 square feet of bed space. Space the plants 18–24 inches apart, planting at the same depth as in the container.

GROWING Give supplemental water during long dry periods. In the fall, after significant frost damage, prune to ground level and add a layer of mulch for winter protection. Feed in the spring with a light application of fertilizer with the emergence of growth and every 6–8 weeks through September. Keep the plant deadheaded to increase flower production. The autumn sage responds well to occasional shearing.

LANDSCAPE USE Use these plants for their beauty but also place very close to plants challenged by deer. Plant autumn sage in informal drifts in the perennial garden among rudbeckias, purple coneflowers, mealy-cup sage, Shasta daisies, Russian sage, and lantanas.

VARIETIES The new 'Navajo' series with cream, dark purple, bright red, pink, white, rose, and salmon-red is bringing a revitalized interest in the plant. Look also for 'Cherry Queen' (red) and 'Dark Dancer' (purple-maroon).

Salvia (SAL-via) guaranitica

Brazilian Sage

FAMILY: *Lamiaceae*
ORIGIN: Brazil, Argentina, Uruguay
RELATIVES: Coleus, Lion's Tail
PROPAGATION: Division,
cutting, seed
ZONE: 7–10
LIGHT: Sun to part shade
WATER: Average
SIZE: 3–6 feet
COLOR: Dark blue, light blue,
dark purple

'Argentina Sky' is a light blue selection of Brazilian sage.

TOUGHNESS The Brazilian sage produces the deepest blue color in the world of flowers and is loved by the ruby-throated hummingbird. The genera was chosen as a Georgia Gold Medal winner, while 'Costa Rica Blue' was chosen as a Mississippi Medallion winner. The plants are resilient in the face of all kinds of weather.

PLANTING The ideal site is full sun, as shade will make the plant a little leggy. The soil should be very well drained. Plant on raised beds or amend heavy soils with the addition of compost or humus. Well-drained soil may encourage a return further north than expected. While preparing the soil incorporate 2 pounds of a slow-release 12-6-6 fertilizer per 100 square feet of bed space. Space the plants 36 inches apart, planting at the same depth as in the container.

GROWING Give supplemental water during long dry periods. In the fall, after frost damage, prune to ground level and add a layer of mulch for winter protection. Feed in the spring with a light application of fertilizer with the emergence of growth and every 6–8 weeks through September. Keep the plant deadheaded to increase flower production. If the bloom becomes sparse, prune back by half in August for a fresh fall display. Divide every 3–4 years.

LANDSCAPE USE The Brazilian sage is a must in the hummingbird garden. Plant with other salvias loved by hummers or against a picket fence adorned by trumpet vine. The deep cobalt blue works in the tropical garden with allamanda, firebush *(Hamelia patens)*, yellow shrimp plant, and 'Sonset' lantana. It can also be the center of the perennial garden. Surround with purple coneflowers, Shasta daisies, or daylilies in pink or yellow.

VARIETIES 'Costa Rica Blue' is a Mississippi Medallion winner. Look also for 'Argentine Sky' (light blue), 'Black and Blue' (black calyx, blue petal), and 'Purple Majesty' (dark purple).

Salvia (SAL-via) leucantha

Mexican Bush Sage

FAMILY: *Lamiaceae*
ORIGIN: Mexico, Tropical America
RELATIVES: Coleus, Ajuga
PROPAGATION: Division,
cutting, seed
ZONE: 7b–10
LIGHT: Sun to part shade
WATER: Average
SIZE: 3–4 feet
COLOR: Lavender, dark purple

The tall purple-flowered Mexican bush sage yields dozens of cut flowers.

TOUGHNESS The Mexican bush sage is a short day or long night bloomer, starting in late summer and blooming through several hard frosts. The purple, fuzzy, velvet spikes with white flowers are produced in huge quantities. The gardener growing this variety could easily harvest a hundred flower stems for the vase. The gray-green foliage provides garden interest, even if the plants aren't blooming.

PLANTING The ideal site is full sun, though a little afternoon shade is tolerated. The soil should be very well drained, as this plant is native to Mexico. Plant on raised beds or amend heavy soils with the addition of compost or humus. Well-drained soil may encourage a return further north than expected. While preparing the soil incorporate 2 pounds of a slow-release 12-6-6 fertilizer per 100 square feet of bed space. Space the plants 24–36 inches apart, planting at the same depth as in the container. Note: do not plant under streetlights or floodlights as these plants bloom in response to number of dark hours.

GROWING Give supplemental water during long dry periods. In the fall, after significant frost damage, prune to ground level and add a layer of mulch for winter protection. Feed in the spring with a light application of fertilizer with the emergence of growth and every 6–8 weeks through September. The Mexican bush sage can be lightly pruned once or twice in late April and early June to increase the number of blooming stems for fall. Harvest several stems and tie with sprigs of rosemary for hanging in the kitchen.

LANDSCAPE USE The Mexican bush sage is primarily a fall bloomer, so plan on combining with other good fall color from Mexican sunflower *Tithonia rotundifolia,* marigolds, lantanas, chysanthemums, angel trumpets, and other salvias.

VARIETIES The Mexican bush sage is mostly sold generically, but 'Midnight' (dark purple) and 'Kab' (dwarf lavender) are choice selections.

Salvia (SAL-via) madrensis

Forsythia Sage

FAMILY: *Lamiaceae*
ORIGIN: Mexico
RELATIVES: Coleus, Basil
PROPAGATION: Division,
cutting, seed
ZONE: 7b–10
LIGHT: Sun to part shade
WATER: Average
SIZE: 6–7 feet
COLOR: Yellow

Forsythia sage is a short day bloomer making the fall garden come alive.

TOUGHNESS The look on the faces of gardeners who see this plant for the first time is priceless. Tough salvia never enters their mind. This short day or long night bloomer reaches 6–7 feet with monolithic proportions, topped by bright yellow blossoms in late summer and fall, reaching 12–24 inches in length. The hummingbirds give the appearance of being in ecstatic bliss when the flowers start blooming. This is a tough, wonderful plant for the patient gardener.

PLANTING The ideal site is full sun, though some shade is tolerated. The soil should be very well drained, as this plant is native to Mexico. Plant on raised beds or amend heavy soils with the addition of compost or humus. Well-drained soil may encourage a return further north than expected. While preparing the soil incorporate 2 pounds of a slow-release 12-6-6 fertilizer per 100 square feet of bed space. Space the plants 24–36 inches apart, planting at the same depth as in the container. Note: do not plant under streetlights or floodlights as these plants bloom in response to number of dark hours.

GROWING Give supplemental water during long dry periods. In the fall, after significant frost damage, prune to ground level and add a layer of mulch for winter protection. Feed in the spring with a light application of fertilizer with the emergence of growth and every 6–8 weeks through September. The forsythia sage can be lightly pruned or pinched once or twice in late April and early June to increase the number of blooming stems for fall. Divide with the emergence of spring growth.

LANDSCAPE USE The forsythia sage is definitely for the back of the border. Plant the indigo spires, bulbous pink sage (*Salvia iinvolucrata*), or pineapple sage in front. The creamy yellow bands of the zebra grass match up well with the forsythia sage.

VARIETIES The forsythia sage is still hard to find and when found is most often generic. The variety 'Dunham' is known for superior cold-hardiness.

Salvia (SAL-via) regla

Royal Sage, Orange Mountain Sage

FAMILY: *Lamiaceae*
ORIGIN: Texas, Mexico
RELATIVES: Coleus, Ajuga
PROPAGATION: Division,
cutting, seed
ZONE: 7b–10
LIGHT: Sun to part shade
WATER: Average
SIZE: 3–4 feet
COLOR: Scarlet-orange

Royal sage produces large 3-inch flowers.

TOUGHNESS Just when the garden is looking its worst for wear, after a long hot summer, the royal sage bursts forth with hundreds of 3-inch tubular scarlet-orange flowers that are among the most unique in the world of salvias. Several references suggest cold-hardiness is zone 9, but salvia lovers everywhere have it return in much colder areas.

PLANTING The ideal site is full sun. The soil should be very well drained, as this plant is native to the Southwest. Plant on raised beds or amend heavy soils with the addition of compost or humus. Well-drained soil may encourage a return further north than expected. While preparing the soil incorporate 2 pounds of a slow-release 12-6-6 fertilizer per 100 square feet of bed space. Space the plants 24–36 inches apart, planting at the same depth as in the container. Note: do not plant under streetlights or floodlights as these plants bloom in response to number of dark hours.

GROWING Give supplemental water during long dry periods. In the fall after significant frost damage, prune to ground level and add a layer of mulch for winter protection. Feed in the spring with a light application of fertilizer with the emergence of growth and every 6–8 weeks through September. Take a few cuttings in the fall to easily over-winter, just in case record cold proves lethal. Divide with the emergence of spring growth.

LANDSCAPE USE Royal sage is another fall bloomer. It combines well with traditional fall colors but can look extremely riotous planted with blue salvias like indigo spires, 'Victoria' blue, or Brazilian sage. A more subdued companion planting might be yellow African marigolds or 'New Gold' lantana.

VARIETIES This one is hard to find and is still most often sold generically, sometimes under the name Hidalgo sage. 'Jame' is a named selection from Dr. Rich Dufrense of Greensboro, N.C.

Salvia (SAL-via) uliginosa

Bog Sage

FAMILY: *Lamiaceae*
ORIGIN: Brazil, Uruguay, Argentina
RELATIVES: Coleus, Agastache
PROPAGATION: Division,
cutting, seed
ZONE: 6–10
LIGHT: Sun to part shade
WATER: Average
SIZE: 6–7 feet
COLOR: Light blue

The name may be lacking but the bog sage will make up for it in garden performance.

TOUGHNESS I suspect many gardeners fail to grow this plant for two reasons: the botanical name and the common name. This is an unequivocal travesty. The plant is one of the most versatile perennials, having cold-hardiness over a huge expanse. Speaking of huge, the plants are large, reaching 6–7 feet and adorned with spikes of light blue flowers, a color that is most rare in the garden.

PLANTING Select a site in full sun. The soil should be very well drained. Plant on raised beds or amend heavy soils with the addition of compost or humus. Well-drained soil may encourage a return further north than expected. While preparing the soil incorporate 2 pounds of a slow-release 12-6-6 fertilizer per 100 square feet of bed space. Space the plants 30–42 inches apart, planting at the same depth as in the container.

GROWING Give supplemental water during long dry periods. In the fall after significant frost damage, prune to ground level and add a layer of mulch for winter protection. Feed in the spring with a light application of fertilizer with the emergence of growth and every 6–8 weeks through September. Keep flowers deadheaded and give the plant a light shearing occasionally to maintain attractive shape. Divide with the emergence of spring growth. The plant spreads by rhizomes, so pay attention to potential invasiveness.

LANDSCAPE USE This is a large salvia that works well with the Brazilian sage in the hummingbird garden. Use it in the cottage garden, in front of a white picket fence, draped by an antique rose like 'Zepherine Droughin.' Plant this salvia in combination with perennial verbenas, yarrow, or coreopsis.

VARIETIES The bog sage is sold generically.

Salvia (SAL-via) van houttei

Wine Sage

FAMILY: *Lamiaceae*
ORIGIN: South America
RELATIVES: Coleus, Basil
PROPAGATION: Division,
cutting, seed
ZONE: (8)–10, annual elsewhere
LIGHT: Morning sun part shade
WATER: Average
SIZE: 4 feet
COLOR: Burgundy

Wine sage is a tender perennial but worthy of growing as an annual.

TOUGHNESS Wine sage is the plant to cause taxonomic brawls over what it really is. Some say it is *Salvia van houttei,* giving it species status. Others say it is one of the first selections of the wild *Salvia splendens.* Gardeners say, "I've got to have it." Whether it is perennial or annual is another fight. Everyone who sees it wants the 4-by-4-foot plant, loaded with spiky, burgundy-wine flowers from spring through frost.

PLANTING The ideal site would be morning sun and afternoon shade. The soil should be very well drained. Plant on raised beds or amend heavy soils with the addition of compost or humus. Well-drained soil may encourage a return further north than expected. While preparing the soil incorporate 2 pounds of a slow-release 12-6-6 fertilizer per 100 square feet of bed space. Space the plants 18–24 inches apart, planting at the same depth as in the container.

GROWING Give supplemental water during long dry periods. In the fall after significant frost damage, prune to ground level and add a layer of mulch for winter protection. Feed in the spring with a light application of fertilizer with the emergence of growth and every 6–8 weeks through September. Keep the flowers deadheaded and give the plant a light shearing if needed to maintain bushiness. Take a few cuttings in the fall to easily over-winter, just in case there is not a spring return. Divide with the emergence of spring growth.

LANDSCAPE USE This one really looks best with afternoon shade protection. The deep burgundy-wine color looks great with yellow-gold from 'Early Sunrise' coreopsis, 'New Gold' lantana, or 'Goldsturm' rudbeckia. Try it also with white flowers like ox-eye or Shasta daisies and angelonia.

VARIETIES The wine sage is usually sold as *Salvia van houttei.*

Salvia (SAL-via) x Indigo Spires

Indigo Spires

FAMILY: *Lamiaceae*
ORIGIN: Texas, Mexico
RELATIVES: Coleus, ajuga
PROPAGATION: Division, cutting, seed
ZONE: 7b–10
LIGHT: Sun
WATER: Average
SIZE: 3–5 feet
COLOR: Violet-blue

Indigo spires was released by the Huntington Botanical Gardens.

TOUGHNESS The world-famous Huntington Botanical Gardens in Pasadena, California, released this hybrid of two salvias, one famous and one obscure (*Salvia farinacea x. S. longispicata*). The indigo spires is one of the most admired of all garden salvias and would qualify as an award winner in every promotional program in the South. It is cold-hardier than most realize, and the violet-blue flowers are borne from spring through frost. The colors intensify in the cooler fall season as the spikes take on a spiraling effect.

PLANTING Select a site in full sun. The soil should be very well drained, as this plant is native to the Southwest. Plant on raised beds or amend heavy soils with the addition of compost or humus. Well-drained soil may encourage a return further north than expected. While preparing the soil incorporate 2 pounds of a slow-release 12-6-6 fertilizer per 100 square feet of bed space. Space the plants 18–24 inches apart, planting at the same depth as in the container. Note: though this plant blooms from the onset of spring through fall I have had it fail to bloom under security lights.

GROWING Give supplemental water during long dry periods. In the fall, after significant frost damage, prune to ground level and add a layer of mulch for winter protection. Feed in the spring with a light application of fertilizer with the emergence of growth and every 6–8 weeks through September. Keep flowers deadheaded and give the plant a light shearing occasionally to maintain attractive shape. Pruning by one-third in early August will make for an incredible show in September and October. Take a few cuttings in the fall to easily over-winter just in case there is not a spring return. Divide with the emergence of spring growth.

LANDSCAPE USE The indigo spires is so versatile it can be used in any type garden. Use in the tropical garden to give color in front of large bananas. Use in the cottage garden with a white picket fence and purple coneflowers, Shasta daisies, 'Goldsturm' rudbeckias, and 'New Gold' lantanas. Some of the best companions are shrub roses like 'Pink Simplicity,' 'Carefree Delight,' and 'Nearly Wild.' Try with 'Hameln' dwarf fountain grass or muhly grass.

VARIETIES The indigo spires is sold generically.

Saponaria (sap-o-NAY-ria) officinalis

Bouncing Bet, Soapwort

FAMILY: *Caryophyllaceae*
ORIGIN: Northern Europe
RELATIVES: Dianthus
PROPAGATION: Division, cutting
ZONE: 4–9
LIGHT: Sun to part shade
WATER: Less than average
SIZE: 2 feet, spreading
COLOR: Pink, white, red

TOUGHNESS Bouncing Bet or soapwort is an old-fashioned southern heirloom plant that the younger generation needs to bring back to popularity. Clusters of white, pink, or rose flowers, complemented by lush, dark green foliage, appear in late spring or early summer and repeat sporadically into fall. The plant is vigorous and spreading, even thriving once abandoned.

PLANTING Bouncing Bet is occasionally found at garden centers and will be worth the search. You may have to get a start from a neighbor. The ideal site is morning sun with a little afternoon shade protection and soil that is fertile and well drained. Bouncing Bet spreads by underground runners and can be a little on the aggressive side in moist, organically rich soils. Amend if necessary to improve drainage. Set out transplants at the same depth as in the container, spacing 24–36 inches apart.

GROWING Bouncing Bet can be divided anytime during the growing season. Watch and keep the plant controlled to the desired area. A midsummer shearing of old blossoms and foliage will keep the plant looking attractive and bushy and producing more blooms.

LANDSCAPE USE Bouncing Bet is at home in a cottage garden with white picket fences, Shasta daisies, purple coneflowers, Brazilian sage, and indigo spires. Bouncing Bet also works well for a tropical look, planted in front of the butterfly ginger or pink cannas.

VARIETIES 'Alba Plena' (double white, pink bud), 'Dazzler' (gold leaf variegation, pink flowers), 'Rose Plena' (double soft pink), and 'Rubra Plena' (double red, aging to pink) are known selections of the bouncing Bet.

Bouncing Bet is an heirloom plant seeing a revival in popularity.

Scabiosa (skab-i-O-sa) columbaria

Pincushion Flower

FAMILY: *Dipsacaceae*
ORIGIN: Europe, Africa, Asia
RELATIVES: Teasel
PROPAGATION: Division, seed
ZONE: 4–8
LIGHT: Sun to part shade
WATER: Less than average
SIZE: 2 feet
COLOR: Pink, white, lavender, blue

Pincushion flower excels in the garden from fall through early summer in much of the South.

TOUGHNESS The pincushion flower became much more prominent when 'Butterfly Blue' was named Perennial Plant of the Year. Flowers almost as intricate as passionflowers and adored by butterflies and bees give welcome blue, lavender, and pink to the garden. The pincushion flower may languish somewhat during the heat of the summer in hotter zones but has surprised all with its ability to bloom during the fall and early winter.

PLANTING Select a site in full sun or morning sun and afternoon shade. The soil must be fertile and well drained. Amend with 3–4 inches of organic matter like compost or humus and till to a depth of 6–8 inches. Plant nursery-grown transplants at the same depth as in the container, spacing 12 inches apart. Apply a layer of mulch after planting.

GROWING Feed with a light application of fertilizer a month after transplanting and every 4–6 weeks during the heavy bloom season. The bloom season is heaviest in the spring and early summer; then the plants start to languish somewhat during the intense heat and humidity. Keeping the plants alive by supplemental water pays dividends as they start to thrive again once temperatures start to moderate. In zones 8 and 9

the fall bloom may surpass that of spring. In mild winters the pincushion flower may bloom heavily right until the next summer. Deadhead as needed to keep flowers producing.

LANDSCAPE USE The pincushion flower needs to be a vital part of the backyard wildlife habitat. Grow in front of the yellow 'Sungold' buddleia. Plant in informal drifts with 'New Gold' lantana, purple coneflower, and yarrow. Use also with 'Early Sunrise' coreopsis and ox-eye daisy.

VARIETIES 'Butterfly Blue,' the Perennial Plant of the Year, is known for the best heat-tolerance. New hybrids like 'Giant Blue' (larger than 'Butterfly Blue'), 'Pink Passion' (compact habit, pink), and 'Samantha's Pink' (large medium pink flowers), and 'Blanca' (small white flowers) are said to be even more heat-tolerant.

Solidago (sol-i-DAY-go) species
and hybrids

Goldenrod

FAMILY: *Asteraceae*
ORIGIN: North America
RELATIVES: Echinacea, Rudbeckia
PROPAGATION: Division, seed
ZONES: 3–9
LIGHT: Sun to part shade
WATER: Less than average
SIZE: 2–6 feet
COLOR: Golden yellow

'Baby Gold' dwarf goldenrod

TOUGHNESS Goldenrod is nothing to sneeze at. Everyone thinks it is the cause of hay fever, but the real culprit is ragweed, which usually blooms at the same time. A look at the roadside should confirm that goldenrod is a carefree perennial with heat- and drought-tolerance. This wonderful plant provides colorful golden yellow flowers during the summer and fall that are perfect for cutting. They are a delight to butterflies and bees and will be to you once you include them in the garden.

PLANTING Goldenrod doesn't require the most luxuriant of soils to perform and put on a show but does require good drainage for a sure-fire spring return. Plant them in full sun for the best flower production. Should your drainage be suspect, plant on raised beds. While preparing the bed, incorporate a pound of a 5-10-5 fertilizer per 100 square feet of bed space. Plant boldly in drifts 18–24 inches apart or as recommended per your selection. This may mean planting to the middle or back of the border. Goldenrod is also easy to grow from seed.

GROWING In the fall, cut back frozen foliage to the ground. Goldenrod is a prolific spreader, sometimes by seed and often from the roots, which is an attribute loved by most gardeners. Pluck unwanted plants and prune to keep within its designated area. If you want to divide, do so with the onset of spring growth.

LANDSCAPE USE Use goldenrods with sea holly, globe thistle, Russian sage, and purple verbenas. Try combining with perennial blue salvias or angelonia. They also work well with drought-tolerant plants like 'Samson' lantana and gomphrena. If you pay attention to the roadside you will learn that the wild ageratum and ironweed make nice companions.

VARIETIES There are a lot of hybrids produced, but few garden centers stock these plants with the undeserved bad reputation. Catalogs, seed racks, and specialty nurseries may be solutions. Leading dwarf varieties are 'Baby Gold,' 'Cloth of Gold,' 'Crown of Rays,' 'Golden Baby,' 'Golden Fleece,' and 'Golden Thumb.' Taller varieties to try are 'Fireworks' and 'Golden Wings.'

Spigelia (spy-JEE-lia) marilandica

Indian Pink

FAMILY: *Loganiaceae*
ORIGIN: Eastern United States
RELATIVES: Carolina Jessamine
PROPAGATION: Division, seed
ZONE: 5–10
LIGHT: Part shade
WATER: Average to above average
SIZE: 2 feet
COLOR: Scarlet with yellow

TOUGHNESS Although called Indian pinks, these are really bright scarlet on the outside. During the months of May and June the scarlet tubular flowers open at the tip into a bursting star-shape, revealing glowing yellow on the inside. This tropical-looking plant is loved by hummingbirds and is native from Maryland to Indiana, Missouri, and Oklahoma, southward to Texas, then eastward to Florida.

PLANTING This is one of those plants usually only offered by nurseries that specialize in native plants and catalog orders. The search will be worth it. Plant yours in part shade, in soil that is moist, fertile, and well drained. Space the plants 12 inches apart, setting out at the same depth as in the containers.

GROWING Indian pink thrives naturally in moist woodland soils and even close to streams. Maintain good soil moisture and mulch, protecting from afternoon sun. Feed with a light application of a slow-release 12-6-6 fertilizer with the emergence of spring growth. Divide clumps in the fall. Seeds can be harvested when mature and planted in the spring.

LANDSCAPE USE Indian pink excels in the naturalistic woodland garden. Plant them boldly in informal drifts along paths. Use in close proximity to wood ferns. The flower form is very tropical looking, ideally suited to be grown with lush foliage like hostas, cast iron plants, caladiums, and elephant ears.

VARIETIES There are no named selections of the native Indian Pink.

Indian pinks are native and are known to be a good source of nectar for hummingbirds.

Stachys (STA-chys) byzantina

Lamb's Ear

FAMILY: *Lamiaceae*
ORIGIN: Iran
RELATIVES: Salvia, Lamium
PROPAGATION: Division
ZONE: 4–8
LIGHT: Sun to part shade
WATER: Less than average
SIZE: 15 inches
COLOR: Grown for silver-gray foliage

TOUGHNESS Beautiful beds of lamb's ear are common in the South, although some references suggest it is not for our climate. Good site selection and soil preparation will yield the striking gray, furry-like foliage that children love to touch. The silver-gray foliage, which looks as if it's coated with shiny wool, stands out in the world so dominated by dark green foliage.

PLANTING The ideal site will have plenty of sun and a little shade protection from midafternoon sun. The soil must drain freely. Plant on raised beds or amend planting area with 3–4 inches of organic matter to improve drainage. While tilling soil incorporate 2 pounds of a 5-10-5 fertilizer per 100 square feet of bed space. Set out nursery-grown transplants at the same depth as in the container, spacing plants 8–12 inches apart. Apply a layer of mulch after planting.

GROWING These are drought-tolerant plants. Water the transplants to get established and then only sparingly or during prolonged dry periods. This is not the best plant for automatic overhead sprinklers. Water in the morning from below with a wand or soaker hose. Purple flowers appear in the spring but are not considered an asset by most gardeners. Sometimes the center of the clump melts out. Divide from the perimeter to fill in these locations.

LANDSCAPE USE This is a wonderful companion used as a border plant with other drought-tolerant selections like gomphrena, salvias, purple heart, pink lantanas or verbenas, and yarrow. Use for spot-planting with sweeping beds of petunias, sweet alyssum, and dianthus. Plant lamb's ear with 'Fragrant Delight' heliotrope and the old-fashioned rose campion.

VARIETIES 'Countess Helene von Stein' (heat- and humidity-tolerant, larger leaves), 'Primrose Heron' (primrose yellow foliage, maturing to silver), and 'Silver Carpet' (doesn't produce flowers) are the leading varieties.

The shiny wool-like foliage of lamb's ear entice children to the garden.

Stokesia (sto-KEE-sia) laevis

Stokes' Aster

FAMILY: *Asteraceae*
ORIGIN: Southeastern United States
RELATIVES: Rudbeckia
PROPAGATION: Division
ZONE: 5–9
LIGHT: Sun to part shade
WATER: Average
SIZE: 18–24 inches
COLOR: Lavender-blue, blue, purple

'Purple Parasols' Stokes' aster

TOUGHNESS Large, 3–4-inch-wide blue-to-purple flowers that are as incredibly intricate as a passionflower adorn this native plant from late spring through summer. The plants are tough, surviving the coldest winters and hottest summers, and yielding bouquets of flowers all season long. The flowers themselves are exceptional, having a long vase life.

PLANTING Choose a site in full sun for best blooming, although this plant tolerates partial shade better than many other perennials. Make your beds well drained by incorporating 3–4 inches of organic matter, like fine pine bark, humus, or compost. Well-drained soil is mandatory if you want a long-lived perennial. Wet winter feet can spell doom. Till your bed to a depth of 8–10 inches and incorporate 2 pounds of a slow-release fertilizer per 100 square feet of planting area. Use a blend like a 12-6-6 with slow-release nitrogen. Plant 6-inch to gallon-size, setting out at the same depth they were growing in the container. The plants reach 18 inches in height. You will want to space them 15–18 inches apart.

GROWING Apply a good layer of mulch and train the roots by watering deeply. When stalks have finished blooming, cut them back to the base, even with the plant. They sometimes rest in summer, to bloom again in the fall. Go into the winter tidy and with a protective layer of mulch. When growth emerges next spring, feed with a light application of fertilizer and again in midsummer. The Stokes' aster is one of those plants that forms large clumps for dividing in early spring.

LANDSCAPE USE Plant them boldly in informal drifts in front of the border, adjacent to large marigolds like 'Antigua' or 'Marvel.' Lantanas like 'Lemon Drop,' 'Silver Mound,' and 'New Gold' also look good with the Stokes' aster. Try massing them with 'Stella d'Oro' daylily for a very nice companion planting, from a color and a perennial standpoint.

VARIETIES The Stokes' aster is often sold generically, but there are some choice named selections like 'Purple Parasols' (large, deep lavender-blue), 'Blue Danube' (lavender-blue), 'Bluestone' (blue), 'Klaus Jelitto' (light blue), and 'Wyoming' (purple).

Tradescantia (trad-ess-KAN-tia) pallida

Purple Heart

FAMILY: *Commelinaceae*
ORIGIN: Eastern Mexico
RELATIVES: Spiderwort
PROPAGATION: Cutting
ZONE: 7–10
LIGHT: Sun to part shade
WATER: Less than average
SIZE: 12 inches
COLOR: Grown for deep purple foliage

The succulent foliage of purple heart contrasts wonderfully with the tall 'Indian Summer' rudbeckia.

as the plant that will grow just about anywhere, if it doesn't get wet feet. In fact, root rot is its number one enemy. A fertile, well-drained bed, having 3–4 inches of organic matter tilled in, will yield an award-winning patch or clump of purple heart.

GROWING   The bushiness of the purple heart can be increased by pinching or cutting back the terminal ends of the plant. These cuttings can also be rooted easily for more plants around the landscape. Remove frost-damaged foliage and put the plant to winter rest by adding a protective layer of mulch. In the spring as growth starts to resume, feed with a light application of a slow-release 12-6-6 fertilizer. Although it is very drought-tolerant, keep mulched and give an occasional soaking.

LANDSCAPE USE If you want to go to Greece for a month but want a pretty and tough flowerbed, plant purple heart with 'New Gold' lantana and add a large rock. All three will be looking good when you return. The vivid purple is outstanding when grown in combination with yellow plants like the 'New Gold' lantana, rudbeckia, and melampodium. Use it with pink flowers like verbenas or 'Coral Nymph' salvia. Use in mixed containers on the porch, patio, or deck, and try indoors.

VARIETIES   Purple heart is sold generically, but try also other species like *T. virginiana* spiderwort and *T. fluminensis* wandering Jew (cold-hardy zone 9–10).

TOUGHNESS   The lush, succulent, dark-purple spreading foliage of the purple heart makes it easy to use in the landscape. The fact that it returns from cold winters and thrives in the hottest summer, despite being virtually abandoned by the homeowner, is a testimony to its ruggedness.

PLANTING   Purple heart prefers a nice, well-drained, organically rich bed but is being touted

Tradescantia (trad-ess-KAN-tia)
virginiana and *T. x andersoniana*

Spiderwort

FAMILY: *Commelinaceae*
ORIGIN: Eastern United States
RELATIVES: Purple Heart,
Blue Ginger
PROPAGATION: Cutting
ZONE: 4–10
LIGHT: Sun to part shade
WATER: Less than average
SIZE: 8–36 inches
COLOR: Purple, blue, white,
lavender, pink, some with lime green
foliage

'Sweet Kate' *T. x andersoniana*

TOUGHNESS When gardeners refer to a plant as invasive, you know it is a tough plant. A little management, however, will keep this plant looking neat and blooming from spring through summer. The unique three-petaled flowers only last a day, but you almost never find them out of bloom. The foliage is handsome, strapped-leafed,

and now offered in chartreuse for a double dose of color.

PLANTING Despite the fact that you see them growing along the roadside, they do not like boggy areas. Select a site with morning sun and part shade in the afternoon. The bed should be fertile, loamy, and well drained. If the soil is heavy and not well drained, amend with 3–4 inches of organic matter. While preparing the site, incorporate 2 pounds of a slow-release 12-6-6 fertilizer per 100 square feet of planting area. Set out nursery-grown plants at the same depth as in the container, spacing 8–15 inches apart depending on variety. Apply a layer of mulch after planting.

GROWING Keep the spiderwort watered during the growing season. Once the flower stalk has finished blooming, remove to keep it from re-seeding. Divide clumps in the fall for the best spring bloom. Once foliage deteriorates in late summer cut back to 8 inches, and new growth will emerge for fall.

LANDSCAPE USE The chartreuse-leafed selections with purple flowers light up the part-shade gardens. Use them with hostas like 'Sum and Substance,' 'Paul's Glory,' and 'Guacamole,' with oxalis like 'Sunset Velvet,' or liriope like 'Silvery Sunproof.' Grow in groups of 3 to 5 for best display.

VARIETIES 'Sweet Kate' (*T. x andersoniana*) with chartreuse leaves and violet-blue flowers is causing gardeners to take notice. Look for 'Purple Dome' (purple flowers, dark lime foliage), 'Innocence' (white flowers), and 'Billberry Ice' (lavender-pink blooms).

Verbena (ver-BEE-na) bonariensis

South American Verbena

FAMILY: *Verbenaceae*
ORIGIN: Argentina, Brazil
RELATIVES: Lantana, Duranta
PROPAGATION: Division, seed
ZONE: 6–9
LIGHT: Sun
WATER: Less than average
SIZE: 4–5 feet
COLOR: Purple

The South American verbena sometimes called "Verbena on a Stick" always commands attention when in bloom.

TOUGHNESS It is rare for plants to bloom all summer in high heat and humidity, but the South American verbena does. It is among the tallest of garden verbenas and produces clusters of purple flowers on plants that reach 3–4 feet in height. These tall plants look delicate, but they are rough and tough in the face of wind and rain.

PLANTING Select a site in full sun with well-drained soil and good air circulation. Plant nursery-grown transplants in the spring after the soil has warmed. These are large plants and will require spacing of 4 feet. This plant is a perennial in zones 6–9 but will reseed in colder areas.

GROWING Cut back frost-damaged foliage in the fall and add a good layer of mulch, like pine straw. In very early spring thin or remove unwanted seedlings, or pot some up, because these great plants are still hard to find. The South American verbena grows vigorously without a lot of fertilizer. Pruning plants in late spring will develop a shrublike form. This verbena is susceptible to powdery mildew and may be treated with a fungicide if the appearance is bothersome; however, if left untreated the plant will stay vigorous and blooming and the symptoms will usually end.

LANDSCAPE USE One of my favorite catalogs calls it "Verbena on a Stick." The tall height does make it a great choice for filling in vertical space in the flower border. Almost any other plant that combines with violet-purple will make a good companion. Purple coneflowers, Shasta daisies, and 'Goldsturm' rudbeckias are all ideal partners.

VARIETIES The *Verbena bonariensis* is sold generically. See other verbenas that follow.

Verbena (ver-BEE-na) canadensis and hybrids

Rose Verbena

FAMILY: *Verbenaceae*
ORIGIN: North America
RELATIVES: Lantana, Duranta
PROPAGATION: Cutting, seed
ZONE: 6–10
LIGHT: Sun
WATER: Less than average
SIZE: 8–12 inches, spreading
COLOR: Many shades and blends except yellow

TOUGHNESS The staggering number of new varieties of this hybrid verbena in the past few years has now made it one of the best perennials for the South. The blooms are larger and more colorful, and the plants are disease-resistant. There is sure to be a color to suit your pleasure. Choose a variety, and if your neighbors don't thank you the swallowtail butterflies will.

PLANTING Select a site in full sun with well-drained soil. Wet, winter, soggy soil is the enemy that can prevent a spring return. Plant nursery-grown transplants in the spring or summer. Plant at the same depth as in the container, spacing 12–18 inches apart depending on the variety. Water to get established, but then sparingly, as dictated by the weather.

GROWING The verbena responds to feeding every 4–6 weeks with a light application of a slow-release 12-6-6 fertilizer. Just as important as feeding is cutting back to rejuvenate vegetative growth and invite more blooms. This verbena rewards those who cut back. Leaving all the old stems because of 4 or 5 flowers will hurt the verbena and make the gardener unhappy with this great plant.

LANDSCAPE USE These are some of the most outstanding plants for the perennial, cottage, or butterfly garden. A few are compact, but most spread with ease. There are so many colors available to accommodate any color scheme. Try blue varieties with orange companions like 'Profusion Orange' zinnia, marigolds, or 'Samson' lantana. Use violet-colored selections with yellow flowers like 'New Gold' lantana, melampodium, and 'Gold Star' esperanza. The verbena is outstanding in mixed baskets and containers.

VARIETIES 'Homestead Purple' is a Louisiana Select and Georgia Gold Medal winner. 'Biloxi Blue' is a Mississippi Medallion winner and a Texas Superstar winner under the name 'Blue Princess.' 'Port Gibson Pink,' with its good fragrance, is a Mississippi Medallion winner. The 'Aztec,' 'Wildfire,' 'Tukana,' and 'Superbena' series offer several colors and are very impressive. The 'Escapade,' 'Lanai,' 'Rapunzel,' and 'Twilight' series with several colors are receiving good comments.

Verbena (ver-BEE-na) tenuisecta
and *hybrids*

Moss Verbena

FAMILY: *Verbenaceae*
ORIGIN: South America
RELATIVES: Lantana, Duranta
PROPAGATION: Cutting,
division, seed
ZONE: 6–10
LIGHT: Sun
WATER: Less than average
SIZE: 6–10 inches, spreading
COLOR: Many shades and blends
except yellow

TOUGHNESS The verbena has undergone quite a revolution in the past decade, giving the gardener a plant that is durable, disease-resistant, and almost ever blooming, from spring through frost. The industry sells virtually all perennial types under the moniker "verbena hybrid." This may have some validity, but one parent or the other may exhibit a dominant trait. The moss verbena has become one of the top performers, giving a blooming groundcover-like habit. They choke out weeds, shade the root zone, keeping it cool, and bloom profusely.

PLANTING Select a site in full sun with well-drained soil. Soggy soil will prevent a spring return. Plant nursery-grown transplants in the spring after the soil has warmed. To call these spreading plants may be an understatement. Plant at the same depth as in the container, spacing 18–24 inches apart. Water to get established, but then sparingly, as dictated by the weather.

GROWING The moss verbena responds to feeding every 4–6 weeks. Feed with a diluted water-soluble fertilizer, pouring it on as a drench or using a hose sprayer. Controlled-release granules can be applied with care. The moss verbena can be cut back at any time to keep confined or as a rejuvenation-type pruning, to stimulate more growth and blooms.

LANDSCAPE USE These are the perfect low-growing border bloomers, although they quickly spread outside their designated area. Try planting with lantanas, melampodiums, rudbeckias, salvias, Shasta daisies, and sun coleus. Grow large drifts of single colors next to each other, letting them gently intermingle.

VARIETIES The variety 'Imagination' (violet) is an All America Selections winner and a Flueroselect winner. The 'Tapien' series is superior and is offered in 'Blue Violet,' 'Pink,' 'Lavender,' 'Salmon,' and 'White.' The 'Babylon' series is most popular with landscapers and is offered in 'Blue,' 'Carpet Blue,' 'Light Blue,' 'Lilac,' 'Neon Rose,' 'Pink,' 'Purple,' 'Red,' and 'White.' This verbena is slightly taller, reaching 10 inches, with the typical lacy foliage.

'Babylon' verbena

"Blue Violet Tapien' verbena and 'New Gold' lantana

'Babylon Red' and 'Tukana White' verbena

Veronica (ver-ON-ik-a) species
and hybrids

Veronica, Speedwell

FAMILY: *Scrophulariaceae*
ORIGIN: Europe
RELATIVES: Snapdragon
PROPAGATION: Cutting
ZONE: 4–8 (9)
LIGHT: Sun to part shade
WATER: Average
SIZE: 10–48 inches
COLOR: Blue, lavender, pink, white

Veronica gives a spiky texture.

TOUGHNESS The veronica is still a rare plant in the southern garden compared to others, but things are changing. Nurseries and garden centers are offering more selections. The impetus for this increase in popularity may have been the selection of 'Sunny Border Blue' as the Perennial Plant of the Year in 1993. Veronicas are showy in the garden with tall spikes of flowers in blue, pink, white, and lilac shades. They are winter tough and perform extremely well in the torrid South, blooming for months when deadheaded.

PLANTING Select a site in full sun, although some afternoon shade is tolerated. The soil should be very well drained. Plant on raised beds or amend heavy soils with the addition of compost or humus. Well-drained soil is critical to encourage a return. While preparing the soil incorporate 2 pounds of a slow-release 12-6-6 fertilizer per 100 square feet of bed space. Space the plants 12–24 inches, depending on variety, and plant at the same depth as in the container.

GROWING Give supplemental water during long dry periods. In the fall, after significant frost damage, prune to ground level and add a layer of mulch for winter protection. Feed in the spring with a light application of fertilizer with the emer-gence of growth and every 6–8 weeks through September. Keep the plant deadheaded to increase flower production.

LANDSCAPE USE The veronica looks like the original cottage garden plant. Combine with white picket fences and antique roses. Plant boldly, as spot-planting doesn't show off the true beauty of the plant. Use with companions like purple coneflowers, Shasta daisies, or its complementary 'Indian Summer' or 'Goldsturm' rudbeckias. Cut back hard to basal foliage after the veronica has completed its bloom cycle in the fall. Divide every 3–4 years in the early spring when growth has resumed.

VARIETIES *V. spicata* 'Blue Bouquet' (lavender-blue), 'Blue Spires' (lavender-blue), 'Lil Corinna' (light blue), and *V. spicata* hybrid 'Sunny Border Blue' (most heat-tolerant, deep blue) are good choices. Try also *V. longiflora* 'Blauriessen' (dark blue), 'Rosalinde' (lilac-pink), and 'Schneeriesen' (white).

BULBS, RHIZOMES, AND TUBERS
Underground Storage Units

I f you asked five ardent gardeners what bulb they felt the most passionate about, you would certainly get an assortment of answers. To the daylily enthusiast there is none other. The iris expert would most certainly take him to task. Another might say those aren't bulbs at all, but a field of jonquils—now those are bulbs! I would probably tout the virtue of gingers. In reality we would all be right.

Bulbs are probably the best perennials for the beginning gardener because of their easy-grow natures. Understanding them, however, is a little more of a challenge. For practical purposes, we group bulbs, rhizomes, tubers, tuberous roots, and corms together. I took the liberty of putting the banana in this chapter because it sometimes seems like a lost puppy without a home.

When I taught Master Gardeners we described the differences of these underground storage units like this: a true bulb is a complete or nearly complete miniature of a plant encased in fleshy modified leaves called scales that contain reserves of food. Corms are the bases of stems that become swollen and solid with nutrients. It has no fleshy scales. The tuber is an underground stem that stores food but differs from a true bulb or corm in that it has no covering of dry leaves and no basal plant from which the roots grow. It has a knobby surface with growth buds, or eyes, from which the shoots of the new plant emerge.

Tuberous roots are actually real roots, and the food supply is kept in root tissue. Rhizomes are sometimes called rootstocks and are thickened stems that grow horizontally, weaving their way along just below the soil surface. Gingers are prime examples of this type of growth.

To most gardeners, there are spring flowering bulbs and summer flowering bulbs. But in addition are those wonderful bulbs grown for exotic summer foliage. Each has a special place in the garden.

Page 143: Red spider lily, *Lycoris radiata*

Opposite: No spring garden is complete without blooming bulbs.

Soil preparation for bulbs is basically the same as for perennials. Regardless of whether they are spring or summer blooming bulbs, they will not survive with wet, soggy, winter soil. Even bananas, which need a lot of water to grow from the ground to 15 feet in one season, hate wet winter feet.

The soil must be amended to improve drainage and aeration. To do this, till or spade 3–4 inches of organic matter to a depth of 8–10 inches. The fertilizer recommendations for the bulbs differ slightly from typical perennial plants. Incorporate 3 pounds of a 5–10–10 fertilizer per 100 square feet. Note the recommendation with each plant, as there is some slight variance.

One of the questions that always arises is how deep to plant the bulb. As a general rule of thumb, you plant bulbs 2½–3 times the diameter of the bulb in depth. Note, however, that gingers are planted shallow, crinums deep, and elephant ears with the top of the bulb one inch below the soil surface. Most of the bulbous plants in this chapter are sold growing in plastic containers at the local garden center. These should be planted so that the top of the soil in the container is even with the soil surface.

Spring flowering bulbs are normally planted in October and November and summer flowering bulbs after the danger of frost has passed in the spring. Apply a good layer of mulch after planting. Mulching is always important for winter protection to prevent the subsequent freezing and thawing of the planting area that can damage bulbs.

After the flowers have faded, deadhead to keep seeds from developing. The developing seeds deplete energy levels of the bulb. Don't trim foliage after the blooms have shriveled. The leaves must remain on the plant until they naturally turn yellow and wither. The leaves act as the energy-gathering device for next year's bloom.

Summer bulbs that cannot take our winters, such as caladiums, can be dug and stored. To do this, dig once the leaves have declined. Let them dry for a week and then remove any remaining foliage. Dust them with a fungicide and place in box of kitty litter or dry peat and store above 60 degrees in a dry environment.

Bulbs alone could comprise a four-season garden, giving beauty and interest. Make sure you have a sufficient quantity to enhance your garden's appeal.

Alocasia (al-o-KAY-sia) macrorrhiza

Giant Taro

FAMILY: *Araceae*
ORIGIN: Tropical Asia
RELATIVES: Philodendron,
Dieffenbachia
PROPAGATION: Division
ZONE: 8–11
LIGHT: Part shade
WATER: Above average
SIZE: 4–6 feet
COLOR: Grown for foliage—green,
purple, variegated

TOUGHNESS The fact that the giant taro generates incredible growth in your garden nonstop for 200-plus days makes this a tough plant, even if gardeners in colder zones will have to make a decision on protecting during the winter. The tropical look is one of the hottest trends in the country, and the giant taro, with its 3-foot leaves on 4-foot petioles is one of the easiest plants to grow. Soon your yard will take on that look of French Martinique.

PLANTING The giant taro can certainly perform in full sun, but in the sultry South, partial shade develops the lush look most seek. Plant the giant taro in well-drained organic-rich beds in the spring after the soil has warmed. This plant can get enormous, so space 4 feet apart. Mulch to conserve valuable moisture and give added winter protection.

GROWING Keep the giant taro growing vigorously with plenty of water and light monthly feedings of a slow-release fertilizer, like a 12-6-6. Remove old, unattractive leaves. Foliage will freeze back below 29 degrees. In zones 8 and 9 plants will return either from the top of the trunk or, if colder, from the base of the clump. Tubers can be dug in the fall just prior to freezing, which will encourage an even larger plant the next season. Shake off soil and store in a warm, dry location until spring.

LANDSCAPE USE Plant anywhere a tropical look is desired. The giant taro combines wonder-fully with bananas, cannas, gingers, and coleus. The coarse-textured leaves can transform a garden from just a flower border to a Caribbean border, so grow giant taro among your favorite flowers.

VARIETIES Look for the variegated form 'Variegata.' *A. plumbea* is similar but dark purple. Choice selections of this species are 'Metallica,' 'Nigra,' and 'Rubra.'

The enormous leaves of the giant taro give a tropical look to this shopping mall.

Alstroemeria (al-stree-MEER-ia)
psittacina

Parrot Lily, Peruvian Lily

FAMILY: *Liliaceae*
ORIGIN: North Brazil
RELATIVES: Daylily, Glory Lily
PROPAGATION: Division
ZONE: 7–10, possibly 6
LIGHT: Sun and afternoon shade
WATER: Average
SIZE: 3 feet
COLOR: Each flower exhibits green, red, maroon to purple

The parrot lily looks tropical when grown with elephant ears.

TOUGHNESS Most gardeners think we can't grow alstroemeria in the South, but the parrot lily not only is hardy and tropical-looking but also has colors exotically indescribable. The 3-foot-tall umbels have 4–6 green blossoms that are overlaid with dark wine red and spotted or streaked with maroon to purple. The plant is so vigorous some consider it invasive, while its suitors are happy to remove the ones they do not want.

PLANTING Searching for the plant will be part of the fun. Once you find it, plant it in fertile, loamy soil in an area that gets morning sun and afternoon shade. If you get a container-grown plant, set in the soil at the same depth it is growing in the pot. If you are getting roots, then plant about 6 inches deep.

GROWING Since the plant grows like it is on steroids, a light application of a balanced fertilizer, timed with the emergence of spring growth, is all that is needed. Remove stalks after flowering, to keep the plants looking tidy.

LANDSCAPE USE The parrot lily has the look of a rare rainforest-type plant. Use it as a lower-level planting with elephant ears, bananas, cannas, or umbrella plants. Grow with yellow flag iris (*Iris psuedocorus*), another high-octane plant. The tall foliage will add interest when the parrot lily starts blooming in June.

VARIETIES Work has begun to incorporate the durability of the *A. psittacina* with modern hybrids, but this will take time. As you shop if you find an alstroemeria labeled *A. pulchella*, rejoice. It most likely is the *A. psittacina*.

Aspidistra (as-pid-ISS-tra) elatior

Cast Iron Plant

FAMILY: *Liliaceae*
ORIGIN: China
RELATIVES: Daylily
PROPAGATION: Division
ZONE: 7–10
LIGHT: Part shade to shade
WATER: Less than average
SIZE: 2–3 feet
COLOR: Grown for dark green foliage, some variegated

Dark green leaves of the cast iron plant rise behind the colorful aucuba adding texture and interest to the shade garden.

TOUGHNESS You don't get the name "cast iron plant" by being a wimp! On the other hand, plant it in the sun and it will disappear. The deep green, glossy leaves give a lush tropical look to the garden. Planted in the right place this plant is virtually indestructible. The cast iron plant develops 2-foot-long, 4-inch-wide leaves, with 15-inch-long petioles. Incredibly, the plant is evergreen, giving a source of needed color and texture during the winter.

PLANTING The cast iron plant is tolerant of a wide variation in soils but does best in fertile, well-drained beds with part shade to shade. Set out nursery-grown plants at the same depth as in the container. Space plants 2–3 feet apart. Add a layer of mulch to keep weeds from competing. Conserve moisture and keep soil temperatures moderate. The dark green, glossy foliage looks even better in contrast with pine bark mulch.

GROWING Feed established clumps in early spring with 1 pound of a slow-release 12-6-6 fertilizer with minor nutrients per 100 square feet of planted area. Although this plant is tough and drought-tolerant, supplemental irrigation during prolonged dry periods keeps it looking its best. Mature clumps respond well to a rejuvenating shearing every 3–5 years. Unsightly foliage can be removed at any time. Divide clumps as needed in the early spring.

LANDSCAPE USE Grow with other shade-loving plants like hostas, ferns, and aucuba. Use along woodland paths and at the base of large trees. Try under stairs leading to the deck. Plant impatiens and begonias as lower-level plants.

VARIETIES Green varieties are mostly offered generically. Look for the variegated selection 'Variegata' and the speckled 'Milky Way.'

Caladium (kal-AY-dium) bicolor

Caladium

FAMILY: *Araceae*
ORIGIN: South America
RELATIVES: Philodendron, Elephant
Ear
PROPAGATION: Division
ZONE: 10
LIGHT: Part shade to shade
WATER: Above average
SIZE: 18–36 inches
COLOR: Grown for variegated foliage
in several shades

TOUGHNESS The words "rugged" and "caladium" may seem incompatible. On the other hand, the fact that this plant produces fancy, colorful, tropical-looking foliage from late spring until cold weather arrives is pretty incredible. High temperatures and humidity don't cause this Amazon native to flinch, as long as there is water.

PLANTING Most gardeners are happy to buy caladiums in 6-inch containers in late spring, while real caladium aficionados buy bulbs in large quantities and start their own transplants. Both are good ideas. Regardless of the method chosen,

the soil needs to be organically rich, well drained, yet moisture-retentive. Amending with several inches of compost or humus will pay big rewards. While amending, incorporate 2 pounds of a slow-release 12-6-6 fertilizer per 100 square feet of bed space. If planting container-grown caladiums, set at the depth as in the containers. If planting bulbs, remove the central eye from the bulb for a bushier plant. Place 3 inches below the soil. Apply a good layer of mulch to hold that moisture.

GROWING Feed in midsummer with a light application of fertilizer. Remove any flowers that develop. To keep over winter, dig tubers as foliage starts to decline. Dry for a week, then remove old foliage, dust with a fungicide, and store in a box with sawdust, kitty litter, or dry peat. Store at temperatures above 60 degrees.

LANDSCAPE USE Caladiums are among the best plants for adding color to the shade garden. Combine with impatiens, gingers, and hostas. Sun-tolerant types work well with cannas and bananas.

VARIETIES 'Fantasy' (white with red veins), 'White Christmas' (white with green margins), 'Carolyn Whorton' (pink with red veins and green splashes), 'Frieda Hempel' (bright red with green margins), and 'Postman Joiner' (pale red with darker veins and green margins) are among the most popular. Those most sun-tolerant are 'Red Flash' (green with red centers and white blotching) and 'Rose Bud' (pink veins and centers fading to white, then green). Try the strapped-leaf varieties with smaller leaves but many to choose from.

White caladiums
combine with red salvia
and blue torenia for a
patriotic look.

Canna (KAN-na) x generalis

Canna Lily

FAMILY: *Cannaceae*
ORIGIN: Tropics
RELATIVES: Indian Shot
PROPAGATION: Division, seed
ZONE: 7–10
LIGHT: Sun to part shade
WATER: Above average
SIZE: 3–6 feet
COLOR: Many shades and blends,
some have variegated foliage

'Bengal Tiger' cannas, coleuses, impatiens, and Joseph's coats create a garden of dazzling beauty.

TOUGHNESS The canna lily produces lush, tropical, banana-like foliage in green, bronze, and various shades of variegation, topped by spectacularly colorful flowers. The plants can thrive from boggy conditions to upland soils.

PLANTING Best blooming occurs in full sun, although part shade is tolerated. The plants can thrive in moist areas but will gain more cold protection in well-drained conditions. Tight clay soils will not allow the canna to reach its potential beauty or size. Improve soils by amending with 3–4 inches of organic matter along with 3 pounds of a 5-10-5 fertilizer per 100 square feet of planted area. Plant the rhizomes 3–5 inches deep and 12–18 inches apart. Plant container-grown cannas at the same depth as in the container.

GROWING Feed established plantings in the spring and again in midsummer with 2 pounds of a slow release 12-6-6 fertilizer per 100 square feet of bed space. Remove seedpods as they develop. Cutting old or damaged stalks at ground level will encourage new basal sprouts to develop quickly. The canna leaf roller, which causes such angst, can be controlled with liquid Sevin dust or Bt.

LANDSCAPE USE Use cannas around water features. Grow in tropical gardens with bananas and elephant ears. Combine with dwarf allamanda. Plant your cannas with sun coleus and Joseph's coat.

VARIETIES Popular variegated varieties are 'Bengal Tiger,' also known as 'Pretoria' (green and yellow variegation and orange blooms) and 'Tropicanna' or 'Phasion' (green, bronze, and pink variegation with orange flowers). 'Cleopatra' (green foliage and bronze stripes, topped with yellow flowers spotted with red) is among the more striking. 'King Humbert' (bronze-red leaves with red-orange flowers) and 'Wyoming' (bronze-red foliage and orange flowers) are seeing a revival. The 'Pfitzer Dwarf' series and the seed-produced 'Tropic' series are industry standards.

Colocasia (col-O-casia) esculenta

Elephant Ear, Taro

FAMILY: *Araceae*
ORIGIN: Tropical East Asia
RELATIVES: Caladiums,
Philodendrons
PROPAGATION: Division
ZONE: 7–11
LIGHT: Sun to part shade
WATER: Above average
SIZE: 6 feet
COLOR: Grown for foliage—green,
purple, some variegated

Elephant ears, 'New Gold' lantana, and purple heart make a winning combination.

TOUGHNESS No plant can transform a garden into a tropical paradise like the elephant ear. Every year garden centers are well stocked with giant bulbs that will grow into plants that reach 5–6 feet in height and defy logic with their 3-foot leaves on 4-foot-long petioles. The plants just get larger as the heat and humidity reach levels that send gardeners indoors to the cool comforts of air-conditioning.

PLANTING Select a site in morning sun and afternoon shade, although fine specimens are often seen in full sun, provided water is readily available. The soil should be fertile and well drained for winter survival. If the soil is tight, heavy clay, amend with 3–4 inches of organic matter. While preparing the soil incorporate 2 pounds of slow-release 12-6-6 fertilizer per 100 square feet of bed space. Plant the large tubers deep enough so the entire bulb is 2 inches below the soil surface.

GROWING Feed with light monthly applications of fertilizer and maintain moisture. Remove tattered and unattractive leaves to keep tidy. Tubers can be dug, separated, dried, and stored for winter protection or left in the ground in warmer zones. In well-drained soil, tubers usually will return with no problem, even in zone 7.

LANDSCAPE USE Grow the elephant ear with other coarse-textured foliage like bananas, cannas, and gingers. They combine well with ornamental grasses and have the ability to work with almost any other garden flower. Use them around water features and to create lush poolside beds.

VARIETIES The green types of elephant ears are sold generically, but specialty varieties, bringing a premium price and look to the garden, are 'Antiquorum,' also sold as 'Illustris' (dark green leaves with maroon to purple markings between the veins), 'Black Magic' (dark purple leaves and petioles), 'Euchlora' (dark green leaves edged in purple), and 'Fontanesii' (dark purple petioles and peduncle).

Crinum (KRY-num)
species and hybrids

Crinum Lily

FAMILY: *Amaryllidaceae*
ORIGIN: Tropical Asia, Africa
RELATIVES: Amaryllis
PROPAGATION: Division
ZONE: 7–10
LIGHT: Sun to part shade
WATER: Average to above average
SIZE: 2–4 feet
COLOR: Burgundy, rose, purple,
pink, white, some striped

TOUGHNESS Fragrant, colorful flowers and exotic, glossy, green, swordlike foliage are produced on the sequoias of the bulb world. Plant the bulb right and it will be here when you are gone. Your great-grandchildren will remember you as they give starts to their kids.

PLANTING Your crinum has the potential of being there a very long time and is somewhat resentful of moving, so prepare your soil right. Organically rich and well drained are two prereq-

uisites. Incorporate 3–4 inches of organic matter along with 3 pounds of a 5-10-5 fertilizer per 100 square feet of planting area. Crinums are large bulbs that should be planted a minimum of 6 inches deep. Deeper planting produces a larger bulb with fewer offsets. Space plants 2–3 feet apart. In colder regions, plant the crinum in a protected area of the landscape, near the home.

GROWING Feed established plantings in spring and midsummer with the above fertilizer. Remove frozen foliage. Apply an extra layer of mulch for winter protection. It is normally several years before crinums need dividing. Some are very finicky about being disturbed, taking several years to bloom again.

LANDSCAPE USE Although most often seen in the middle of the landscape as proud specimens, crinums look best mixed in the flower border. Their leaf texture and bloom allow them to work in the tropical, cottage, or perennial garden. In the tropical garden, use crinum lilies with bananas and elephant ears. In the cottage garden, use crinums with daylilies, Asian lilies, and Japanese irises. Crinums also look exceptional in close proximity to water gardens.

VARIETIES The most cold-hardy species is *Crinum bulbispermum*. *C. moorei* (long neck crinum) and the *C. powellii* hybrids can be grown throughout the South. 'Bradley' (wine), 'Elizabeth Traub' (rose), 'Ellen Bousanquet' (reddish-purple), and 'Walter Flory' (pink) are also known for beauty and cold-hardiness.

Crinum lilies survive for years, making them the sequoias of the bulb world.

Crocosmia (cro-COS-mia)
x crocosmiiflora

Crocosmia or Monbretia

FAMILY: *Iridaceae*
ORIGIN: South Africa
RELATIVES: Gladiola
PROPAGATION: Divison
ZONE: 5–10
LIGHT: Sun to part shade
WATER: Less than average
SIZE: 3–4 feet
COLOR: Red, orange, yellow

TOUGHNESS If you think you can't grow tropical plants, try the crocosmia. Mature clumps of this South African native produce 8–10 stems, 3–4 feet long, bearing sprays of 2-inch red, orange, or yellow blossoms, from deep green, swordlike foliage. They are incredibly cold-hardy.

PLANTING Select a site with sun or morning sun and afternoon shade. The soil should be fertile and well drained. Prepare the planting bed by mixing 3–4 inches of organic matter and 3 pounds of a 5-10-5 fertilizer per 100 square feet of planting area. Space clumps of corms 2 inches deep and 12 inches apart. If purchasing nursery-grown plants, set out at the same depth as in the containers.

GROWING Crocosmias are vigorous and some say invasive; therefore, only a light application of fertilizer in the early spring is required. When the clump gets too large, divide in the fall or early spring. Remove old foliage in the fall and add a protective layer of mulch.

LANDSCAPE USE The croscosmia is most often spot-planted but really shows best when planted boldly. Some of the prettiest displays are in tropical gardens, mass-planted in front of bananas, giant taro, or saddle-leafed philodendrons. In a more typical garden, use croscosmia with blue-to-purple angelonias for an unbelievably bright and cheerful look.

VARIETIES The most well-known selection is 'Lucifer,' bearing brilliant orange-red flowers. 'Jenny Bloom,' 'Jupiter,' and 'Venus' (yellow), 'Bressingham Beacon' (orange and yellow bi-colored), 'Bressingham Blaze' (orange-red), and 'Spitfire' (orange-red) are worth searching for.

Monbretia or crocosmia is related to the gladiola and makes a great cut flower.

Curcuma (ker-KEW-ma) petiolata

Hidden Ginger, Hidden Lily

FAMILY: *Zingiberaceae*

ORIGIN: Malaysia

RELATIVES: Edible Ginger

PROPAGATION: Division

ZONE: 7–10

LIGHT: Part shade

WATER: Average

SIZE: 3 feet

COLOR: Yellow with purple, pink, white bracts

The hidden lily looks like a rare flower from Bora Bora but is among the most cold-hardy gingers for the South.

TOUGHNESS Gardeners in zone 7 probably wouldn't dream they could grow ginger with a flower so exotic and appealing it looks as though it came from Tahiti or Bora Bora. The 8-inch bloom is composed of purple, pink, and white bracts with yellow flowers, coupled with wide, sheathlike, tropical-looking leaves. The hidden ginger has a built-in defense mechanism that sends it into dormancy with the short days of fall.

PLANTING The hidden ginger performs best in morning sun, afternoon shade, or part shade. The soil must be organically rich and well drained for return from cold winters. Plant nursery-grown plants at the same depth as in the container. If rhizomes are purchased, plant shallow just below the soil surface and cover lightly.

GROWING Feed in the spring with a light application of a slow-release fertilizer with a 2-1-2 ratio or balanced 8-8-8 containing minor nutrients. Feed again in midsummer. A diluted water-soluble 20-20-20 fertilizer applied monthly also works well. Keep well watered during the growing season. Once the leaves turn yellow in the fall, remove and add a layer of mulch. Clumps can easily be divided in the spring. The rhizomes are easily dug and stored for winter protection in colder zones.

LANDSCAPE USE Plant the hidden ginger boldly in informal drifts, with wood fern, autumn fern, and hostas. Lilac or pink impatiens make nice companion flowers. Gingers also work well around bananas.

VARIETIES Hidden ginger is sold mostly generically, although 'Emperor,' a variegated form, is offered in catalogs. 'Jewel of Thailand,' a Florida Plant of the Year often sold as *C. cordata,* is more striking in that the flowers are larger and produce higher on the plant. Nomenclature references suggest *C. cordata* is really *C. petiolata,* but it may lack the cold-hardiness.

Hedychium (hed-IK-ium) coccineum

Scarlet Ginger

FAMILY: *Zingiberaceae*
ORIGIN: Himalayas
RELATIVES: Edible Ginger
PROPAGATION: Division
ZONE: 7–10
LIGHT: Part shade
WATER: Above average
SIZE: 6–7 feet
COLOR: Red, orange, yellow

TOUGHNESS *Hedychium* gingers are some of the most cold-hardy enjoyed by gardeners throughout the South. The scarlet ginger with its foot-long spikes of red and orange flowers and hybrids of all colors rank among the most beautiful and exotic in the world and offer the gardener a tropical Jamaican look. The striking foliage and fragrant flowers, enticing to butterflies, are just a couple of the outstanding traits.

PLANTING Select a site in partial shade and plant after the last frost of spring. The soil should be moist, fertile, and yet well drained. Plant nursery-grown transplants at the same depth as in the container. Rhizomes are often for sale and can be planted with good success. Plant the rhizome shallow by laying flat with the eyes up and covering lightly with soil. Mulch to conserve moisture.

GROWING Moisture and fertilizer will keep the scarlet ginger growing with vigor. Feed in early spring with a slow-release fertilizer like a 10-5-10 or a 12-6-6 ratio with minor nutrients prior to shoot emergence in the spring and again in midsummer. Avoid letting the fertilizer touch the stalks. Remove stalks once frozen and add mulch to assist with winter protection. Divide clumps every 3–5 years or as needed.

LANDSCAPE USE The scarlet gingers are among the tallest in the landscape. Grow to the back of the border. They are well suited placed behind evergreen shrubs like fatsia so that when frozen back in the winter they will not be missed. Orange and red impatiens are good companions, as are hostas and ferns.

VARIETIES 'Tara' (bright-orange, possibly *H. densiflorum*) and 'Disney' (orange-red) are leading varieties. 'Peach' or 'Peach Delight' is often sold as *H. angustifolium*. It has yellow blossoms that age to peach with dark orange stamens and great fragrance. 'Flaming Torch' (orange) *Hedychium coccineum* var. *aurantiacum* is an outstanding selection from Tony Avent, Plant Delights Nursery. The Kahili ginger *H. gardnerianum* grown by many in zone 7 may be the most beautiful of all, with yellow flowers, dark orange-red stamens, and an enticing fragrance.

The scarlet ginger forms large clumps of tropical-looking foliage and blooms but is cold-hardy to zone 7.

Hedychium (hed-IK-ium) coronarium

Butterfly Ginger

FAMILY: *Zingiberaceae*
ORIGIN: India
RELATIVES: Edible Ginger
PROPAGATION: Division
ZONE: 7–10
LIGHT: Part shade
WATER: Above average
SIZE: 3–6 feet
COLOR: White, yellow

The glistening white blooms of the butterfly ginger have a tropical look and a tantalizing fragrance. They are very cold-hardy.

TOUGHNESS The butterfly ginger is among the most cold-hardy gingers for the South and can be grown much further north than most gardeners realize. The foliage is lush and tropical-looking and yields white flowers that exude a tantalizing fragrance, reminiscent of the gardenia. This is one of the favorite blossoms used for leis in Hawaii.

PLANTING The ginger prefers an organically rich, fertile, well-drained soil in part shade. Plant nursery-grown transplants at the same depth as in the containers. Rhizomes can be planted shallow and covered lightly with soil. In zone 6 or colder areas of zone 7, plant the butterfly ginger in a protected area of the landscape. Apply mulch after planting.

GROWING Feed in early spring with a slow-release 2-1-2 ratio fertilizer, like a 10-5-10 or a 12-6-6 ratio with minor nutrients, prior to shoot emergence in the spring and again in midsummer. Avoid letting the fertilizer touch the stalks. Remove stalks once frozen and add mulch to assist with winter protection. Divide clumps every 3–5 years or as needed.

LANDSCAPE USE The butterfly ginger excels in the garden designed for the tropical look. Combine with bananas, elephant ears, ferns, and hostas. Flowers, like impatiens, begonias, crossandra, and Brazilian plume flower *Justicia carnea* all enhance the tropical garden with the butterfly ginger. Use along water features for an extra-special appeal.

VARIETIES The butterfly ginger is sold generically, but there are many hybrids with *H. coronarium* as a parent. One such is 'F. W. Moore,' an *H. coccineum* x *H. coronarium* hybrid that is amber yellow.

Hemerocallis (hem-er-o-KAL-is) hybrids

Daylily

FAMILY: *Liliaceae*
ORIGIN: East Asia, China, Japan
RELATIVES: Hosta, Liriope
PROPAGATION: Division
ZONE: All zones
LIGHT: Sun to part shade
WATER: Average
SIZE: 1–6 feet
COLOR: All shades except blue

'Spiderman' daylily

TOUGHNESS There are thousands of spectacular daylilies for sale, some even approaching the price of my first car. One thing all gardeners will admit is there is nothing prettier than a daylily garden that changes colors like a kaleidoscope. Nothing can perform like a daylily garden. Daylilies are deciduous, semi-evergreen, or evergreen, meaning there are daylilies for everyone. Daylilies are mostly worry-free.

PLANTING Best results are obtained from planting on raised beds rich in organic matter receiving at least 6 hours of sun per day. Although a disease called rust has infected plants in some regions, the majority of gardeners' problems begin with daylilies planted in soggy soils. Daylilies are best planted in the early spring or fall, although container-grown plants can be planted throughout the growing season with outstanding success. While preparing the soil incorporate 2 pounds of a 1-2-2 ratio fertilizer per 100 square feet of bed space. Add a good layer of mulch to hold moisture, keep the soil cool, and prevent weeds.

GROWING To keep energy going to flower production, keep seed pods picked off and feed with a complete and balanced fertilizer every 4–6 weeks. Give supplemental water during prolonged dry periods. Feed with a light application of the fertilizer in September. Most daylilies need dividing every 3 years. For the best spring bloom, divide in the fall.

LANDSCAPE USE Daylilies work well in special gardens alone or as part of the perennial border when combined with flowers like purple coneflowers, Shasta daisies, and rudbeckias. Plant yellow or pink selections in drifts with perennial salvia like 'Victoria' blue or indigo spires. Daylilies look at home when combined in beds with ornamental grasses like fountain or maiden grass and are breathtaking when planted in front of evergreen shrubs like hollies or junipers.

VARIETIES When choosing daylily varieties, be aware of the fact that some bloom early, some midseason, some late. Many repeat bloom, which is an ideal trait from a landscape standpoint. Visit with your local daylily society or a farm near you to find regional favorites. 'Spiderman,' 'Crimson Pirate,' and 'Beelzebub' are favorite red selections. 'Leeba Orange Crush' (orange), 'Judith' (pink), and 'Bitsy' (yellow) were 2002 All America Daylily Selections.

Hosta (HOS-ta) species and hybrids

Hosta, Plantain Lily

FAMILY: *Liliaceae*
ORIGIN: China, Japan
RELATIVES: Daylily
PROPAGATION: Division, seed
ZONE: 3–9
LIGHT: Part shade to shade
WATER: Moderate
SIZE: 1–4 feet
COLOR: Grown for foliage—green,
blue, gold, veriegated with lavender or
white flowers

TOUGHNESS Not many perennials thrive from the cold in zone 3 to the sweltering heat in the South, but the hosta does, which makes it a must-have plant for any garden. This easy-to-grow herbaceous groundcover has become the number one shade perennial throughout the United States.

PLANTING Hostas can be planted any time during the growing season. Buy nursery-grown transplants and choose from literally thousands of varieties. Incorporate 3–4 inches of peat or compost to insure drainage and aeration. A shady or partially shady location will produce the best results. Blue varieties normally prefer more shade while gold ones tolerate some sun. Dig a hole in your prepared soil slightly larger than your pot. Remove entire soil clump from pot, placing the plant's crown slightly above the soil. Space the hostas 1–3 feet apart, depending on variety. Young hostas need a minimum of two seasons in one location to mature to their adult potential. Water thoroughly and mulch. After your plants are established, a weekly soaking will do.

GROWING Hostas need to be watered until established and during dry periods. Feed with light applications of a 12-6-6 slow-release fertilizer, every 6–8 weeks. Clumps may be divided in the spring after plants have reached their maturity. If needed, treat for slugs and snails with baits or sprays.

LANDSCAPE USE Hostas bring a beauty and calmness to your garden unequaled by other plants. They make great border plants for woodland trails or may be used as a focal point to brighten dark areas of the garden. Try hostas in the tropical garden, planted with bananas, elephant ears, or gingers.

VARIETIES Slug-resistant varieties include 'Big Daddy,' 'Hadspen Blue,' 'Sum and Substance,' 'Inniswood,' and 'Fragrant Blue.' Try also 'Blue Angel,' 'Guacamole,' 'Paul's Glory,' and 'Paul Revere.' Visit with your local hosta society about regional favorites.

'Guacamole' was the
2002 Hosta of the Year.

'Frosted Jade' hosta offers colorful variegation to the shade garden.

Hymenocallis (hy-men-o-KAL-is) species

Spider Lily

FAMILY: *Amaryllidaceae*
ORIGIN: Southeastern United States
RELATIVES: Amaryllis
PROPAGATION: Division, seed
ZONE: 7–10
LIGHT: Sun to part shade
WATER: Average
SIZE: 2 feet
COLOR: White

TOUGHNESS White, spidery-looking flowers are borne from deep green, swordlike foliage. The 2-foot-tall stems usually bear 2–9 fragrant flowers. The foliage gives added texture in the garden. It is okay for these natives to be in the ditches and swamps of the South, but they need to be in the garden too.

PLANTING Choose a site with full sun to part shade. The spider lily is a plant that can tol-erate those wet feet areas, but your choice companion plants may not. Since it performs just as well in fertile, well-drained soil, prepare the bed by incorporating 3–4 inches of organic matter. Set the bulbs with the tips one inch below the soil surface, spacing your plants 12–24 inches apart.

GROWING Feed with a light application of a slow-release 12-6-6 fertilizer in spring with the emergence of growth and about every 4–6 weeks until midsummer. Keep the plants well watered, especially during the bloom period. Once the foliage turns brown in late summer or fall it may be removed.

LANDSCAPE USE In the landscape, spider lilies are perfect around water features. They also excel in a tropical garden with bananas and elephant ears and ferns. Those of you who are passionate about Louisiana iris may want to have bold drifts of white spider lilies separating some of the bright purples, blues, or yellows.

VARIETIES *Hymenocallis liriosome, H. caroliniana, H. choctawensis,* and *H. crassiflolia* are species native to the Southeast. Try *H. narcissifolia,* known as Peruvian daffodil; it is deciduous, allowing it to be grown over most of the South.

The native spider lily offers one of the most exotic blooms for the garden.

Iris (EYE-ris) species and hybrids

Louisiana Iris

FAMILY: *Iridaceae*
ORIGIN: Louisiana,
Southeastern United States
RELATIVES: Bearded Iris
PROPAGATION: Division
ZONE: 6–10
LIGHT: Sun to part shade
WATER: Average to above average
SIZE: 2–5 feet
COLOR: All shades and blends

TOUGHNESS The popularity of the Louisiana iris has steadily risen in the past decade as home gardeners and commercial landscapers alike come to realize this group affords much in the way of texture and beauty. The habit is graceful and the flowers exquisite in shades of burgundy, pink, blue, purple, lavender, white, and yellow. The semi-evergreen foliage is a garden asset almost year-round.

PLANTING Louisiana irises perform best with at least 6 hours of sunlight per day. The soil should be fertile and organically rich. Tight, compacted soil yields an inferior plant. Amend the soil with 3–4 inches of organic matter and till to a depth of 6–8 inches. While tilling incorporate 3 pounds of a 5-10-5 fertilizer per 100 square feet of planting area. Rhizomes are best planted in the fall, setting just below the soil surface. Container-grown plants can be set out anytime during the growing season, planting at the same depth as in the container. Space the plants 2 feet apart.

GROWING Feed with light applications of fertilizer in the fall and late winter, and give supplemental water should rains be sparse. If foliage becomes unattractive in late summer, trim back for a new fall flush of leaves.

LANDSCAPE USE The Louisiana iris complements the water garden, ponds, and creek beds, whether they are dry or flowing. Those grown in water usually maintain very attractive foliage. The swordlike leaves look striking in the tropical garden when combined with elephant ears, ferns, and bananas. Use also with cannas and gingers.

VARIETIES Four species and their hybrids make up the group known as Louisiana irises, *I. fulva, I. brevecaulis, I. nelsonii,* and *I. giganti-caerulea. I. psuedacorus,* which is outstanding in the southern garden too, is sometimes called a Louisiana iris because it has naturalized, but it is from Europe. A few of the favorite Louisiana iris varieties are 'Creole Fantasy' (purple), 'Cajun Country' (deep burgundy-red), 'Marie Caillet' (purple), 'Sun Fury' (yellow), and 'Acadian Sunset' (burgundy and yellow). The Siberian iris *Iris siberica* x *I. sanguinea* hybrids are equally outstanding in the South.

Iris (EYE-ris) ensata

Japanese Iris

FAMILY: *Iridaceae*
ORIGIN: Japan, China
RELATIVES: Louisiana Iris
PROPAGATION: Division
ZONE: 4–9
LIGHT: Sun to part shade
WATER: Average to above average
SIZE: 24–30 inches
COLOR: Most shades and blends

TOUGHNESS Southern gardeners are just now waking up to the fact that this is one of the best species of iris. It complements the Louisiana and Siberian iris with toughness, beauty, and blooms that are born in glorious summer displays after the others are finished. The Japanese iris produces the largest blossoms in shades of blue, pink, white, and purple, with bicolored stripes, veins, and blotches. They are available in single, double, and peony flower forms. These are a must for extending your iris season. The foliage is equally attractive, bright green with a prominent rib.

PLANTING Japanese irises perform better with at least 6 hours of sunlight per day. The soil

should be fertile, organically rich, and acidic. Tight, compacted soils yield an inferior, stunted plant. Amend the soil with 3–4 inches of organic matter and till to a depth of 6–8 inches. While tilling incorporate 3 pounds of a 5-10-5 fertilizer per 100 square feet of planting area. Plant the rhizomes in the fall, setting just below the soil surface. Container-grown plants can be set out anytime during the growing season, planting at the same depth as in the containers. Space the plants 12–18 inches apart.

GROWING Japanese irises are heavy feeders, so give light applications of a 12-6-6 fertilizer in the early spring and every 4–6 weeks through summer. Take care not to let your plants dry out after fertilizing, as this will quickly burn plant roots. Keep evenly moist during the growing season. Best blooming occurs on 2- and 3-year-old clumps. Plants under good culture require dividing every 3–4 years. This can be done in the spring or fall. Maintain a good layer of mulch year-round to conserve moisture and moderate soil temperatures.

LANDSCAPE USE The Japanese iris complements the water garden, ponds, and creeks and can actually be grown in water. They do just as well in fertile upland soils. Plant the Japanese iris boldly in informal drifts. Some of the prettiest displays are with other Japanese irises, in groups of differing colors. The large leaves look striking in the tropical garden when combined with elephant ears, ferns, and bananas and in front of larger ornamental grass.

VARIETIES The Japanese iris varieties are many, yet still a little on the rare side at the local garden center. Check specialty catalogs for more varieties than you ever guessed existed. Favorites are 'Cry of Rejoice' (purple with yellow center), 'Diomedes' (blue), 'Rikki-Pikki' (white), 'Loyalty' (violet-blue double, yellow striping on the falls), and 'Sapphire Star' (pale lavender with white veins).

'Diomedes' Japanese iris

Iris (EYE-ris) pseudacorus

Yellow Flag

FAMILY: *Iridaceae*
ORIGIN: Europe, Turkey, Iran
RELATIVES: Louisiana Iris
PROPAGATION: Division, seed
ZONE: 4–9
LIGHT: Sun to part shade
WATER: Average to above average
SIZE: 4–5 feet
COLOR: Yellow, gold, tan, some with dark veins

TOUGHNESS If you chose an iris for its foliage, this would be the first choice. The tall, 4–5-foot foliage is outstanding almost year-round in the South. The spring yellow blooms are pretty, but the texture of the foliage is magnificent. This iris is aggressive, maybe to a fault, but controlling the spread isn't any harder than simply sticking in a shovel and thinning or removing. If you live on a waterway you should probably choose another selection, as the seeds can be carried downstream. The yellow flag is cold-hardy, heat- and humidity-tolerant, and can be grown in a bog as well as an upland perennial garden.

PLANTING The yellow flag performs admirably in part shade but blooming is best when it receives at least 6 hours of sunlight. The soil should be fertile, organically rich, and acidic. Tight, compacted soil yields a stunted, inferior plant. Amend the soil with 3–4 inches of organic matter and till to a depth of 6–8 inches. While tilling incorporate 3 pounds of a 5-10-5 fertilizer per 100 square feet of planting area. The yellow flag is so resilient that rhizomes or plants can be planted or transplanted just about anytime. If planting rhizomes, set just below the soil surface. If planting container-grown plants set at the same depth as in the containers. Space the plants 18–24 inches apart.

GROWING There is certainly nothing hard about growing this iris other than managing its spread. Since the yellow flag is so vigorous, fertilization other than at the time of planting is not normally needed. Divide every 3–4 years. If growing from seed it will take a couple of years to bloom. Cut the foliage back when it becomes untidy. New shoots will quickly return.

LANDSCAPE USE Use the yellow flag around water gardens, dry creek beds, and in tropical gardens with ferns, elephant ears, bananas, and umbrella plants *(Cyperus alternifolius).* Grow with hostas and *Hedychium* ginger species.

VARIETIES The garden centers selling *Iris pseudacorus* usually offer it generically. 'Holden Clough' (tan with maroon veins) and 'Phil Edinger' (golden yellow with brown veins) are two of the better-known hybrids.

Lycoris (LY-ko-ris) radiata

Spider Lily

FAMILY: *Amaryllidaceae*
ORIGIN: Japan
RELATIVES: Amaryllis
PROPAGATION: Division
ZONE: 6–9
LIGHT: Part shade
WATER: Average
SIZE: 18 inches
COLOR: Red, white, yellow

TOUGHNESS Every year around September something almost magical happens across the South. Red spider lilies with long, tropical-looking stamens pop up, surprising everyone who had forgotten about them. They were out of sight, out of mind. The red spider lily naturalizes with ease and brings color and beauty to the landscape trying to recover from weeks of oppressive heat.

PLANTING Plant red spider lily bulbs in the spring, in fertile, organically rich, well-drained beds in sun or part shade. Place the bulbs 3–4 inches deep, spacing 6–8 inches. They can be planted in straight lines in a formal look but they are usually better in bold, informal drifts.

GROWING Keep the spider lilies watered while they are in bloom to keep the floral show as long as possible. Once the flower is finished the foliage arises and will be making food for the bulb from the fall or winter through late spring. The temptation is to mow those that have naturalized or cut back for a tidy look, but this will do harm to the next season's bloom. Divide in the spring as the foliage starts to turn yellow.

LANDSCAPE USE The red spider lily bloom is not all that long and therefore is a great addition to a bed with a groundcover like ivy. The flowers will emerge above the groundcover and then will not be missed when they retreat back to the ground. The long stamens give a very tropical appearance that allows them to be used in and around bananas and elephant ears. Use them under rice paper plants, or plant drifts among blue-green hostas.

VARIETIES In addition to the red spider lily, look for 'Alba' (white), *L. aurea* (yellow gold, zone 8–10), and *L. squamigera,* often referred to as naked lady (pink summer blooming, more cold-hardy).

Red spider lily blooms are among the most exotic looking in the world of gardening.

Musa (MEW-sa) basjoo

Japanese Fiber Banana

FAMILY: *Musaceae*
ORIGIN: Japan
RELATIVES: Edible banana
PROPAGATION: Division, seed
ZONE: (5) 6–10
LIGHT: Sun to part shade
WATER: Average to above average
SIZE: 10 feet
COLOR: Grown for coarse-textured foliage

The Japanese fiber banana is the most cold-hardy species known.

TOUGHNESS Japanese fiber bananas are the most cold-hardy banana species known. Unfortunately, most gardeners do not know about them. This cold-hardiness makes it possible to grow bananas throughout the South allowing all gardens to take on the look of the West Indies. Though it may seem unbelievable, well-mulched Japanese fiber bananas have been known to return from minus 20 degrees. The flowers are among the most beautiful and exotic.

PLANTING Plant the Japanese fiber banana in the spring after the soil has warmed and the threat of freezing weather has past. Full sun and fertile, well-drained, organically rich soil are needed for both vigor and cold-hardiness. Amend the soil if needed with 3–4 inches of compost or humus and till to a depth of 8–10 inches. While preparing the soil incorporate 3 pounds of a slow-release fertilizer with a 2-1-2 or 2-1-3 ratio per 100 square feet of bed space. If it is unavailable use 3 pounds of a 12-6-6. Plant the banana at the same depth it is growing in the container.

GROWING Bananas are heavy feeders and need light monthly applications of fertilizer and plenty of moisture. Keep them well mulched.

Trim leaves as needed to keep attractive. In the fall once the foliage has been frosted, trim and add an extra layer of mulch. If the soil stays soggy during the winter a spring return will be in jeopardy. Divide as needed in early summer.

LANDSCAPE USE Use the Japanese fiber banana to add coarse-textured foliage to the perennial or cottage garden, transforming it into the look of the islands. Plant them around swimming pools and water gardens and next to the deck, porch, or patio. Grow with other tropicals like elephant ears, hibiscus, and allamandas.

VARIETIES The Japanese fiber banana is sold generically. Look also for the yellow Chinese wax banana *Musella lasciocarpa,* cold-hardy throughout zone 7.

Musa (MEW-sa) ornata

Flowering Banana

FAMILY: *Musaceae*
ORIGIN: Bangladesh, Burma
RELATIVES: Edible Banana
PROPAGATION: Division, seed
ZONE: (7) 8–10
LIGHT: Sun to part shade
WATER: Average to above average
SIZE: 8–10 feet
COLOR: Grown for foliage with flowers—purple, red, lavender, cream

TOUGHNESS References that are among the most scientific and honored list this banana as a zone 10 in cold-hardiness. It is indeed cold-hardy in this zone, but as I travel throughout the South I have seen it at numerous homes in zone 7, not only growing but blooming too! Some were in protected microclimates and others in the open. Without a doubt this is a beautiful banana that blooms with ease and suckers freely, which may enhance its ability to return from cold winters. The flowering banana can transform a mundane garden into a Jamaican paradise.

PLANTING Select a site in full sun, though a little afternoon shade is certainly tolerated. The soil must be fertile, organically rich, and very well drained. Amend the soil with 3–4 inches of organic matter and till to a depth of 8–10 inches. While preparing the soil incorporate 3 pounds of a slow-release fertilizer with a 2-1-2 or 2-1-3 ratio per 100 square feet of bed space. If it is unavailable use 3 pounds of a 12-6-6. Plant the banana at the same depth as it is growing in the container. If you live in zone 6 or 7, err on the side of caution and plant in a protected microclimate or the warmest area of the landscape. This is often on the east-

ern, southeastern, or southern exposure of the home, where the plant will be protected from cold north winds.

GROWING Bananas are heavy feeders, needing light monthly applications of fertilizer and plenty of moisture. Keep them well mulched. Trim leaves as needed to keep attractive. In the fall, once the foliage has been frosted or stalks have frozen, cut back and add an extra layer of mulch. If the soil stays soggy during the winter a spring return may not occur. Divide as needed in early summer.

LANDSCAPE USE The banana's coarse leaf texture transforms the perennial or cottage garden to the look of a Costa Rican plantation. Plant the flowering banana around swimming pools, water gardens, and next to the deck, porch, or patio. Grow with other tropicals like elephant ears, cannas, hibiscus, and allamandas.

VARIETIES The species form may be the more cold-hardy. Named selections are 'African Red' (red), 'Royal Purple' (pale purple), 'Lavender Beauty' (lavender), and 'Milky Way' (off-white).

Musa (MEW-sa) velutina

Velutina Banana

FAMILY: *Musaceae*
ORIGIN: Northeast India
RELATIVES: Edible Banana
PROPAGATION: Division, seed
ZONE: (7) 8–10
LIGHT: Sun to part shade
WATER: Average to above average
SIZE: 5–8 feet
COLOR: Grown for foliage with hot
pink flowers

The velutina banana is perfect for the tropical garden or
can be easily grown in containers.

TOUGHNESS The velutina banana is one anyone can grow if for no other reason than they are small and will grow in a container. They are more cold-hardy than references suggest and deserve to be much more widely planted. The flowers are deep rose and followed by hot pink bananas that look like they have been coated with velvet fabric.

PLANTING Select a site with at least 6 hours of sun. A little afternoon shade is tolerated and appreciated. The soil must be fertile, organically rich, and very well drained. Amend the soil with 3–4 inches of organic matter and till to a depth of 8–10 inches. While preparing the soil incorporate 3 pounds of a slow-release fertilizer with a 2-1-2 or 2-1-3 ratio per 100 square feet of bed space. If it is unavailable, use 3 pounds of a 12-6-6. Plant the banana at the same depth it is growing in the container. If you live in zone 7, plant in a protected microclimate or the warmest area of the landscape. This is often on the eastern, southeastern, or southern exposure of the home, where the plant will receive protection from cold north winds. If growing in containers it will need to be moved indoors for winter protection.

GROWING Bananas are heavy feeders that need light monthly applications of fertilizer and plenty of moisture. Keep them well mulched. Trim leaves as needed to keep attractive. In the fall, once the foliage has been frosted or stalks have frozen, cut back and add an extra layer of mulch. Soggy, cold winter soil will most likely prevent a spring return. Divide as needed in early summer.

LANDSCAPE USE Since the velutina appreciates afternoon shade, it can be wonderfully combined with elephant ears, ferns, impatiens, Louisiana irises, and gingers, all of which are cold-hardy too. Plant the velutina banana around swimming pools, water gardens, along creeks whether flowing or dry, and next to the deck, porch, or patio.

VARIETIES The *Musa velutina* banana is sold generically. Try the 'Super Dwarf Cavendish' (zone 8 in the landscape) in containers around the pool.

Narcissus (nar-SIS-us) species
and hybrids

Narcissus, Daffodil

FAMILY: *Amaryllidaceae*
ORIGIN: Europe, Mediterranean,
China, Japan, N. Africa
RELATIVES: Spider Lily
PROPAGATION: Division
ZONE: 5–9
LIGHT: Sun to part shade
WATER: Average
SIZE: 8–16 inches
COLOR: Pink, yellow, white, orange,
two-toned

Narcissus are among the easiest bulbs to grow and naturalize in the garden.

TOUGHNESS Each spring all across the South you can tell where old homes once stood. No, you aren't looking at concrete slabs, although maybe an old chimney still exists. The real signs are the fields of daffodils that have naturalized. If the narcissus have made themselves at home in this abandoned site, perhaps planted in the late 1800s or during the depression, we can all rest assured that the daffodil or narcissus is a perennial we can rely on too!

PLANTING Select a site in full sun to partial shade or the filtered light under tall deciduous trees. Prepare the planting area by amending the soil with 3–4 inches of organic matter like compost or humus. Incorporate 3 pounds of a 5-10-5 fertilizer per 100 square feet of planting area, tilling the soil to a depth of 8–10 inches. Plant the bulbs 3–6 inches deep, spacing 6–8 inches.

GROWING The foliage plays an important role in the next season's bloom. The leaves must remain on the daffodil for at least 6–8 weeks or until yellowing. Feed the bulbs with an application of a slow-release 12-6-6 fertilizer once the blooms have faded. When the clumps get crowded or the blooms have become sparse, divide and reset in the spring as the leaves start to turn yellow.

LANDSCAPE USE Unlike tulips, daffodils or narcissus look best if planted in random, informal groups or drifts. Plant them boldly with redbuds, dogwoods, azaleas, and Louisiana phlox to make an incredible spring display. Interplant in the fall with pansies, violas, or flowering kale and cabbage.

VARIETIES A look at bulb catalogs will make you almost crazy with anticipation. By all means try new ones and share your success or failure reports with others. Those plants you see at the abandoned home sites are outstanding. Many daffodils known for naturalizing are in the Tazetta class. Look for 'Ziva,' 'Galilee,' 'Grand Monarque,' and 'Grand Soleil d'Or.' Jonquilla varieties and hybrids also naturalize well. Look for 'Campernelle,' 'Trevithian,' and 'Golden Scepter.' 'Barrett Browning,' 'Ice Follies,' 'Fortune,' and 'Carlton' remain among the top daffodil choices for the South.

Oxalis (ox-AY-lis) regnellii

Purple Oxalis

FAMILY: *Oxalidaceae*
ORIGIN: South America
RELATIVES: Wood Sorrel, Star Fruit
PROPAGATION: Division
ZONE: 6–8
LIGHT: Sun to part shade
WATER: Average
SIZE: 8 inches
COLOR: Grown for purple foliage
with pink to lilac flowers

TOUGHNESS Mention oxalis and the word "tough" probably does come to mind—tough to kill or eradicate. But take a deep breath and consider the beauty of the purple oxalis with large triangular leaves of deep purple and flowers approaching 1 inch that are pink to lilac. Though they are tough they are not invasive like the ones you have been trying to kill. These are true garden assets.

PLANTING Purple oxalis is so pretty you will want to prepare a good home. Amend the soil with 3–4 inches of organic matter like compost or humus and till to a depth of 6–8 inches. While you are preparing the bed incorporate 2 pounds of a slow-release 12-6-6 fertilizer per 100 square feet of bed space. Set out plants at the same depth as in the container and space 8–12 inches. Apply a layer of mulch after planting.

GROWING At any time during the growing season should the foliage look less than desirable, oxalis can be cut back. New growth will quickly emerge. Feed with a light application of fertilizer a month after transplanting and then every 4–6 weeks through the growing season. Start feeding established plants in the spring with the emergence of growth and continue through the summer. In colder areas apply an added layer of mulch once frost damage has occurred.

LANDSCAPE USE The purple oxalis is a wonderful border plant for the shade to part-shade garden. There are positive reports back from gardeners growing the purple oxalis in full sun. Combine with wood ferns, hostas, and cast iron plants. Grow under gingers for an extra-special lush look. Grow also with pink or lilac impatiens and in front of hydrangeas.

VARIETIES *O. regnelli* is often sold as *O. triangularis*. Try also *O. siliquosa* variety 'Sunset Velvet' (chartreuse and coppery maroon leaves with yellow flowers). The cold-hardiness of the latter is still under question.

The purple oxalis foliage is exceptionally beautiful and the flowers offer extra incentive.

Tulbaghia (tul-BAG-ia) violacea

Society Garlic

FAMILY: *Liliaceae*
ORIGIN: South Africa
RELATIVES: Onion
PROPAGATION: Division
ZONE: 7–11
LIGHT: Sun to part shade
WATER: Average
SIZE: 18–24 inches
COLOR: Lilac-pink

Society garlic is an heirloom plant being rediscovered by many younger gardeners.

TOUGHNESS This old heirloom plant is experiencing a revival in home landscapes and garden centers too! A new generation is learning about this plant from our grandparents' gardens. Oddly, many books say it is a tropical that needs to be brought indoors. But all over the South, even in zone 7, they are blooming in gardens where they have been for years. Never-ending lilac-pink blossoms and foliage the culinary expert will want to use to flavor dishes make the society garlic an all-purpose plant.

PLANTING Select a site with at least 4 hours of direct sun, the more the better. The soil should be fertile and well drained. Amend heavy, poorly drained soil, with the addition of 3–4 inches of organic matter. While preparing the soil incorporate 2 pounds of a slow-release 12-6-6 fertilizer per 100 square feet of planting area. Plant at the same depth as in the container.

GROWING Keep the plants watered during the growing season. Feed with light monthly applications of fertilizer. The bulbs multiply rapidly. Divide in the spring once the clumps become too crowded. Remove flower stalks that have finished blooming. In colder areas the bulbs can be lifted and stored under cool, dry conditions.

LANDSCAPE USE The society garlic flowers standing tall above the foliage are reminiscent of a small agapanthus. The garlicky fragrant foliage lends a nice texture to the landscape. Use in rock gardens and along dry creek beds. Group them in clusters between plantings of verbena or lantana. Grow with 'Blackie' sweet potato, purple heart, or 'Purple Knight' alternanthera.

VARIETIES The society garlic is mostly sold generically. 'Silver Lace' is a variegated white-striped selection. 'Tri-color' has blue-gray foliage with white margins and lilac-pink flowers. 'Variegata' produces creamy striped variegation.

ORNAMENTAL GRASSES

Magical Garden Plants

O rnamental grasses are easy to grow, but there is a mystique that surrounds their use in the landscape. The mystery is all in the imagination of the gardener who has yet to try them.

When the gorgeous blooms start to appear all over the South on various grasses in home and commercial landscapes, the gardeners who have not tried ornamental grasses start to get a little testy. It may be that their best friend in the neighborhood has them blooming profusely. Where did their friend learn such a complicated design plan?

Once the grasses are in the landscape and blooming, a new dimension has been added. Vines add a vertical element, but grasses do something few people think about—they move. A garden planted with several species of grasses in close proximity to each other performs a dance in the wind that no choreographer could duplicate. Back and forth they move as the wind dictates, slow and gentle, fast and swirling. They mesmerize everyone who is watching.

They do something else that is incredible. When placed in the background, backlit from the setting sun or landscape lighting, they glisten as if with a thin coat of ice. And speaking of ice, the frosty kiss of those cold mornings of fall makes the ornamental grass the prettiest plant in the landscape.

The truth is there is no design school that you have to enroll in to learn how to use ornamental grass. The use is almost as simple as digging a hole, planting the grass, and tucking in few of your favorite blooming flowers, like mums, lantanas, zinnias, or salvias. The list is almost endless, but the real key is doing it. Then the strutting can begin for the ornamental grass grower.

But you might be wondering, "Where do I start?" Consider starting with one or two of the *Miscanthus* varieties. *Miscanthus* gives us some of

Page 173: Coleus, chrysanthemums, and 'Hameln' dwarf fountain grass create a fall garden to envy.

Opposite: 'Strawberries and Cream' ribbon grass, 'Babylon' verbenas, and a purple picket fence create a showy display.

175

our prettiest choices of ornamental grasses, the maiden grass green-foliage types and the variegated versions, such as Japanese silver grass and zebra grass.

The fountain grasses, or *Pennisetums,* are certainly not outdone, as they have some of the most eye-catching foliage and flowers for the landscape. 'Hameln' is a dwarf form reaching only 24–30 inches tall and has showy plumes from midsummer through fall. 'Moudry' has black, 12-inch plumes on 24-inch-tall plants.

The most popular is purple fountain grass, *Pennisetum setaceum,* an annual grass for most of the South whose purple foliage and arching plumes make it worth every cent. New grasses are showing up every year, giving more choice than even the ardent grass lover could have dreamed. The Mexican feather grass and 'Red Bunny Tails' fountain grass are two prime examples. And who would have ever thought that a black or purple millet called 'Purple Majesty' would become an All America Selections winner?

Regardless of the grass you choose, plant nursery-grown transplants into loose, well-prepared beds, rich in organic matter. To accomplish this, incorporate 3–4 inches of peat or compost, to improve drainage and aeration. While tilling, add 2 pounds of a 12-6-6 slow-release fertilizer with minor nutrients per 100 square feet.

It is more important with ornamental grasses than with almost any other plant to remove competing vegetation before planting. There have been many disgruntled gardeners who find that aggressive Bermuda grass or vines make themselves at home intermingled in the middle of the ornamental grass clump. Apply a nonselective herbicide or remove with a hoe. It may take a second herbicide application.

Plant at the same depth as in the container, placing the crown of the plant slightly above the soil line. Water the grass thoroughly after planting to remove any air pockets and to settle the soil. Add a good layer of mulch after planting to prevent a rapid loss of moisture from evaporation and to prevent many weed seeds from germinating.

Cut back the grass in February before any new growth has begun. Trim back from ground level to 6 or 12 inches, depending on the grass. Side-dress with an application of the 12-6-6 fertilizer after you cut back, and then again in midsummer. Keeping the bed well mulched and watered during the summer pays off with a healthier, happier-looking plant.

Since the grasses are perennials (purple fountain excluded), they offer wonderful opportunities to propagate by dividing in early spring. Ornamental grasses have the ability to catch the eye and hold attention in the landscape even when not in bloom. Their leaf texture is unmatched. If you are not growing them, consider it today.

Grasses add a new dimension of movement as they move gracefully in the wind.

Acorus (AK-or-us) gramineus

Dwarf Sweet Flag

FAMILY: *Araceae*
ORIGIN: Japan
RELATIVES: Calla Lily
PROPAGATION: Division
ZONE: 5–9
LIGHT: Part shade to sun
WATER: Above average
SIZE: 12 inches
COLOR: Grown for variegated foliage

TOUGHNESS Wet feet will not be a challenge for the dwarf sweet flag. It tolerates excess moisture and thrives near water features, yet is resilient enough to be grown in upland garden soil too. Dwarf sweet flag is grown for its striking variegated, grasslike foliage that lights up a bubbling brook, garden, or a large mixed container. Solid green selections are also available.

PLANTING Choose a location with filtered light or morning sun and afternoon shade. The soil should be fertile, organically rich or loamy, and moisture retentive. Tight clay soils will not

make you, or the sweet flag, very contented. Amend with 3–4 inches of organic matter like compost or humus if needed. Space green selections 12–18 inches apart and variegated forms 10–14 inches apart.

GROWING Given adequate moisture, the dwarf sweet flag is an easy plant to grow, so use supplemental water during drought periods. Feed in late winter with a light application of a slow-release fertilizer such as a 12-6-6 containing minor nutrients. Should foliage get unattractive cut back in late winter prior to the new spring growth. In moist soils sweet flag will spread much like an iris, so divide as needed. Variegated forms spread more slowly.

LANDSCAPE USE Dwarf sweet flags work well tucked among rocks in creek beds, whether dry or flowing with water. Plant them also next to water gardens or ponds. They are choice plants for pocket-planting in mixed containers. Try combining with bamboo, umbrella plants, and Louisiana iris.

VARIETIES 'Ogon' with bright gold and green variegated leaves and 'Variegatus' with creamy white variegation are the most popular selections. 'Licorice,' a release from the U.S. National Arboretum, gives off an anise aroma when handled.

The versatile dwarf sweet flag is a striking landscape feature, whether planted along a bubbling brook (facing page) or tucked within a shell planter.

Calamagrostis (ka-la-ma-GROST-is) x acutifolia 'Karl Foerster'

Feather Reed Grass

FAMILY: *Gramineae*
ORIGIN: Europe and Asia
RELATIVES: Fountain Grass,
Maiden Grass
PROPAGATION: Division
ZONE: 6–9
LIGHT: Sun
WATER: Average
SIZE: 3–5 feet
COLOR: Grown for foliage with light
pink flowers

'Karl Foerster' feather reed grass is complemented by Joe Pye weed and pink chelone.

TOUGHNESS 'Karl Foerster,' also known as 'Stricta,' is a feather reed grass of rugged durability and was given the award of Perennial Plant of the Year. The feather reed grass is low-maintenance and tough in bad weather. In heavy winds and rains the stems dip and droop in all directions but return to vertical as soon as the storm passes. The deep green, shiny foliage appears in early spring and lasts until early winter. Loose, feathery flowers appear in June and are initially light pink in color.

PLANTING 'Karl Foerster' grows best in well-drained, fertile soils with sufficient moisture, but tolerates tighter soils in drier sites. Feed with a fertilizer such as a 12-6-6 to produce the maximum height. Low fertility will result in shorter plants. Incorporate 2 pounds per 100 square feet during bed preparation. 'Karl Foerster' has a narrow, tight habit and forms an 18-inch-wide clump.

GROWING Little maintenance is required except to cut back the stems to about 6 inches in late winter or early spring. Established clumps can be divided in the fall or early spring. The larger the transplanted portion, however, the faster you

get rewarded with those gorgeous plumes. 'Karl Foerster' is sterile, eliminating the prospects of unwanted seedlings.

LANDSCAPE USE Some call this the perpetual motion grass. The slightest breeze sets it in motion. The graceful movement is a highlight for any landscape. It is excellent as a specimen plant or as a vertical accent in the landscape. Use it for creating a fast-developing screen. It can be grown in patio pot containers and will survive the winter without protection. A combination of feather reed grass with other perennials makes a dramatic effect in the landscape. Choice perennials to use are coreopsis, purple coneflowers, black-eyed Susans, and 'Victoria' blue salvias. Stems cut before the flowers mature will maintain the golden tan color for months in an arrangement .

VARIETIES In addition to 'Karl Forester' try 'Overdam,' which is variegated with white stripes.

Chasmanthium (chas-MAN-the-um)
latifolium

Northern Sea Oats

FAMILY: *Gramineae*
ORIGIN: Eastern United States,
Northern Mexico
RELATIVES: Fountain Grass
PROPAGATION: Division
ZONE: 5–11
LIGHT: Sun to part shade
WATER: Average
SIZE: 2–3 feet
COLOR: Grown for foliage with
green aging to copper flowers

TOUGHNESS There isn't another grass with the appearance of the northern sea oats. The growth habit is upright and arching. The leaves are bamboolike and topped by silvery green flower spikes that resemble clusters of flattened oats. The foliage changes from green to copper to rich brown in the fall. It is superb for winter contrast. The northern sea oats are very cold hardy and are stalwart performers in the hot sweltering summer. This is an environmentally friendly grass with virtually no pests or diseases.

PLANTING Select a site in full sun, although a little light shade is tolerated. The bed should be fertile, organically rich, and well drained. Amend the soil if needed with 3–4 inches of organic matter and till to a depth of 8–10 inches. While preparing the soil incorporate 2 pounds of a slow-release 12-6-6 fertilizer per 100 square feet of bed space. Plant nursery-grown transplants at the same depth as in the container, with the crown slightly above the soil profile. Space plants 12–18 inches apart. Apply a good layer of mulch after planting.

GROWING In late winter cut the foliage back to the ground before spring growth has resumed. Apply a light application of the fertilizer at the time of pruning and again in midsummer. Keep the grass watered during the summer for the best appearance. Divide clumps in early spring when they have become crowded or flowering becomes sparse. Northern sea oats do reseed aggressively, so watch for seedlings and pluck the ones you do not want. Someone will be happy to take them.

LANDSCAPE USE The northern sea oats are striking planted alone or in large masses or drifts. This is another great choice for placing where the sun can backlight them. Use along dry streambeds or close to water features. Grow with other ornamental grasses like the Mexican feather grass. They are well suited to the meadow look, planted in drifts with rudbeckias and purple coneflowers.

VARIETIES These plants are finally being produced in large quantities and being promoted as northern sea oats. They have been for sale sparingly under the names inland sea oats and river oats.

The blooms of northern
sea oats age to copper in
the fall.

Cortaderia (kor-ta-DEER-ia) selloana

Pampas Grass

FAMILY: *Gramineae*
ORIGIN: South America
RELATIVES: Maiden Grass
PROPAGATION: Division
ZONE: 5–10
LIGHT: Sun
WATER: Average
SIZE: 8–10 feet
COLOR: Grown for foliage with white
or pink flowers

The white blooms of the pampas grass are long-lasting and highly ornamental.

TOUGHNESS This Argentina native can survive on just about any amount of water. It will come back from wildfires or burning by gardeners. Yet it produces fountainlike foliage and feathery, plumelike flowers that are perhaps the most attractive in the world of grasses. Pampas grass is cold-, heat-, and drought-tolerant and has virtually no insect or disease problems.

PLANTING Select healthy, growing nursery transplants and set out in the spring into well-prepared beds free from weeds, especially Bermuda grass. Container-grown grass can be successfully planted at any time during the summer. Plant at the same depth it is growing in the container. Planting too deep will prove lethal. If planting as a screen, space 8 feet apart. After planting, water thoroughly to get the roots established, and then only sparingly or during prolonged dry periods.

GROWING Remove old flowers in early spring. The pampas grass is considered evergreen, but once foliage is unattractive or has had freeze damage cut back in mid-February to near ground level. The leaves are very sharp and can easily cut hands. After cutting back, feed with a light application of a lawn-type fertilizer.

LANDSCAPE USE As a screen the pampas grass is unsurpassed. Use at the entry to large gates or driveways. Plant them to the back of the border, allowing plenty of room. Try dwarf pampas grass with other grasses like muhly and tough roses like 'Carefree Delight' or 'Nearly Wild.'

VARIETIES Leading selections are 'Marabout' and 'Sunningdale Silver.' Choice variegated forms are 'Sun Stripe,' 'Silver Comet,' and 'Variegata.' Some of the best pink-bloomed varieties are 'Rosea,' 'Rubra,' and 'Carnea.' Choice dwarf varieties are 'Pumila,' 'Bertini,' and a variegated form called 'Gold Band.'

Liriope (li-ri-O-pe) muscari

Liriope, Lily Turf

FAMILY: *Liliaceae*
ORIGIN: China, Taiwan, Japan
RELATIVES: Daylily
PROPAGATION: Division, seed
ZONE: 6–10
LIGHT: Part shade
WATER: Average
SIZE: 8–24 inches
COLOR: Grown for foliage with lilac, purple, or white flowers

TOUGHNESS Whether you call it lily turf, liriope, or monkey grass, everyone will agree it is one of our best plants. Even though most gardeners grow liriope for the foliage it does produce gorgeous lavender, purple, or white flower spikes. The showy blooms last for weeks, providing welcome color during one of the hottest times of the year. Taller selections can be used as cut flowers.

PLANTING Liriope, like most other plants, prefers a well-drained, well-prepared, organically rich bed. Tight, compacted clay seldom lets the liriope reach its potential in size and beauty. Loosen the soil and increase the fertility by adding 3–4 inches of organic matter, tilling to a depth of 6–8 inches. Incorporate 2 pounds of a slow-release 12-6-6 fertilizer per 100 square feet of planting area. Plant at the same depth it is growing in the container. Space the plants as recommended per your variety.

GROWING The cultural techniques of growing liriope are very simple. Prune back established clumps in late winter before new growth resumes. After pruning the liriope side-dress it with a light application of a lawn-type fertilizer. Pruning after the growth has resumed yields ragged, torn leaf blades for the rest of the season. Many gardeners ask about getting rid of Bermuda grass in the liriope. Herbicides with the active ingredient *sethoxydin* will eliminate the Bermuda without damaging the liriope. Follow label directions.

LANDSCAPE USE *Liriope muscari* is often used as border plant for shrub or flower beds or as a clumping groundcover when mass-planted. It excels in full sun, and the variegated forms give color and interest to the shade garden. Combine with aucuba, hostas, ginger, and chartreuse forms of oxalis.

VARIETIES *Liriope muscari* is clump forming and comes in green and variegated varieties. Choice green selections are 'Big Blue' (12–15 inches), 'Majestic' (15–18 inches), 'Evergreen Giant' (24 inches, zones 8–10), 'Lilac Beauty' (15–18 inches), and 'Samantha' (10 inches). Variegated forms do best with afternoon shade protection; 'Silvery Sunproof' (gold variegation, 12–15 inches) and 'Variegata' (creamy variegation, 12–15 inches) are the leading selections. *Liriope spicata,* known as creeping liriope, spreads rapidly by rhizomes.

'Silvery Sunproof' liriope and purple heart make an interesting combination.

Miscanthus (mis-KAN-thus) sinensis

Maiden Grass, Silver Grass, Eulalia Grass

FAMILY: *Gramineae*
ORIGIN: East Asia
RELATIVES: Muhly Grass
PROPAGATION: Division
ZONE: 4–9
LIGHT: Sun to part shade
WATER: Average
SIZE: 5–6 feet
COLOR: Grown for foliage with pink, white, or silver flowers

Ornamental grasses can give a bold look to the landscape.

TOUGHNESS The genus and species *Miscanthus sinensis* deserves a book on its own. It is a great starting place for those gardeners who have not yet tried ornamental grass. *Miscanthus* is a survivor in cold temperatures and thrives in extreme heat and humidity. No plant can make a statement in a large border like one of these ornamental grasses. The blooms are wonderful and move gracefully in the wind but are just an added bonus to the color and texture of the foliage. The long arching leaves come in green-silver variegation or creamy yellow horizontal bands.

PLANTING Select a site in full sun, though a little light shade is tolerated. The bed should be fertile, organically rich, and well drained. Amend the soil if needed with 3–4 inches of organic matter and till to a depth of 8–10 inches. While preparing the soil incorporate 2 pounds of a slow-release 12-6-6 fertilizer per 100 square feet of bed space. Plant the grass at the same depth it is growing in the container, with the crown slightly above the soil profile. Space plants 4–6 feet apart. Apply a good layer of mulch after planting.

GROWING In late winter cut the foliage back to the ground before spring growth has resumed.

Apply a light application of the fertilizer at the time of pruning and again in midsummer. Keep the grass watered during the summer for the best appearance. Clumps can be divided in early spring.

LANDSCAPE USE These large grasses can be planted as an accent, specimen, or screen. If you are creating a new flower border, make it large enough to accommodate a large grass. Many gardeners feel there is some magic formula to using maiden grass. Here is the formula. Plant the grass and then use your favorite sun-loving flowers in front of it. You will look like a design pro. Use in combination with water features or along dry creek beds.

VARIETIES An in-depth listing of varieties could cover pages. *M. sinensis* 'Variegatus' is known as Japanese silver grass. Choice selections are 'Silberfeder,' 'Cabaret,' and 'Cosmopolitan.' Look also for 'Adagio' (gray foliage, pink flowers aging white), *M. sinensis* var. *Zebrinus* zebra grass (creamy yellow horizontal bands pink aging to white plumes), 'Gracillimus' maiden grass (green foliage with white mid-rib reddish-pink plumes), and 'Graziella' (narrow green leaves, silver plumes).

Zebra grass

Japanese silver grass

Muhlenbergia (moo-len-BUR-jee-uh)
capillaris

Muhly Grass

FAMILY: *Gramineae*
ORIGIN: Southeastern United States
RELATIVES: Zebra Grass
PROPAGATION: Division
ZONE: 5–9
LIGHT: Sun to part shade
WATER: Less than average
SIZE: 2–4 feet
COLOR: Grown for foliage with rose-pink flowers

TOUGHNESS Muhly grass was little known a few years ago even though it is native to much of the South. Today it ranks as one of the most popular. Its virtues are many. It is able to return from cold blustery winters and thrives in high heat and humidity. The foliage has a unique spiky texture, and the plant finishes the season with the Grand Finale, the bloom. The bloom gives the appearance of a billowy cloud of rose-pink that moves back and forth dictated by the breeze. The blooms persist until freezing weather arrives.

PLANTING Select a site in full sun, with fertile, organically rich soil. Amend the soil as needed with 3–4 inches of organic matter like compost and humus. Till the soil to a depth of 8–10 inches and incorporate 2 pounds of a slow-release 12-6-6 fertilizer. Dig the planting hole 2–3 times as wide as the root ball but no deeper. Plant the muhly grass at the same depth it is growing in the container, with the crown slightly above the soil profile. Space plants 24–36 inches apart. Apply a layer of mulch after planting.

GROWING In late winter cut the foliage back to the ground before spring growth has resumed. Apply a light application of the fertilizer at the time of pruning and again in midsummer. Keep the grass watered during the summer for the best appearance. Clumps can be divided in early spring.

LANDSCAPE USE Muhly grass is at home in any type of garden. Grow in beds with deep pink shrub-type roses. Place in front of other grasses like dwarf pampas, purple fountain, or black bamboo. Muhly grass is exceptional with 'Clara Curtis' chrysanthemums.

VARIETIES Muhly grass is sold generically and sells out quickly.

Muhly grass forms large billowy, cotton-candy-like blossoms in the fall.

Nassella (nas-SEL-a) tenuissima

Mexican Feather Grass

FAMILY: *Gramineae*
ORIGIN: Texas, New Mexico,
Mexico, Argentina
RELATIVES: Muhly Grass
PROPAGATION: Division
ZONE: (6) 7–11
LIGHT: Sun to part shade
WATER: Average
SIZE: 12–18 inches
COLOR: Grown for foliage with
cream flowers

Mexican feather grass moves with the gentle breeze.

TOUGHNESS The Mexican feather grass is mounding with needlelike leaves forming bright green clumps. The flowers are silky hairlike and glisten in the light. They move gracefully back and forth with the gentle breeze. This outstanding grass is new to most gardeners but will become an instant hit. It has shown good cold-hardiness and is likewise a trooper in the hot sweltering summer. This is an environmentally friendly grass with virtually no pests or diseases.

PLANTING Select a site in full sun, though a little light shade is tolerated. The bed should be fertile, organically rich, and well drained. Amend the soil if needed with 3–4 inches of organic matter and till to a depth of 8–10 inches. While preparing the soil incorporate 2 pounds of a slow-release 12-6-6 fertilizer per 100 square feet of bed space. Plant at the same depth as in the container, with the crown slightly above the soil profile. Space plants 12–18 inches apart. Apply a good layer of mulch after planting.

GROWING In late winter cut the foliage back to the ground before spring growth has resumed. Apply a light application of the fertilizer at the time of pruning and again in midsummer. Keep the grass watered during the summer for the best appearance. Clumps can be divided in early spring.

LANDSCAPE USE The Mexican feather grass is striking planted alone or in large masses or drifts. The blooms are almost indescribable when backlit by the setting sun or landscape lighting. Use with other ornamental grasses like muhly, purple fountain, or 'Karl Foerster' feather reed grass. They are quite at home in the perennial garden with the black-eyed Susan, purple coneflower, and salvia.

VARIETIES Mexican feather grass is sometimes sold as Texas needle grass. Try also *N. gigantea*, giant feather grass.

*Pennisetum (pen-i-SEE-tum)
alopecuroides*

Fountain Grass, Chinese Pennisetum

FAMILY: *Gramineae*

ORIGIN: East Asia, West Australia

RELATIVES: Muhly Grass

PROPAGATION: Division

ZONE: 6–9

LIGHT: Sun to part shade

WATER: Average

SIZE: 12–48 inches

COLOR: Grown for foliage with flowers—white, black, pink, bronze-purple

---

TOUGHNESS Fountain grass is among the most beautiful grasses in the world. Graceful arching stems topped by plumes reminiscent of a fox's tail stir with the slightest breeze, giving a new dimension to the garden, that of movement. Fountain grass is cold-hardy, returning in the spring and then flourishing in the torrid heat and humidity.

PLANTING Select a site in full sun, though a little light shade is tolerated. The bed should be fertile, organically rich, and well drained. Amend the soil if needed with 3–4 inches of organic matter and till to a depth of 8–10 inches. While preparing the soil incorporate 2 pounds of a slow-release 12-6-6 fertilizer per 100 square feet of bed space. Plant at the same depth as in the container, with the crown slightly above the soil profile. Space plants 18–36 inches apart as dictated by the variety. Apply a good layer of mulch after planting.

GROWING In late winter cut the foliage back to the ground before spring growth has resumed. Apply a light application of the fertilizer at the time of pruning and again in midsummer. Keep the grass watered during the summer for the best appearance. Clumps can be divided in early spring.

LANDSCAPE USE Fountain grasses can be planted as an accent, as a specimen, or in odd-numbered groupings. If you are creating a new flower border, make it large enough to accommodate ornamental grass. Dwarf varieties excel in gardens with fall-blooming chrysanthemums and burgundy-leafed varieties of coleus. Use with flowering kale and cabbage. Fountain grasses of all types work in perennial gardens with black-eyed Susans, purple cone-flowers, and salvias.

VARIETIES 'Hameln' is a champion, (dwarf, 24–30 inches). 'Moudry' (dwarf, black plumes, 24 inches) and 'Little Bunny' (dwarf, 12 inches) are among the best.

Fountain grasses have an exceptionally long blooming season.

Pennisetum (pen-i-SEE-tum) glaucum

'Purple Majesty'

FAMILY: *Gramineae*
ORIGIN: North America
RELATIVES: Muhly Grass
PROPAGATION: Division
ZONE: Annual all zones
LIGHT: Sun for best color
WATER: Average
SIZE: 4–5 feet
COLOR: Grown for purple foliage
with purple flowers

'Purple Majesty,' an award-winning millet with a grasslike texture, is wonderfully ornamental.

TOUGHNESS The gardening world in the United States is coming of age. How do we know? 'Purple Majesty,' which is millet, was declared a 2003 All America Selections Gold Medal Winner. Even before the public was aware that it was a winner they were craving it and buying up the limited quantities. As an annual it thrives in our summer heat and produces deep, dark purple leaves topped by equally dark plumes. It will stand out in gardens wherever it is planted.

PLANTING Select a site in full sun for the showiest color. The bed should be fertile, organically rich, and well drained. Amend the soil if needed with 3–4 inches of organic matter and till to a depth of 8–10 inches. While preparing the soil incorporate 2 pounds of a slow-release 12-6-6 fertilizer per 100 square feet of bed space. Plant at the same depth as in the container, with the crown slightly above the soil profile. Space plants 10–12 inches apart. Transplant to the garden before 'Purple Majesty' gets root-bound in the container. Apply a good layer of mulch after planting.

GROWING Apply a light application of the fertilizer a month after transplanting and again 6–8 weeks later. Keep the grass watered during the summer for the best appearance. Avoid drying to the wilting point. The plumes, which are a lot like cattails, are great for using in the vase and drying too.

LANDSCAPE USE 'Purple Majesty' looks its best when grown informally in groups or clusters of 5–9 plants. Spot-planting one simply doesn't do the plant justice. Use the grass as a backdrop in the border and plant 'Hameln' dwarf fountain grass in front. Try 'Purple Majesty' with 'Indian Summer' or 'Goldsturm' rudbeckia for an exceptional display. Purple coneflowers, Russian sage, and 'Autumn Joy' sedum would make nice companion plants too.

VARIETIES 'Purple Majesty' is the *Pennisetum glaucum* of choice for the garden.

Pennisetum (pen-i-SEE-tum) messiacum

'Red Bunny Tails'

FAMILY: *Gramineae*
ORIGIN: Southwest Asia, Australia
RELATIVES: Muhly Grass
PROPAGATION: Division
ZONE: 7–11
LIGHT: Sun to part shade
WATER: Average
SIZE: 18–36 inches
COLOR: Grown for foliage with
reddish purple flowers

TOUGHNESS 'Red Bunny Tails' is a new *Pennisetum* that will delight the home gardener. Red flower plumes reminding you of rabbits' feet are produced in contrast with attractive glossy green foliage that has burgundy overtones. The blooms remain on the plant all season and are even effective once frost has kissed them. 'Red Bunny Tails' is cold-hardy to zone 7 and thrives in southern heat and humidity.

PLANTING Select a site in full sun, though a little light shade is tolerated. The bed should be fertile, organically rich, and well drained. Amend the soil if needed with 3–4 inches of organic matter and till to a depth of 8–10 inches. While preparing the soil incorporate 2 pounds of a slow-release 12-6-6 fertilizer per 100 square feet of bed space. Plant nursery-grown transplants at the same depth as in the container, with the crown slightly above the soil profile. Space plants 18–24 inches apart. Apply a good layer of mulch after planting.

GROWING In late winter cut the foliage back to the ground before spring growth has resumed. Apply a light application of the fertilizer at the time of pruning and again in midsummer. Keep the 'Red Bunny Tails' watered during the summer for the best appearance. Clumps can be divided in early spring when needed.

LANDSCAPE USE 'Red Bunny Tails' is really another species of fountain grass and can be planted as an accent, as a specimen, or in odd-numbered groupings. Since it is relatively dwarf it will excel in gardens with fall-blooming chrysanthemums and burgundy-leafed varieties of coleus. Use with flowering kale and cabbage. Fountain grasses of all types work in perennial gardens with the black-eyed Susan, purple coneflower, and salvia. Some of the most striking plantings are with other grasses like muhly grass or Mexican feather grass.

VARIETIES 'Red Bunny Tails' is the only selection of *P. messiacum* available in the United States at this time.

They may be small, but the blooms of the 'Red Bunny Tails' are effective in the landscape.

Pennisetum (pen-i-SEE-tum) setaceum

Purple Fountain Grass

FAMILY: *Gramineae*
ORIGIN: Tropical Africa,
Southwest Asia
RELATIVES: Muhly Grass
PROPAGATION: Division
ZONE: 9–11, annual elsewhere
LIGHT: Sun to part shade
WATER: Average
SIZE: 18–48 inches
COLOR: Grown for foliage with
purple-pink flowers

Purple fountain grass is an annual in all but the coastal South and rewards all who grow it with incredible beauty.

TOUGHNESS The purple fountain grass is an asset in the garden from the day it is planted until freezing weather takes it out months later. Though it is an annual, it is an outstanding purchase because of the striking purple foliage and scores of coppery pink-purple flowers. The purple fountain thrives in the worst of heat and humidity, making the amateur gardener look like a professional landscape designer.

PLANTING Select a site in full sun, though a little light shade is tolerated. The bed should be fertile, organically rich, and well drained. Amend the soil if needed with 3–4 inches of organic matter and till to a depth of 8–10 inches. While preparing the soil, incorporate 2 pounds of a slow-release 12-6-6 fertilizer per 100 square feet of bed space. Plant at the same depth as in the container, with the crown slightly above the soil profile. Space plants 24–36 inches apart. Apply a good layer of mulch after planting.

GROWING If living in zone 9 or further south, cut the foliage back to the ground in late winter before spring growth has resumed. Apply a light application of the fertilizer at the time of pruning and again in midsummer. If growing as an annual, feed a month after transplanting and again 6–8 weeks later. Keep the grass watered during the summer for the best appearance. In zones 8 and colder, clumps can be lifted and divided for over-wintering in a protected area. I find it easier to simply buy new ones in the spring.

LANDSCAPE USE The purple fountain grass is perfect for combining with rudbeckias like 'Indian Summer,' petunias like 'Tidal Wave Silver,' or coleus. Use also with purple-leafed cannas, purple coneflowers, and 'Autumn Joy' sedum.

VARIETIES 'Rubrum' is the industry standard. Look also for the dwarf 'Little Red Riding Hood.'

Phalaris (FAL-a-ris) arundinacea

Ribbon Grass

FAMILY: *Gramineae*
ORIGIN: North America, South Africa
RELATIVES: Bamboo
PROPAGATION: Division
ZONE: 4–11
LIGHT: Sun to part shade
WATER: Above average
SIZE: 18–36 inches
COLOR: Grown for variegated foliage

TOUGHNESS Ribbon grass is described as tenacious, bamboolike, and aggressive—in other words, it is no wimp. The variegated types are amongst the prettiest selections and thrive in areas that are too moist to grow many other plants. Ribbon grass makes a great groundcover and contrasts wonderfully with the dark green of nearby St. Augustine or centipede grass. The showy soft white flowers rise 6–12 inches above the plant and remain attractive even after freezing weather.

PLANTING Ribbon grass thrives just about anywhere other than tight, dry clay. Before planting apply a nonselective herbicide to kill existing vegetation. This may take more than one application. Plant in moist, fertile areas with a plan in mind about how far you will let it spread. Space transplants 12–15 inches apart, mass-planting in informal drifts. This isn't a border-type plant but will fill in the designated groundcover area. Make sure you have a large mowed buffer area between the grass and flowerbeds.

GROWING Control the spread of ribbon grass by mowing. In late winter mow or trim the grass near ground level before growth has resumed. After mowing the ribbon grass, feed with a lawn-type fertilizer. Ample moisture keeps the ribbon grass growing vigorously and looking its best.

LANDSCAPE USE Use the ribbon grass as a large groundcover for moist, boggy areas. Create islands of the groundcover in the turf. The ribbon grass is not without good companions. Combine variegated varieties with native wood fern, autumn fern, and Louisiana iris. Use ribbon grass as under-story plantings to bamboo. The ribbon grass lends great texture in mixed containers.

VARIETIES The species with green leaves is most aggressive. Look also for 'Picta' (variegated green and white stripes). Varieties known to be less aggressive are 'Dwarf Carters' (12–15 inches, white stripes), 'Mervyn Freesey' (18–36 inches, white stripes blushed pink), and 'Strawberries and Cream' (18–36 inches, white stripes blushed pink).

Ribbon grass makes an excellent variegated groundcover.

Phyllostachys (fill-OS-tak-is) nigra

'Henon' Black Bamboo

FAMILY: *Gramineae*
ORIGIN: China
RELATIVES: Zebra Grass
PROPAGATION: Division
ZONE: 7–10
LIGHT: Sun to part shade
WATER: Average
SIZE: 50 feet
COLOR: Grown for dark green canes

TOUGHNESS For the Japanese or tropical garden, no plant can replace the bamboo. 'Henon' is a variety of black bamboo, although it isn't black but green and is much larger than typical black bamboo. It is also one of the finest. The plants are evergreen and the canes measure over 3 inches in diameter. One look at it and you get a sense of being in the presence of a plant of rare, exotic beauty.

PLANTING 'Henon' bamboo performs best given afternoon shade. Bamboo grows best in fertile, well-drained soils that are slightly acidic with a pH of 6–6.5. Add dolomitic lime if soil pH is very acidic. Loosen tight clay soil by incorporating 3–4 inches of organic matter, tilling or shoveling to a depth of 8–12 inches. Dig the planting hole twice as large as the root ball but no deeper. Plant at the same depth it is growing in the container. Space plants 12–15 feet apart. Though the plant is drought–tolerant, keep the area moist until established. This may take 3–6 months. To prevent the spread of running bamboo put down a barrier prior to planting. First choose how large a bamboo area or grove you want. Then dig a trench 36 inches deep around the perimeter. In this trench place a barrier of rolled fiberglass, 40 ml polypropylene, or aluminum flashing. The barriers should extend above the soil profile at least 2 inches.

GROWING Feed in late winter with an application of a lawn-type fertilizer and every 6 weeks during the growing season. If no barrier was placed in the ground, the bamboo can be controlled by mowing around the grove. This will only work, however, if a large turf area surrounds the grove; otherwise, it will come up in shrub beds, the neighbor's backyard, etc. The large, aggressive types can send up shoots 20–30 feet away. Propagate by making large divisions in the spring.

LANDSCAPE As a screen the 'Henon' bamboo is one of the finest, so don't be fearful—plant a large grove. Use in Japanese or tropical gardens or anywhere you want to create your private retreat. Grow in close proximity to ponds or small lakes where the bamboo can reflect off the water. Very striking combinations can be made with bald cypress, which gives a fine leaf texture in contrast with the 'Henon.'

VARIETIES In addition to the smaller black species and 'Hernon,' try *P. edulis,* known as 'Moso' bamboo.

*Phyllostachys (fill-OS-tak-is)
sulphurea* var. *viridis*

'Robert Young'

FAMILY: *Gramineae*
ORIGIN: East China
RELATIVES: Timber bamboo
PROPAGATION: Division
ZONE: 7–10
LIGHT: Sun to part-shade
WATER: Average
SIZE: 25–40 feet
COLOR: Grown for golden yellow canes

TOUGHNESS The words "tough" and "aggressive" apply to many bamboos, but the one known as 'Robert Young' has a rare beauty to add to the list of virtues. Golden yellow canes 3 inches in diameter reach 25–40 feet in height. They stand out in dramatic fashion against the backdrop of green leaves from nearby trees. 'Robert Young' bamboo is a running bamboo that is cold-hardy and thrives in the southern heat and humidity.

PLANTING 'Robert Young' bamboo performs best when grown in afternoon shade. Plant the bamboo in well-drained soil that is slightly acidic with a pH of 6–6.5. Add dolomitic lime if soil pH is very acidic. Loosen tight clay soil by incorporating 3–4 inches of organic matter, tilling or shoveling to a depth of 8–12 inches. Dig the planting hole twice as large as the root ball but no deeper. Plant at the same depth it is growing in the container. Space plants 12–15 feet apart. Keep the young plants moist until established, which may take 3–6 months. To prevent the spread of running bamboo, put down a barrier prior to planting. First, choose how large a bamboo area or grove you want. Then dig a trench 36 inches deep around the perimeter. In this trench place a barrier of rolled fiberglass, 40 ml polypropylene, or aluminum flashing. The barriers should extend above the soil profile at least 2 inches.

GROWING Feed in late winter with an application of a lawn-type fertilizer and every 6 weeks during the growing season. If no barrier was placed in the ground, the bamboo can be controlled by mowing around the grove. This will only work, however, if a large turf area surrounds the grove; otherwise, it will come up in shrub beds, flower beds, and the neighbor's backyard. The large, aggressive types can send up shoots 20–30 feet way. Propagate by making large divisions in the spring.

VARIETIES In addition to *Phyllostachys sulphurea* var. *viridis* 'Robert Young,' try also Japanese giant timber bamboo, *Phyllostachys bambusoides*. It has been recorded at 70 feet tall in the United States with culms 6 inches in diameter. It may lose leaves below 10 degrees and die back at zero, but it will return faithfully in the spring. Suppliers offer several selections from this species.

VINES AND CLIMBERS
Going Vertical

Like trees, shrubs, and groundcovers, vines are important to the interest of any garden landscape. Vines provide vertical dimension and may be the key ingredient to making a garden. Like hanging a mirror on the living room wall, adding an arbor gives depth and yet closure, helping form an outdoor room. In fact, placing climbers on iron trellises is a quick and easy way to screen and make a series of outdoor privacy areas for relaxing or entertaining.

Distinctive characteristics make each species and variety of vine well adapted to certain locations in the garden. Vines can be used to frame a doorway, relieve the monotony of a large wall, or dramatically change a fence. Using those known for bloom, however, makes the effect even more special.

Perennial vines will be around a long time, so planning is very important. Is this where you really want the vine? Do you have a support structure large enough and sturdy enough to hold the weight of the vine once it matures and develops a more woody nature?

Planting a perennial vine is like planting a shrub. Prepare the planting location by amending with 3–4 inches of organic matter and turning to a depth of 8–10 inches. Prepare the area 2–3 feet outward. While preparing the planting area incorporate one cup of a slow-release 12-6-6 fertilizer. Give another light application a month after transplanting.

Dig the planting hole 2–3 times as wide as the root ball but not deeper. Plant the vine at the same depth it is growing in the container. If the vine is attached to a stake or small trellis with tendrils, leave it in and place it against the new permanent support structure. Water thoroughly and apply a layer of mulch.

Annual vines are also exceptional in the landscape. These plants grow with unbelievable vigor, covering a trellis in a couple of months and actually covering a pergola in one season. The tropical vines that we

Page 195: Clematis and a white picket fence, two Southern standards

Opposite: Hyacinth bean, an old-fashioned climber grown from seed, can cover a trellis or fence in one season.

Two 'Tangerine Beauty' cross-vines give blooms numbering in the thousands.

mostly treat as annuals, such as the mandevilla, bloom from the minute you get them in late April until November or the first hard freeze. This is why these are among the best values for the landscape dollar.

Annual vines are much like perennial vines except many of them can be grown from seed, such as the morning glory or moonflower. Many of these seed-grown vines give a perennial-like performance as they reseed every year. They may or may not reseed where you want them, such as against the trellis, but they are easily transplanted.

These high-octane plants will need feeding with light monthly applications of fertilizer and supplemental water during prolonged dry periods.

Some vines climb easily by twining, others attach with tendrils, and then there are those that are called climbers but are tied and trained along the fence or trellis. If you need more basal branches, pinch or lightly prune terminal shoots frequently.

Don't forget about the possibilities of using vines in containers and baskets. Instead of using an evergreen shrub or grass as the center plant in a large container, try a vine on a tower, which may work just as well and offer a unique bloom. Plant large baskets and let tropicals like mandevillas climb the chains while other plants cascade over the rim.

Once you start growing "up," you have arrived in the gardening world. Your neighbors begin to suspect that that weekend when you were supposed to be at Grandma's, you were really at a landscape design seminar that cost a pretty penny. Things like this are bound to happen when you are no longer vertically challenged.

Allamanda (al-am-AN-da) cathartica and *A. schottii*

Golden Trumpet

FAMILY: *Apocynaceae*
ORIGIN: Tropical America
RELATIVES: Mandevilla
and Oleander
PROPAGATION: Cutting, layering
ZONE: Perennial in 10–11, annual
elsewhere
LIGHT: Sun to part shade
WATER: Average
SIZE: 10–15 feet
(50 feet in frost-free areas)
COLOR: Golden yellow

TOUGHNESS The 5-inch golden yellow trumpet flowers are produced almost nonstop from spring until frost. When the family is seeking shelter in the comfortable air-conditioned home, the allamanda is outside in the sweltering heat making the landscape look like Jamaica. Insect pests and diseases are practically nonexistent. The allamanda is poisonous if eaten.

PLANTING If the allamanda has a threat it is wet feet, so plant in fertile, well-drained soil. Incorporate 3–4 inches of organic matter to improve drainage and aeration. Select a site in full sun or morning sun and afternoon shade. Plant in the spring after the last frost when the soil has warmed. If growing as a vine, use a sturdy support structure like a fence, arbor, or trellis. The allamanda will need to be tied.

GROWING Keep the soil moist and the plant growing vigorously by feeding with light monthly applications of a slow-release, balanced fertilizer like a 10-10-10 or 12-6-6 containing micronutrients. If it is grown in containers, use controlled-release granules per label directions. Diluted water-soluble fertilizers also work quite well. Allamandas will only survive the winter in south Florida, so treat as an annual, protect from freezing, or take cuttings for over-wintering.

LANDSCAPE USE Allamandas excel for adding a touch of the Caribbean around the pool, patio, or deck, yet look at home against a white picket fence and grown in combination with mandevillas. Use as under-story plantings to large bananas and plants like the princess flower *(Tibouchina urvilleana)*. Bush forms are well suited to be grown with annual red salvias and cannas.

VARIETIES Look for 'Williamsii,' dwarf forms 'Hendersonii Dwarf,' 'Hendersonii Compacta,' 'Dwarf Discovery,' and the bush form *A. schottii*.

Golden allamanda is tropical in nature but blooms nonstop during the growing season.

Bignonia (big-NOH-nee-ah) capreolata

Cross-vine, Trumpet Flower

FAMILY: *Bignoniaceae*
ORIGIN: North America
RELATIVES: Trumpet creeper,
cape honeysuckle
PROPAGATION: Seed,
cutting, layering
ZONE: Perennial in 6–9
LIGHT: Sun to part shade
WATER: Average
SIZE: Climbing 20–30 feet
COLOR: Red, orange, red-purple

'Tangerine Beauty' cross-vine yields more flowers per square foot than any other vine.

TOUGHNESS In the spring this evergreen to semi-evergreen native produces more flowers per square foot than any other vine. An arbor, fence, or trellis may have brilliant tangerine flowers numbering in the thousands. Cold-hardiness and heat- and humidity-tolerance make this vine most welcome throughout the South. Many older gardeners admit they smoked cross-vine in their youth!

PLANTING Select a site in full sun for best bloom. Improve tight soil with 3–4 inches of compost or humus for better drainage and aeration. This is a large vine, so provide a sturdy support structure like an arbor or pergola for climbing. The vine climbs by tendrils and has small disks that allow it to climb a wall or fence much like a Virginia creeper. Most garden centers stock a selection of quality plants. Plant at the same depth as in the container, spacing 10–15 feet apart. Apply a good layer of mulch after planting.

GROWING Feed with a light application of 5-10-5 fertilizer in late winter and a slow-release 12-6-6 in midsummer. Remove up to two-thirds of the previous season's growth after the spring bloom. Cut back as needed to maintain shape and keep contained.

LANDSCAPE USE The major bloom is in April and May with light flowering throughout the growing season. Use the cross-vine on a fence behind old-fashioned blue larkspurs, Brazilian sage, or indigo spires salvia. The trumpet-shaped flowers look tropical when mixed with coarse-textured foliage from bananas or elephant ears.

VARIETIES 'Tangerine Beauty' (reddish-tangerine), 'Atrosanguinea' (red-purple), and 'Shalimar Red' (red) are the most prized selections.

Campsis (KAMP-sis) radicans

Trumpet Vine

FAMILY: *Bignoniaceae*
ORIGIN: North America
RELATIVES: Cross-vine
PROPAGATION: Cutting, layering,
seeds, suckering
ZONE: Perennial in 4–9
LIGHT: Sun to part shade
WATER: Less than average
SIZE: 20–40 feet
COLOR: Red, yellow, orange

TOUGHNESS Bright orange-red trumpet flowers, 3 inches long, are borne in clusters of 6–12 and produced all summer long. These flowers are a favorite of the ruby-throated hummingbird. The vine is drought- and cold-tolerant, thrives in heat and humidity, and is aggressive. For the gardener who tends his landscape this vine is hard to beat.

PLANTING Garden centers are finally stocking selections, testifying to their appeal. Plant the trumpet vine alongside a strong support structure for climbing. Fences, arbors, and pergolas are among the best. Set plants at the same depth as in the container.

GROWING Many gardeners consider the plant invasive. Mowing or cutting with a string trimmer keeps them under control. Plants are normally vigorous enough without fertilizer. Cut back as needed in late winter to keep contained.

LANDSCAPE USE The trumpet vine is a prolific bloomer, perfect in a tropical garden or on a picket fence in a cottage garden. Blue flowers, such as the 'Coast Rica Blue' variety of Brazilian sage, complement the orange-red flowers as does the salvia indigo spires. Use agapanthus or lily of the Nile in front of the structure holding the trumpet vine. If well managed the trumpet vine is ideal for climbing pine trees. Let the vine get no taller than you can easily prune to keep from escaping.

VARIETIES 'Crimson Trumpet' (red), 'Flava' (yellow), and 'Praecox' (scarlet) are named selections. Try also 'Madame Galen,' a *C. x tagliabuana* hybrid with salmon flowers. *C. grandiflora*, Chinese trumpet creeper, has much larger flowers.

'Madame Galen,' a hybrid, is less invasive and produces larger blooms than the native trumpet vine.

Clematis (KLEM-at-is) species and hybrids

Clematis

FAMILY: *Ranunculaceae*
ORIGIN: Asia and Himalayas
RELATIVES: Columbine,
Delphinium
PROPAGATION: Layering, cutting
ZONE: Perennial in 4–9
LIGHT: Sun to afternoon shade
WATER: Average
SIZE: 10–20 feet
COLOR: Several shades and blends

TOUGHNESS Scores of books instruct amateur horticulturists to do this and that to have success with clematis. Every year, however, they are found blooming on mailboxes, trellises, and arbors at homes of gardeners who do nothing more than look the other way. The clematis is tougher than you think. The flowers are among the largest of any vine and the colors so rich they look as if they were designated for royalty.

PLANTING Prepare the planting area by making it organically rich and very well drained, amending with compost, humus, or very fine pine bark. Incorporate a light application of a slow-release 12-6-6 fertilizer while preparing the soil. Plants will need a support structure to climb. Select healthy, nursery-grown clematis and plant at the same depth as in the container.

GROWING Feed established plantings in late winter and midsummer with fertilizer. Pruning is often confusing. Spring-flowering clematis bloom on old wood and should be pruned right after blooming. Summer- and fall-flowering types bloom on new wood and should be pruned in early spring. If the clematis blooms in the spring on old wood, and again in the fall on new wood, only light pruning to shape should be done, either in the spring or fall.

LANDSCAPE USE The clematis is perfect for the cottage garden picket fence or the tropical garden where it can be combined with mandevillas. Make unique combinations with climbing roses like 'New Dawn.' Clematis is the ideal vine for old "Victorian style" towers.

VARIETIES The white-flowered 'Henryi' produces enormous blooms. Other white selections are 'Candida' and 'Gillian Blades.' Choice pink selections are 'Comtesse de Blouchard' and 'Lincoln Star.' For red to burgundy 'Red Kardinal,' 'Niobi,' and 'Mme. Edouard Andre' are among the most popular. 'Lady Betty Balfour,' 'Prince Philip,' and 'Star of India' are choice selections in the blue-violet-purple range.

'Nelly Moser' is one of the most popular selections of clematis.

Whether you have a trellis, split rail fence, or mail box, the clematis would make a superb choice.

This trellis with moonflower, mandevilla, and Brazilian sky flower offers beauty day and night.

Ipomoea (eye-po-MEE-a) alba

Moonflower

FAMILY: *Convolvulaceae*

ORIGIN: Tropical America

RELATIVES: Morning Glory

PROPAGATION: Seed, cutting

ZONE: Perennial in 8–10, annual elsewhere

LIGHT: Sun

WATER: Average

SIZE: 15–30 feet

COLOR: White

TOUGHNESS The moonflower is the kind of plant that makes memories for your children. It is an heirloom vine in the South that all children—and adults, for that matter—need to experience. Large, pristine white, fragrant flowers open in the afternoon and reflect moonlight all night long. This nightly occurrence happens from midsummer through fall. If your are fortunate, a luna moth will visit, making the whole experience one to reminisce about with the family.

PLANTING Select a site in full sun. The soil should be fertile and organically rich, so amend with 3–4 inches of compost or humus. While preparing the site incorporate a cup of a 5-10-5 fertilizer. Transplants aren't available at all garden centers, but seeds are easy to find. Start seeds in a container or plant at the site. Scratch the seed coat with sandpaper lightly a few times and soak the seeds overnight. Plant ½-inch deep next to a sturdy structure for climbing.

GROWING Keep the moonflower watered through the summer and fed every 4–6 weeks with a light application of a slow-release 12-6-6 fertilizer. Should the vine get too vigorous, pinch or prune to keep confined. Occasionally spider mites become a problem; pay attention and treat early if needed.

LANDSCAPE USE Since it is showiest at night, combine it with something colorful for the daytime, such as its cousin the morning glory or the pink 'Alice du Pont' mandevilla.

VARIETIES 'Giant White' is the standard variety.

Any bird would be at home in this house flanked by the 'Giant White' moonflower.

Ipomoea (eye-po-MEE-a) lobata

Exotic Love, Spanish Flag

FAMILY: *Convolvulaceae*

ORIGIN: Mexico

RELATIVES: Morning Glory

PROPAGATION: Seed, cutting

ZONE: Perennial in 8–10, annual elsewhere

LIGHT: Sun

WATER: Average

SIZE: 10–20 feet

COLOR: Each flower exhibits red, orange, yellow, cream

Exotic love grown from seed can cover a pergola with blooms in approximately 135 days.

TOUGHNESS You will gaze in awe at the almost indescribable spikes of flowers borne by the hundreds, showing red, orange, yellow, and cream all at the same time. Whether you find it as exotic love or Spanish flag, you will want it. This vigorous vine, grown mostly as an annual, covers an arbor or trellis and blooms in the fall from seed planted in the spring.

PLANTING The press has been good on the exotic love vine, but it is still rare to find it in the local garden center. It is easy to locate seeds from specialty companies. Seeds should be planted in well-drained soil about ½ inch deep. Amend the planting area with organic matter and a cup of a 5-10-5 fertilizer. Provide a structure for the vine to climb. Germination normally takes place in 10–16 days. Thin the seedlings to a spacing of 18 inches. Blooming should occur about 135 days after the date of planting. Starting seeds indoors several weeks in advance will give a longer bloom period.

GROWING Feed every 4–6 weeks with a light application of a slow-release 12-6-6 fertilizer.

This vine will grow a long time so supplement water during the season. Water deeply when needed and maintain a layer of mulch. Occasionally spider mites become a problem; pay attention and treat early if needed.

LANDSCAPE USE Exotic love is definitely a conversation item when in bloom. Use it to cover a pergola, trellis, or fence. New marigolds that are off-white, such as 'Sweet Cream' or 'French Vanilla,' and annual red salvia planted in front of the vine would be most striking. Try also with burgundy coleus varieties like 'Mississippi Summer,' 'Plum Parfait,' and 'Burgundy Sun.'

VARIETIES Exotic love or Spanish flag is sold generically and oftentimes under the old botanical name *Mina lobata*.

Ipomoea (eye-po-MEE-a) purpurea

Morning Glory

FAMILY: *Convolvulaceae*

ORIGIN: Mexico, Central America

RELATIVES: Sweet Potato

PROPAGATION: Seed

ZONE: Perennial in 9–11, mostly grown as annuals

LIGHT: Sun

WATER: Average

SIZE: 20–40 feet

COLOR: Several shades and blends

Morning glories are popular again as this mail box will attest.

TOUGHNESS Gardeners everywhere love the morning glory with its large trumpet- or funnel-shaped, colorful blossoms that look as tropical as a mandevilla. Then there are those who hate it because they have let it escape with abandon—or should we say *by* abandon. Well managed, this vigorous vine is an asset to landscapes anywhere in the country.

PLANTING The morning glory is in vogue again in the United States. So much so that many garden centers now offer large transplants. If yours doesn't, don't fret because they most likely have them in seed packets. The soil should be fertile and organically rich, so amend with 3–4 inches of compost or humus. While preparing the site incorporate a cup of a 5-10-5 fertilizer. Start seeds in a container or plant at the site. Scratch the seed coat with sandpaper lightly a few times and then soak the seeds overnight. Plant ½-inch deep next to a sturdy structure for climbing, the larger the better.

GROWING A copious quantity of fertilizer is not recommended unless you want the vine to cover your neighbor's house. Though this might be tempting in some instances, just give a light application of a slow-release 12-6-6 fertilizer in midsummer. Supplement the vine with water during prolonged dry periods. Should the vine get too vigorous, pinch or prune to keep confined. Occasionally spider mites become a problem; pay attention and treat early if needed. Enjoy the flowers in the morning because when you come home from work they will be closed.

LANDSCAPE USE Whatever you want to cover, the morning glory can do the job. From mailboxes to pergolas, arbors, and lattice structures, the morning glory will climb with vigor. Use at the entrance to the topical or cottage garden. Combine with the moonflower or mandevilla.

VARIETIES 'Star of Yelta' (deep purple with darker star), 'Crimson Rambler' (dark crimson with white throat), 'Milky Way' (white with purple star), *I. nil* 'Scarlet O'Hara,' *I. tricolor* 'Heavenly Blue' (sky blue with pale center), and 'Wedding Bells' (rose-lavender) are some of the best.

Ipomoea (eye-po-MEE-a) quamoclit

Cypress Vine

FAMILY: *Convolvulaceae*
ORIGIN: Mexico, Tropical America
RELATIVES: Morning Glory
PROPAGATION: Seed
ZONE: Annual all zones
LIGHT: Sun
WATER: Average
SIZE: 10–20 feet
COLOR: Red

TOUGHNESS The cypress vine is a vigorous climber with airy, fernlike foliage and 1½-inch scarlet-red flowers. The blooms are produced all summer and in prolific quantities for gardeners to enjoy and for the feasting ruby-throated hummingbird. Some view it as weedy, but most gardeners consider it a treasure.

PLANTING The cypress vine is an annual, but it reseeds with ease. It has naturalized as far north as zone 6. Seed catalogs or volunteers from a neighbor are the most likely sources. This may be where you have to get your start. Plant seeds in fertile, well-drained soil adjacent to a structure for climbing. Thin seedlings to 15 inches. Germination occurs in as little as 4 days.

GROWING The cypress vine is drought-tolerant, but many more flowers are produced on vines given supplemental water during the growing season. Once seedlings are 8–12 inches tall, side-dress with a light application of a 5-10-5 or 10-20-10 fertilizer.

LANDSCAPE USE The cypress vine is picturesque climbing among white lattice that shows off the foliage and bloom. Use also on split-rail or picket fences. Good companion plants are bright red or yellow cannas, 'New Gold' lantana, and 'Vista Red' scarlet sage.

VARIETIES 'Cardinalis' is a named selection. Look also for *I. x sloteri (I. coccinea x I quamoclit)*, known as 'Cardinal Climber.'

Cypress vine produces fern-like foliage and hundreds of scarlet flowers loved by hummingbirds.

Lablab (LAB-lab) purpureus

Hyacinth Bean

FAMILY: *Fabaceae*
ORIGIN: Tropical Africa
RELATIVES: Green Bean
PROPAGATION: Seeds
ZONE: Perennial in 9–11, annual
elsewhere
LIGHT: Sun
WATER: Average
SIZE: 10 feet
COLOR: Lilac-purple, white with
purple pods

The hyacinth bean is attractive with blooms and shiny purple pods.

TOUGHNESS This favorite of Thomas Jefferson will be yours as well once you start growing it. Even as an annual vine the hyacinth bean is quick-covering, producing fragrant lilac-purple and white flowers in staggering numbers. Attractive glossy purple bean pods follow bloom. Insect and disease pressures are low, and the vigor is high, making this an easy vine for anyone to grow.

PLANTING Select a site in full sun with fertile, organically rich soil. One of the key criteria is very good drainage. If drainage is suspect and the soil is heavy clay, amend the planting site with 3–4 inches of organic matter. While working the soil, incorporate 2 pounds of a 5-10-5 fertilizer per 100 square feet of planting area. Plant the seed adjacent to a structure for climbing such as a fence, trellis, or pergola. Plant 1 inch deep and cover. Water thoroughly and apply mulch. The seeds should germinate in 10–14 days. Group 4 seedlings at intervals 36 inches apart if planting along a fencerow.

GROWING The hyacinth bean will be growing a long time to reach maturity. Feed every 4–6 weeks with a light application of a slow-release 12-6-6 fertilizer. Keep well watered during the growing season. If growing in warmer zones, apply a layer of mulch for winter protection and it may return. The pods are edible and considered a staple in Indian and Asian food markets. Before cooking, inquire on the correct method of processing.

LANDSCAPE USE The hyacinth bean is a good quick cover and blooms when the days are shorter in the fall. Good companions for the season are mums, salvias, and marigolds. The vine is a landscape asset to the cottage, perennial, or tropical garden.

VARIETIES There are no named selections of hyacinth bean.

Lonicera (lon-ISS-er-a) x heckrottii

'Gold Flame' Honeysuckle

FAMILY: *Caprifoliaceae*
ORIGIN: Hybrid
(*L. sempervirens* x *L. x americana*)
RELATIVES: Abelia, Viburnum
PROPAGATION: Cutting, layering, seed
ZONE: Perennial in 5–9
LIGHT: Sun to part shade
WATER: Less than average
SIZE: 12–15 feet
COLOR: Each flower exhibits yellow, purple, pink

TOUGHNESS Mention the word "honeysuckle" and many gardeners get an immediate escalation of their blood pressure. The trepidation comes from the imported Japanese honeysuckle that has escaped and is a close second to kudzu as a hated plant. The 'Gold Flame,' however, is tame and has flowers of rare beauty that are yellow on the inside and flushed with purple-pink. Blooms cycle from spring through frost.

PLANTING Select a site in full sun for the most prolific bloom, though performance is acceptable in part shade. The soil should be fertile and well drained. Tight clay stunts the 'Gold Flame' and keeps it from reaching its potential. Amend if necessary with 3–4 inches of compost or humus. It is best planted in the spring, but container-grown plants can be set out anytime during the growing season. Place next to a sturdy structure for climbing.

GROWING Feed the 'Gold Flame' in late winter with an application of a slow-release, balanced fertilizer. Prune as needed to keep tidy and confined within the designated area. Keep the 'Gold Flame' on the dry side until blooms begin, and then keep evenly moist. Powdery mildew rarely attacks; if it occurs it is easy to control with a fungicide. This is a very disease-resistant hybrid and considered one of the finest selections.

LANDSCAPE USE Use the 'Gold Flame' on split-rail fences, picket fences, trellises, arbors, gazebos, latticework, and even old-fashioned towers. Grow where it can climb on the porch or patio. The colorful yellow, purple, and pink blooms blend wonderfully in the perennial garden with blue salvias, daylilies, iris species, yarrow, and verbenas. The 'Gold Flame' looks at home in the tropical setting too.

VARIETIES In addition to 'Gold Flame,' try 'Pink Lemonade.'

'Gold Flame' honeysuckle is beautiful but not the least bit invasive.

Lonicera (lon-ISS-er-a) sempervirens

Coral Honeysuckle

FAMILY: *Caprifoliaceae*
ORIGIN: Eastern and
Southern United States
RELATIVES: Abelia, Viburnum
PROPAGATION: Cutting,
layering, seed
ZONE: Perennial in 4–9
LIGHT: Sun to part shade
WATER: Less than average
SIZE: 10–20 feet
COLOR: Red, yellow, orange

Coral honeysuckle is an outstanding native and a good source of nectar for hummingbirds.

TOUGHNESS The native coral honeysuckle offers much in comparison to the invasive Japanese honeysuckle. It is well behaved and offers both unique foliage that is semi-evergreen in zones 8b and 9 and outstanding red, yellow, or orange blooms. The flowers are an important source of nectar for the hummingbird, and cardinals and purple finches eat the fruit.

PLANTING Select a site in full sun for the most prolific blooming, though the coral honeysuckle performs admirably in part shade. The soil should be fertile and well drained. Tight clay stunts the growth of the coral honeysuckle, keeping it from reaching its potential. Amend if necessary with 3–4 inches of compost or humus. It is best planted in the spring. Container-grown plants can be set out anytime during the growing season with good success. Place next to a sturdy structure for climbing.

GROWING Feed the coral honeysuckle in late winter with an application of a slow-release, balanced fertilizer. Prune as needed to keep tidy and confined within the designated area. Keep the honeysuckle on the dry side until blooms begin, and then keep evenly moist. Powdery mildew occasionally attacks in the early spring but is easy to control with a fungicide.

LANDSCAPE USE Use the coral honeysuckle on picket fences, trellises, arbors, or towers. The bloom is heaviest in the spring and coincides well with other flowers like coreopsis, ox-eye daisies, yarrow, and lantana. The trumpet-shaped flowers look good in a tropical garden too.

VARIETIES The coral honeysuckle is often sold generically. Good named selections are 'Alabama Scarlet' (scarlet), 'John Clayton' (yellow), 'Magnifica' (red), and 'Sulphurea' (yellow). Look also for *L. x brownii* 'Dropmore Scarlet' with a longer season of bloom.

Mandevilla (man-dev-ILL-a) x amablis

Mandevilla, Brazilian Jasmine

FAMILY: *Apocynaceae*
ORIGIN: Brazil
RELATIVES: Oleander
PROPAGATION: Cutting, layering
ZONE: Perennial in (9) 10–11, annual elsewhere
LIGHT: Sun to part shade
WATER: Average
SIZE: 10–20 feet
COLOR: Pink, red, white

'White Delight' mandevilla

TOUGHNESS This is the best buy in tropical plants for everyone living in areas where it freezes. The mandevilla blooms from the moment you buy in April until the first hard freeze in October or November. The flowers are large and trumpet-shaped in shades of pink, red, and white. The mandevilla is superior, thriving in high heat and humidity even when planted at the streetside or on a wall.

PLANTING Select a location with at least 6 hours of sun. As tough as it is, the mandevilla has an Achilles heel—drainage. It cannot tolerate wet feet; it will rot. Prepare the bed by adding 3–4 inches of organic matter and plant next to a support structure for climbing. A gallon-sized container-grown specimen will quickly climb to 8 feet.

GROWING Feed monthly with light applications of a slow-release, balanced fertilizer containing minor nutrients. Feed those growing in containers with controlled-release granules per directions. Keep in mind that daily watering combined with warm soil temperatures usually means more frequent feeding. Another good option is to use a diluted water-soluble fertilizer

such as a 20-20-20 every 2 weeks. Keep the soil moist; avoid letting the mandevilla dry to the wilting point. To over-winter container-grown plants, cut back to a manageable size and place in a bright area indoors. Reduce water and fertilizer until spring. Watch for mealy bugs and spider mites once inside.

LANDSCAPE USE The mandevilla is a versatile plant that adds beauty wherever it is grown. In the tropical garden, combine with allamandas. Clematis makes an unusual companion, providing a double dose of colorful blooms. Once the clematis is finished it will not be missed because the mandevilla will keep blooming for months. Grow in a very large hanging basket, allowing it to climb the chains while 'Pink Frost' sweet potato cascades over the rim of the basket.

VARIETIES 'Alice du Pont' (hot pink) is the leading selection. 'Best Red' (red), 'Ruby Star' (red), 'White Delight' (white-blushed pink), 'Monte' (white-blushed pink), 'Moonlight Parfait' (semi-double pink with white throat), and 'Pink Parfait' (double pink) are worth searching for and buying.

Passiflora (pass-i-FLO-ra)
incarnata hybrid

'Incense' Passionflower

FAMILY: *Passifloraceae*
ORIGIN: Eastern United States
RELATIVES: Edible Passion Fruit
PROPAGATION: Cutting, layering
ZONE: Perennial in 6–10
LIGHT: Sun
WATER: Average
SIZE: 20–30 feet
COLOR: Purple

TOUGHNESS Today's gardeners are searching out vines for that special fence, trellis, or arbor, and one of the best is the passionflower. The native passionflower *Passiflora incarnata* was used in breeding, and the result is an improved, cold-hardy, exotic-looking flower known as 'Incense.' 'Incense' produces 5-inch-wide, fragrant, royal purple flowers with a lacy corolla overlaying the petals. Unbelievably, 'Incense' has been known to survive in zone 5 with protection.

PLANTING Passion vines require good drainage and plenty of sunlight to be prolific bloomers. Improve the planting area if needed by amending with organic matter like compost or humus. Dig the planting hole twice as wide as the root ball but no deeper. Plant at the same depth as in the container and adjacent to a good support structure for climbing. Water to get the vine established and maintain a layer of mulch. Feed with a light application of a 12-6-6 fertilizer a month after transplanting.

GROWING After a couple of years these vigorous vines will need thinning by cutting in the late winter. Prune back to the base or to major branches. The passionflower is so vigorous it normally doesn't need a lot of fertilizer. A light application of a 12-6-6 fertilizer in late spring should suffice. Do give supplemental water during the long summer season. The gulf fritillary butterfly likes the passionflower as a host plant, so put up with a few holes when it happens.

LANDSCAPE USE There may not be a quicker cover for a trellis or arbor. In the landscape, it is hard to beat a well-managed 'Incense' passionflower draped on a fence behind yellow shrimp plants, bush allamandas, or lantanas like 'New Gold,' 'Sonset,' and 'Sonrise.'

VARIETIES The *Passiflora incarnata* and the *P. incarnata* hybrid 'Incense' are superior in bloom and cold-hardiness. *P. caerulea,* blue passionflower, is striking in bloom and cold-hardy to zone 7. The red passionflower *P. coccinea* can be grown in zones 8b–11.

'Incense' passionflower is extremely cold-hardy and vigorous, easily covering an arbor or trellis.

Thunbergia (thun-BER-ja) alata

Black-eyed Susan Vine

FAMILY: *Acanthaceae*
ORIGIN: Tropical Africa
RELATIVES: Ruellia
PROPAGATION: Seed,
cutting, layering
ZONE: Perennial in 9–10, annual
elsewhere
LIGHT: Sun to part shade
WATER: Average
SIZE: 8–10 feet
COLOR: Yellow, orange, white

'Sunny Orange Wonder' and 'Sunny Lemon Star'

TOUGHNESS The black-eyed Susan vine can cover a trellis in one season from seed. From a distance the flowers do resemble the black-eyed Susan, but a closer inspection reveals that the flowers are tubular with a dark purple throat. The flowers may be orange, white, or yellow. The vine is perennial in zone 9 and 10 and often reseeds in other zones.

PLANTING Choose a site in full sun to partial shade and plant after the last frost of the year. Prepare the soil deeply by adding 3–4 inches of composted pine bark and humus. Till to a depth of 8–10 inches. While tilling, incorporate 2 pounds of a slow-release 12-6-6 fertilizer per 100 square feet of bed space. Plant at the same depth as in the container, adjacent to a support structure for climbing. The black-eyed Susan vine is easy to grow from seed. Sow three seeds about ¼ inch deep, water, and cover with mulch. Germination takes 10–21 days. Remove the weakest seedling by cutting.

GROWING Feed with a light application of fertilizer every 4–6 weeks. Keep well watered to maintain vigorous growth. The black-eyed Susan vine climbs effortlessly. Prune or pinch to keep

in bounds. Occasionally spider mites will become a problem, so treat early if needed and the problem will not get out of hand.

LANDSCAPE USE The black-eyed Susan vine is perfect at the entrance to the cottage garden or as a bright addition to the tropical garden. Grow them over an arbor or along a fence. They will also work on the mailbox. For the tropical garden try combining with the princess flower, *Tibouchina urvilleana*, or red cannas and in proximity to the bold foliage of bananas and elephant ears. Some of the prettiest companion plants in the cottage garden are perennial blue salvias such as 'Victoria' blue, salvia indigo spires, or the blue anise sage. Try 'AngelMist' angelonias as lower-level plants. Tall perennial summer phlox planted in front also makes an impressive show.

VARIETIES 'Susie' is the most recognized variety and comes in yellow, orange, and white. 'Angel Wings' has white flowers and an ever-so-light fragrance. Two new varieties, 'Sunny Orange Wonder' and 'Sunny Lemon Star,' have quickly gained acceptance by gardeners everywhere.

When in Doubt
Go with a Winner!

Garden centers today are stocked with large selections of high-quality plants. Many of these plants may seem unfamiliar but could be the best performers for your region of the country. When in doubt about what plants to choose, go with a winner.

Several state nursery associations have promotional programs in which plants are designated as award winners based on trials or past performance in that state. These award winners are listed on the following pages.

ARKANSAS SELECT WINNERS

1998

Lady in Red Salvia *Salvia coccinea*
Crystal White Zinnia *Zinnia angustifolia*
Dwarf Fountain Grass *Pennisetum alopecuroides*
May Night Meadow Sage *Salvia x sylvestris*

1999

Melampodium *Melampodium paludosum*
Purple Coneflower *Echinacea purpurea*
Scaevola *Scaevola aemula*
Variegated Solomon Seal *Polygonatum odoratum* 'Variegatum'
Oakleaf Hydrangea *Hyndrangea quercifolia*

2000

New Gold Lantana *Lantana camara*
Pink Diamond Hydrangea *Hydrangea paniculata*
Siskiyou Pink Gaura *Gaura lindheimeri*
Russian Sage *Perovskia atriplicifolia*
Summer Wave Torenia *Torenia x hybrida*

2001

Arkansas Blue Star *Amsonia hubrictii*
Homestead Purple Verbena *Verbena canadensis*
Dragonwing Begonia *Begonia x hybrida*
Million Bells *Calibrachoa x hybrida*
Japanese Snowbell *Styrax japonica*

2002

Dynamite Crape Myrtle *Lagerstroemia indica* 'Whit II'
Vera Jameson Stonecrop *Hylotelephium ssp. maximum* 'Atropurpureum' x 'Ruby Glow'
Yellow Queen Columbine *Aquilegia chrysantha*
Streptocarpus *Streptocarpus saxorum*
Butterfly Pentas *Pentas lanceolata*

FLORIDA PLANTS OF THE YEAR

1998

Hilo Princess *Angelonia angustifolia*
Autumn Fern *Dryopteris erythrosora*
Firebush *Hamelia patens*
Peacock Ginger *Kaempferia species*
Acoma Crape Myrtle *Lagerstroemia indica x L. fauriei*
Sioux Crape Myrtle *Lagerstroemia indica x L. fauriei*
Pink Loropetalum *Loropetalum chinense* var. 'Rubrum'
Firepower Dwarf Nandina *Nandina domestica*
Alusion Series Nephthytis *Syngonium species*

1999

Cross-vine *Bignonia capreolata*
Snailseed *Cocculus laurifolius*
Blackie Sweet Potato *Ipomoea batatas*
Margarita Sweet Potato *Ipomoea batatas*
Lake Tresca Ligustrum *Ligustrum japonicum*
Desert Cassia *Senna polyphylla*
Winged Elm *Ulmus alata*
Firespike *Odontonema strictum*
B. J. Freeman Aglaonema *Aglaonema species*

2000

Red Buckeye *Aesculus pavia*
Yellow Barleria *Barleria micans*
Golden Jasmine *Cestrum aurantiacum*
White Geiger *Cordia boissieri*
Mahogany Fern *Didymochlaena truncatula*
Pineapple Guava *Acca sellowiana* (formerly known as *Feijoa*)
Henery's Garnet Virginia Willow *Itea virginica*
Silver Saw Palmetto *Serenoa repens* (silver form)
Alii Ficus *Ficus binnendijkii*
Midnight Ficus *Ficus benjamina*
Toolittle Ficus *Ficus benjamina*

2001

Mexican Bush Sage *Salvia leucantha*
Blue Anise Sage *Salvia guaranitica*
Salvia Indigo Spires *Salvia farinacea x S. longispicata*
Japanese Cleyera *Ternestroemia gymnanthera*
Domino Spathiphyllum *Spathiphyllim species*
Dwarf Variegated Asian Jasmine *Trachelospermum asiaticum* 'Tricolor'
Emerald Gem *Homalomena* 'Emerald'
Fringe Tree *Chionanthus virginicus*
Ribbon Palm *Livistona deciplens*
Lindley's Butterfly Bush *Buddleia lindleyana*
Summer Wave Torenia *Torenia x hybrida*
Profusion Zinnias *Zinnia x hybrida*
Evergreen Red Wisteria *Millettia reticulata*

2002

Compact Walter's Viburnum *Viburnum obovatum*
Perennial Peanut *Arachis glabrata*
Oakleaf Hydrangea *Hydrangea quercifolia*
Simpson's Stopper *Myrcianthes fragrans* 'Compacta'
Bismarck Palm *Bismarckia nobilis*
Orange Plume *Justicia spicigera*
Robin Holly *Ilex x Robin*
Giant Plume Ginger *Curcuma elata*
Hidden Ginger *Curcuma zeodoaria*
Jewel of Thailand Ginger *Curcuma cordata* (petiolata)
"ZZ" *Zamioculcas zamiifolia*
Mammy Croton *Codiaeum* 'Mammy'

GEORGIA GOLD MEDAL PLANTS

1994

Homestead Purple Verbena *Verbena canadensis*
Bath's Pink Dianthus *Dianthus gratianopolitans*
Mt. Airy Fothergilla *Fothergilla major*
Japanese Plum Yew *Cephalotaxus harringtonia*

1995

New Gold Lantana *Lantana camara*
Blue Anise Sage *Salvia guaranitica*
Annabelle Hydrangea *Hydrangea arborescens*
Athena Elm *Ulmus parvifolia*

1996

Purple Wave Petunia *Petunia x hybrida*
Wild Indigo *Baptisia* species
Hummingbird Clethra *Clethra alnifolia*
Lipan Crape Myrtle *Lagerstroemia indica x
    L. fauriei*
Sioux Crape Myrtle *Lagerstroemia indica x
    L. fauriei*
Tonto Crape Myrtle *Lagerstroemia indica x
    L. fauriei*
Yuma Crape Myrtle *Lagerstroemia indica x
    L. fauriei*

1997

New Wonder Scaevola *Scaevola aemula*
Three-Lobed Coneflower *Rudbeckia triloba*
Pink Chinese Loropetalum *Loropetalum chinense*
    var. *rubrum*
Yoshino Japanese Cedar *Cryptomeria japonica*

1998

Athens Gem Plectranthus *Plectranthus* species
Japanese Aster *Kalimeris pinnatifida*
Bottlebrush Buckeye *Aesculus parviflora*
Trident Maple *Acer buergeranum*

1999

Nova Pentas *Pentas lanceolatas*
Lenten Rose *Helleborus orientalis*

Mohawk Viburnum *Viburnum x burkwoodii*
American Yellowwood *Cladrastis kentuckea*

2000

Sun Loving Coleus *Solenostemon scutellariodes*
David Phlox *Phlox paniculata*
Robert Poore Phlox *Phlox paniculata*
Alice Oakleaf Hydrangea *Hydrangea quercifolia*
Little Gem Magnolia *Magnolia grandiflora*

2001

Ornamental Sweet Potato *Ipomoea batatas*
Autumn Fern *Dryopteris erythrosora*
Inkberry *Ilex glabra*
Chastetree *Vitex agnus-castus*

2002

Lady in Red Salvia *Salvia coccinea*
Blue Mist Bluebeard *Caryopteris x clandonensis*
Purple Beautyberry *Callicarpa dichotoma*
Forest Pansy Redbud *Cercis canadensis*
Texas White Redbud *Cercis canadensis*
Oklahoma Redbud *Cercis reniformis*

LOUISIANA SELECT WINNERS

1996

Mayhaw *Cratageus opaca* or *Cratgeus aestivalis*
New Orleans Red Coleus *Solenostemon
    scutellariodes*
Homestead Purple Verbena *Verbena canadensis*
Telestar Dianthus *Dianthus chinensis x barbatus*
Watchet Azalea *Rhododendron* x Robin Hill Hybrid
Henry's Garnet Virginia Willow *Itea virginica*

1997

Bald Cypress *Taxodium distichum*
New Wonder Scaevola *Scaevola aemula*

1998

Lantana *Lantana camara hybrids*

1999

Lady in Red Salvia *Salvia coccinea*
Foxy Foxglove *Digitalis purpurea*

2000

Goldsturm Rudbeckia *Rudbeckia fulgida var. sullivantii*

2001–2002

No plants chosen

2003

Natchez Crape Myrtle *Lagerstroemia indica x L. fauriei*
Profusion Zinnia *Zinnia x hybrida*

MISSISSIPPI MEDALLION WINNERS

1996

Blue Daze Evolvulus *Evolvulus pilosus*
New Gold Lantana *Lantana x camara*

1997

Melampodium *Melampodium paludosum*
New Wonder Scaevola *Scaevola aemula*
Little Gem Magnolia *Magnolia grandiflora*

1998

Narrow Leaf Zinnias *Zinnia angustifolia*
Victoria Blue Salvia *Salvia farinacea*
Natchez Crape Myrtle *Lagerstroemia indica x L. fauriei*

1999

Indian Summer Rudbeckia *Rudbeckia hirta*
Biloxi Blue Verbena *Verbena x hybrida*
Tonto Crape Myrtle *Lagerstroemia indica x L. fauriei*
Sioux Crape Myrtle *Lagerstroemia indica x L. fauriei*

2000

Petunia Wave Series *Petunia x hybrida*
Yellow Shrimp Plant *Pachystachys lutea*
Oakleaf hydrangea *Hydrangea quercifolia*
Blood Good Japanese Red Maple *Acer palmatum*
Panola Panache *Viola x wittrockiana x V. cornuta*

2001

Butterfly Pentas *Pentas lanceolata*
Burgundy Fringe Flower *Loropetalum chinense*
Kathy Ann Yaupon Holly *Ilex vomitoria*
Bouquet Purple Dianthus *Dianthus x hybrida*

2002

Shishigashira *Camellia sasanqua*
Lilac Chastetree *Vitex agnus-castus*
Dragon Wing Red Begonia *Begonia x hybrida*
Mississippi Summer Sun Coleus *Solenostemon scutellarioides*

2003

Autumn Blaze Red Maple *Acer x freemanii*
Edward Goucher Abelia *Abelia x grandiflora x A. schumannii*
Costa Rica Blue *Salvia guaranitica*
Sonset Lantana *Lantana camara*

2004

Port Gibson Pink Verbena *Verbena canadensis*
Krauter Vesuvius Purple Leaf Plum *Prunus cerasifera*

OKLAHOMA PROVEN AWARD WINNERS

1999

Oakleaf Hydrangea *Hydrangea quercifolia*
Purple Fountain Grass *Pennisetum setaceum 'Rubrum'*
Chinese Pistache *Pistacia chinensis*
Powis Castle Artemisia *Artemisia x Powis Castle*

2000

Bald Cypress *Taxodium distichum*
Magic Carpet Spiraea *Spiraea japonica*
Homestead Purple Verbena *Verbena canadensis*
Scaevola Fan Flower *Scaevola aemula*

2001

Siskiyou Pink *Gaura lindheimeri*
Deciduous Holly *Ilex decidua*

2002

Bur Oak *Quercus macrocarpa*
Margarita Sweet Potato *Ipomoea batatas*

TENNESELECT AWARD WINNERS

1999

Basil *Ocimum species*
Threadleaf Coreopsis *Coreopsis verticillata*
Wave Petunias *Petunia x hybrida*
Sunny Border Blue Veronica *Veronica x hybrida*
Narrow Leaf Zinnia *Zinnia angustifolia*

2000

Tardiva Hydrangea *Hydrangea paniculata*
Oakleaf Hydrangea *Hydrangea quercifolia*
Annabelle Hydrangea *Hydrangea arborescens*
Melampodium *Melampodium paludosum*
Purple Coneflower *Echinacea purpurea*
Eastern Redbud *Cercis Canadensis*
Rosemary *Rosmarinus officinalis*

2001

Lantana *Lantana camara*
Goldsturm Rudbeckia *Rudbeckia fulgida var. sullivantii*
Sweet Bay Magnolia *Magnolia virginiana*
Thyme *Thymus species*
Shasta Viburnum *Viburnum x burkwoodii*
Conoy Viburnum *Viburnum x burkwoodii*
Mohawk Viburnum *Viburnum x burkwoodii*

2002

Sun Loving Coleus *Solenostemon scutellariodes*
Butterfly Blue Scabiosa *Scabiosa columnaria*
Milky Way Kousa Dogwood *Cornus kousa*
Winterberry Holly *Ilex verticillata*
Garden Sage *Salvia officinalis*

2003

Butterfly Bush *Buddleia* species and hybrids

TEXAS SUPERSTAR AWARD PROGRAM

Texas Bluebonnet *Lupinus texensis*
Texas Maroon Bluebonnet *Lupinis texensis*
Burgundy Sun SuperSun Coleus *Solenostemon scutellariodes*
Plum Parfait SuperSun Coleus *Solenostemon scutellariodes*
Texas Gold Columbine *Aquilegia chrysantha hinckleyana*
Gold Star Esperanza *Tecoma stans*
Firebush *Hamelia patens*
Flare Rose Mallow *Hibiscus* species
Lord Baltimore Rose Mallow *Hibiscus* species
Moy Grande Texas Giant *Hibiscus* species
Deciduous Holly *Ilex deciduas*
Pam's Pink Honeysuckle *Lonicera x Americana*
New Gold Lantana *Lantana camara*
Blue Bunny Bloom Larkspur *Consolida ambigua*
Pink Bunny Bloom Larkspur *Consolida ambigua*
Satsuma *Citrus reticulata*
Shantung Maple *Acer truncatum*
Antigua Mari-mum Fall Planted Marigold *Tagetes erecta*
Lacey Oak *Quercus glaucoides*
Laura Bush Petunia *Petunia x violacea*
VIP Petunia *Petunia violacea (Petunia integrifolia)*
Dwarf Mexican Petunia *Ruellia brittoniana*
John Fanick Phlox *Phlox paniculata*
Victoria Perennial Phlox *Phlox paniculata*

Chinese Pistache *Pistacia chinensis*
Yubi Portulaca *Portulaca oleracea*
Belinda's Dream *Rosa x hybrida*
Marie Daly Rose *Rosa x polyantha*
Mexican Bush Sage *Salvia leucantha*
New Wonder Scaevola *Scaevola aemula*
Blue Princess *Verbena x hybrida*

For more information about plant trials or state promotional programs contact the following:

Alabama Nurserymen's Association
P.O. Box 9
Auburn, AL 36831-0090

Arkansas Nurserymen's Association
P.O. Box 21715
Little Rock, AR 72221

Florida Nurserymen & Growers Association
5401 Kirkman Road, Suite 650
Orlando, FL 32819-7911

Georgia Green Industry Association
P. O. Box 369
Epworth, GA 30541

Louisiana Nursery and Landscape Association
P.O. Box 25100
Baton Rouge, LA 70894-5100

Mississippi Nursery and Landscape Association
P.O. Box 5385
Miss. State, MS 39762-5385

North Carolina Association of Nurserymen
P.O. Box 400
Knightdale, NC 27545-0400

Oklahoma State Nurserymen's Association
400 N. Portland
Oklahoma City, OK 73107-6110

South Carolina Nurserymen's Association
2541 Glenwood Road
Columbia, SC 29204

Tennessee Nurserymen's Association
115 Lyon St.
P.O. Box 57
McMinnville, TN 37110-0057

Texas Nursery and Landscape Association
7730 South IH-35
Austin, TX 78745-6621

Bibliography

Armitage, Allan M. *Armitage's Garden Perennials A Color Encyclopedia*. Portland, Ore.: Timber Press. 2000.

———. *Armitage's Manual of Annuals, Biennials, and Half-Hardy Perennials*. Portland, Ore.: Timber Press. 2001.

———. *Herbaceous Perennial Plants*. Champaign, Ill.: Stipes Publishing. 1997.

Cathey, Dr. H. Marc, with Linda Bellamy. *Heat Zone Gardening*. New York: Time Life Books. 1998.

Dirr, Michael A. *Manual of Woody Landscape Plants: Their Identification, Ornamental Characteristics, Culture, Propagation and Uses*. Revised 4th ed. Champaign, Ill.: Stipes Publishing. 1990.

Hill, Madalene, and Gwen Barclay, with Jean Hardy. *Southern Herb Growing*. Fredericksburg, Tex.: Shearer Publishing. 1987.

Hutson, June, with Ruth Rogers Clausen. *Annual Gardening*. New York: Pantheon Books. 1995.

Mathias, Mildred E. *Flowering Plants of the Landscape*. Berkeley and Los Angeles: University of California Press. 1982.

McDonald, Elvin. *The 400 Best Garden Plants: A Practical Encyclopedia of Annuals, Perennials, Bulbs, Trees, and Shrubs*. Edison, N.J.: Chartwell Books. 2002.

The New Royal Horticultural Society Dictionary of Gardening. New York: Stockton Press. 1992.

Odenwald, Neil, and James Turner. *Identification, Selection, and Use of Southern Plants for Landscape Design*. 3rd ed. Baton Rouge, La.: Claitor's Publishing Division. 1996.

Perry, James. Revised by John Davis. *Selecting Landscape Plants*. Mississippi State University Extension Service, Publication 666. 1999.

The Southern Living Garden Book. Birmingham, Ala.: Oxmoor House. 1998.

Sperry, Neil. *Texas Gardening*. 2nd ed. Dallas: Taylor Publishing. 1991.

Welch, William C. *Perennial Garden Color*. Dallas: Taylor Publishing. 1989.

Winter, Norman L. *Mississippi Gardener's Guide*. Franklin, Tenn.: Cool Springs Press. 2000.

———. *Paradise Found: Growing Tropicals in Your Own Backyard*. Dallas: Taylor Publishing. 2001.

Watkins, John V., and Thomas J. Sheehan. *Florida Landscape Plants, Native and Exotic*. Revised edition. Gainesville: University Presses of Florida. 1980.

Index